MW00668101

Employee Stock Options

Exercise Timing, Hedging, and Valuation

Modern Trends in Financial Engineering

ISSN: 2424-8371

This new book series, Modern Trends in Financial Engineering, publishes monographs on important contemporary topics in theory and practice of Financial Engineering. The series' objective is to provide cutting-edge mathematical tools and practical financial insights for both academics and professionals in Financial Engineering. The modern trends are motivated by recent market phenomena, new regulations, as well as new financial products and trading/risk management strategies. The series will serve as a convenient medium for researchers, including professors, graduate students, and practitioners, to track the frontier research and latest advances in the field of Financial Engineering.

Published

More information on this series can also be found at http://www.worldscientific.com/series/mtfe

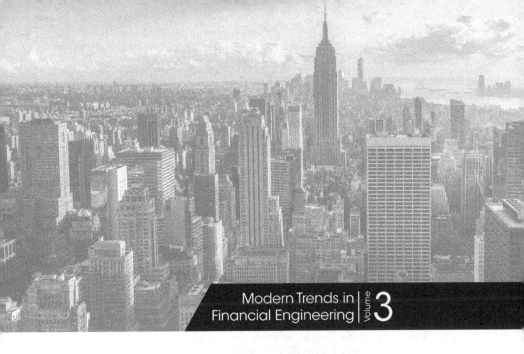

Modern Trends in Financial Engineering | Volume 3

Employee Stock Options

Exercise Timing, Hedging, and Valuation

Tim Leung
University of Washington, USA

 **World Scientific**

NEW JERSEY · LONDON · SINGAPORE · BEIJING · SHANGHAI · HONG KONG · TAIPEI · CHENNAI · TOKYO

Published by

World Scientific Publishing Co. Pte. Ltd.

5 Toh Tuck Link, Singapore 596224

USA office: 27 Warren Street, Suite 401-402, Hackensack, NJ 07601

UK office: 57 Shelton Street, Covent Garden, London WC2H 9HE

Library of Congress Cataloging-in-Publication Data
Names: Leung, Tim, author.
Title: Employee stock options : exercise timing, hedging, and valuation /
    Tim Leung, University of Washington, USA.
Description: New Jersey : World Scientific, [2022] | Series: Modern trends in financial engineering,
    2424-8371 ; Volume 3 | Includes bibliographical references and index.
Identifiers: LCCN 2021003542 | ISBN 9789813209633 (hardcover) |
    ISBN 9789813209640 (ebook) | ISBN 9789813209657 (ebook other)
Subjects: LCSH: Employee stock options.
Classification: LCC HD4928.S74 L48 2022 | DDC 331.2/1649--dc23
LC record available at https://lccn.loc.gov/2021003542

British Library Cataloguing-in-Publication Data
A catalogue record for this book is available from the British Library.

For any available supplementary material, please visit
https://www.worldscientific.com/worldscibooks/10.1142/10437#t=suppl

Desk Editor: Jiang Yulin

Typeset by Stallion Press
Email: enquiries@stallionpress.com

To my children

Preface

Employee stock options (ESOs) are an integral component of compensation in the US. In fact, almost all S&P 500 companies grant options to their top executives, and the total value accounts for almost half of the total pay for their chief executive officers (CEOs). In view of the extensive use and significant cost of ESOs to firms, the Financial Accounting Standards Board (FASB) has mandated expensing ESOs since 2004. This gives rise to the need to design a reasonable valuation method for these options for most firms that grant ESOs.

Most ESOs come with several common features, such as vesting and early exercise, while the ESO holders (employees) face various constraints and sources of risks. All these present major challenges to companies that seek to evaluate the cost of these options. Hence, it is an important active research area, not only in Accounting and Corporate Finance, but also in Computational Finance and Risk Management.

In this book, practical and challenging problems surrounding ESOs are discussed from a financial mathematician's perspective. This book begins with a systematic overview of the main characteristics of ESOs and related problems on hedging strategies, exercise timing, and valuation, along with a up-to-date literature review. The subsequent chapters, different valuation approaches based on stochastic modeling and optimal control, along with option pricing theory, are presented. In particular, this book highlights the connections and combined effects of different ESO features, constraints, and sources of risks on the timing of exercise and value of ESOs.

The book is arranged based on a series of papers on ESOs by the author. While there is a recurring theme (ESO valuation) throughout the entire book, each chapter is intended as a separate stand-alone study, often with a distinct approach or stochastic model for ESO valuation. As such, the notations in each chapter are intended for that chapter only. This allows the reader to jump into any chapter of interest and alleviates the reader's burden to look for definitions or notations in earlier chapters.

The book is designed with the hope that it will be useful for graduate students, advanced undergraduates, and researchers in financial engineering/mathematics, especially those who specialize in derivatives pricing and hedging and, of course, employee stock options and executive compensation. For practitioners, there are formulas and numerical schemes for fast implementation of the valuation models and explicit hedging strategies for ESOs.

Finishing this book marks the end of a decade-long journey. The authors would like to express their gratitude to several people who have helped make this book possible. A few chapters in this book are based on research conducted in collaboration with my mentors Ronnie Sircar and Thaleia Zariphopoulou. My students Haohua Wan and Yang Zhou have contributed significantly to Chapters 2 and 3 of the book respectively. My research is partially supported by NSF grant DMS-0908295 and has also benefited from the helpful remarks and suggestions from many colleagues over the year. Last, but certainly not least, we thank Rochelle Kronzek and Max Phua of World Scientific for encouraging us to pursue this book project.

Tim Leung
Boeing Professor of Applied Mathematics
University of Washington
Seattle, WA
June 2021

Contents

Chapter 1

Introduction

Employee Stock options (ESOs) are call options granted by a firm to its employees as a form of compensation and incentive. The primary objective is to align the interests between the employees and the firm. As such, they are often used for recruiting and retaining employees. Since the mid-1980s, stock options have become an integral component of compensation in the United States.[1] According to Table 1.1, the percentage of S&P 500 companies granting ESOs was as high as over 94% in 2001 and remained above 72% in the following decade.

Typically, ESOs are long-dated early exercisable call options written on the company stock. To maintain the incentive effect, the firm usually imposes a *vesting period* that prohibits the employee from exercising the option. During the vesting period, the employee's departure from the firm will result in forfeiture of the option (i.e. it becomes worthless). After the vesting period, when the employee leaves the firm, the ESO will expire though the employee can choose to exercise if the option is in the money.[2] Table 1.1 summarizes the average vesting period and average maturity of ESOs granted by S&P 500 companies over 2000–2011. As we can see, the vesting period has been consistently close to 2 years, while the average maturity has decreased from 9–10 years to 8 years over a decade.

Due to the extensive use of ESOs, the Financial Accounting Standards Board (FASB) has become concerned about the cost of these options to shareholders. In the past decade, the reporting of the granting cost of such

---

[1] Empirical studies by Hall and Murphy (2002); Frydman and Jenter (2010) estimate that the total value of ESOs accounts for 25–47% of total pay for the CEOs from 1990s to 2000s.

[2] See, for example, "A Detailed Overview of Employee Ownership Plan Alternatives" by The National Center for Employee Ownership, available at http://www.nceo.org.

Table 1.1. Summary of ESO compensation during 2000–2011.[a]

Year	% of S&P500 companies granting ESOs	Avg. vesting period (years)	Avg. maturity (years)
2000	92.98%	2.00	9.24
2001	94.35%	2.22	9.28
2002	93.56%	2.18	9.53
2003	89.59%	2.18	10.17
2004	88.09%	2.03	8.66
2005	75.34%	2.16	8.61
2006	81.30%	2.12	7.86
2007	77.33%	2.18	8.14
2008	76.31%	2.38	7.35
2009	75.30%	2.16	8.41
2010	72.69%	2.32	8.71
2011	73.39%	2.16	8.07

[a]*Source*: Thomson Reuters Insider Trading database and Compustat Exe-cuComp database.

options has changed from optional to mandatory. In 2004, under *Statement of Financial Accounting Standards No. 123 (revised)*, FASB required firms to estimate and report "the grant-date fair value" of the ESOs issued.[3] Opponents of expensing ESOs often argue that calculating the fair values at the time they are granted is very difficult. This gives rise to the need to design a valuation method that is "practical, easy to implement, and theoretically sound," according to Hull and White (2004a).

1.1. Main Characteristics of ESOs

In order to determine the cost of ESOs to the firm, it is important to understand the characteristics of ESOs, and distinguish them from market-traded options. Typically, ESOs are American call options (i.e. they can be exercised at any time during the exercise window), with long maturity ranging from 5 to 15 years. In most cases, the ESOs are not immediately exercisable. The firm usually wants to maintain the incentive effect by prohibiting the employee holders from exercising during a certain period from the grant date. This period is called the *vesting* period. During the vesting period, the holder's departure from the firm, voluntarily or forced, will lead to forfeiture of his option (i.e. it becomes worthless).

---

[3]The Statement is available at https://www.fasb.org/pdf/fas123r.pdf.

Once endowed with an ESO, the employee cannot sell it, or hedge against his position by short-selling the company stock, but he can partially hedge his position by trading other securities, for example, the S&P 500 index.[4] The sale and hedging restrictions may induce the employee to exercise the ESO early and invest the option proceeds elsewhere. The employee's risk preference and his available investment opportunities directly affect his exercise behavior.

Another vital feature for ESO valuation is the possibility that the employee will leave the firm before the ESO matures. At any time, an employee could be fired by the employer, or leave the firm voluntarily for various reasons, such as retirement. If the departure happens during the vesting period, then the option is forfeited, and the ESO costs the firm nothing in this case. If the ESO holder leaves after the vesting period, then, at the time of departure, the holder may exercise the option, and the firm pays the proceeds, if any.

All these features — vesting, sale and hedging restrictions, the employee's exercise behavior and the risk of sudden job termination — have significant bearing on the fair value of ESOs. Hence, FASB requires valuation models to capture the unique characteristics of ESOs.[5] Our primary objective in this paper is to provide a model that can accommodate all these characteristics and determine the cost of ESOs to the firm. Moreover, we want to address the challenging question: how do these characteristics influence the employee's exercise policy and the firm's granting cost? The employee's hedging and exercising strategies depend on the contract features and various sources of risk. They in turn affect the cost of the ESO to the firm. Our model will be useful not only in improving the precision of ESOs expensing, but will also shed light on executives' exercising behavior.

1.2. Exercise Timing

As empirical studies on ESOs suggest, the majority of ESOs holders tend to exercise early, often right after the vesting period. For instance, Hemmer

---

[4]According to Section 16(c) of the U.S. Securities Exchange Act, executives are precluded from short-selling the shares of their employer. The FASB statement 123R (see paragraph B80) indicates that "many public entities have established share trading policies that effectively extend that prohibition to other employees." This short sales restriction has been adopted in the literature on ESOs; e.g. Huddart (1994), Carpenter (1998), and Olagues and Summa (2010).

[5]See *Appendix A: Implementation Guideline* in the FASB statement 123R.

et al. (1996), Huddart and Lang (1996), Marquardt (2002), and Bettis *et al.* (2005) have shown that employees tend to exercise their options very early, often soon after the vesting period. For ESOs with 10 years to maturity, the average exercise time is between 4 and 5 years.

There are several reasons that an employee may voluntarily exercise an ESO early. These include retirement, liquidity needs, risk exposure control, and portfolio diversification/optimization. The inability to sell or perfectly hedge the ESOs gives the employee an incentive to exercise the options earlier to lock in profits, rather than waiting for future uncertain though possibly higher returns (Bova and Vance, 2019). Klein and Maug (2010) estimate a hazard model from a large data set of almost 200,000 option packages to identify the main drivers for early exercises. They find that stock price behaviors and contract features (vesting dates, grant dates, blackout periods) strongly influence the executives' timing decisions. Monoyios and Ng (2011) discuss how insider information may affect the timing of ESO exercises.

On the other hand, the vesting period prohibits voluntary exercise but may lead to forfeiture of the options if the employment is terminated. Several studies (Grasselli and Henderson, 2009; Leung and Sircar, 2009a; Rogers and Scheinkman, 2007) have attempted to rationalize this *early exercise phenomenon* by showing that risk aversion and job termination risk can induce the employee to adopt a more conservative exercising strategy, accelerating the option exercises. This is an important issue since early exercises generally imply a significantly lower ESO cost to the firm.

Other exercise patterns have also been investigated. For perpetual options, Grasselli and Henderson (2009) show that the phenomenon of early "block exercises" (exercising multiple options simultaneously) will occur under transaction costs. In the finite-maturity case, simultaneous early exercises may also happen when the financial market regime changes, as shown in Leung (2010).

The early exercise phenomenon deviates from the prediction made by no-arbitrage pricing theory. For instance, in the case of an American call written on a non-dividend paying underlying stock, no-arbitrage pricing models conclude that the holder should never exercise early. This early exercise phenomenon indicates that no-arbitrage theory is inadequate for determining the exercise policy for ESOs.

To account for the employee's early exercise, FASB proposes an expensing approach by adjusting the Black–Scholes (B–S) model (for European call options). In particular, it recommends substituting the option expiration date with the expected time to exercise. Although this expensing method is very simple and convenient, it is far from accurate. Jennergren and Naslund (1993), Hemmer *et al.* (1994), and Huddart and Lang (1996) conclude that this adjusted B–S model fails to capture the employee's exercise behavior and overstates the cost of the ESOs to the firm. Since ESOs are early exercisable, a better approach is to treat ESOs as American options and determine the holder's optimal exercise strategy. The job termination risk also may lead to involuntary exercise, and therefore, shorten the life of an ESO. The corresponding valuation is more complicated than the simplistic B–S model, but the computation is straightforward and accurate, as studied by Leung and Wan (2015).

1.3. Valuation Methodologies

As required by FASB, firms face the recurring challenge to estimate and report the costs of their ESO grants. The cost of an ESO to the firm depends crucially on the price level and time at which the option is exercised. Therefore, it is important to model the exercise timing of ESOs in order to accurately estimate their costs to the firm.

The wide use of ESOs has led to a growing literature on their valuation. Typically, ESO valuation models can be categorized into risk-neutral models and utility-based models.

Among risk-neutral models, one approach is to prescribe an *ad hoc* ESO exercise boundary. Hull and White (2004b) and Cvitanic *et al.* (2008) are examples of this approach. Hull and White propose that the employee's exercise boundary be flat. Cvitanic *et al.* (2008) propose an exponentially decaying barrier. This approach, while simple, comes with several shortcomings. First, there is no *optimality* justification for the employee's exercise policy. Moreover, the exercise time does not interact with the employee's risk attitude, hedging strategies, job termination risk, or the firm's stock price dynamics. In fact, the *ad hoc* exercise boundaries do not depend on the stock price model parameters. In contrast, we will find in all models studied in this book that the employee's exercise boundary changes considerably with model parameters and contract features.

One enhancement to the risk-neutral approach is to accurately recognize the early exercise feature and determine the employee's optimal timing strategy while accounting for other major characteristics and sources of risk, including job termination. Following this direction, we first present a valuation framework that incorporates the common ESO features of vesting period, early exercise and job termination risk, while allowing for different price dynamics with jumps.

In Chapter 2, we model the arrival of the employment shock by an exogenous jump process, and formulate the American-style ESO as an optimal stopping problem with possible forced exercise prior to expiration date. Our valuation problem is studied under a wide class of stock price models (exponential Lévy price processes), rather than limiting to the geometric Brownian motion model commonly found in the literature (see, e.g., Hull and White, 2004b; Cvitanic *et al.*, 2008; Carpenter *et al.*, 2010). Under constant or stochastic job termination intensity assumptions, we analyze the corresponding optimal timing problem to determine the optimal exercise and option value. Mathematically, this leads us to analyze several free boundary problems in terms of their inhomogeneous partial integro-differential variational inequalities (PIDVIs), and discuss the computational methods to solve them. Analytically and numerically, we find that with higher job termination risk it is optimal for the holder to voluntarily accelerate ESO exercise. For risk analysis, we also apply our numerical schemes to calculate the probability of cost exceedance and the probability of contract termination under various scenarios.

To account for the multiple random exercises associated with each ESO grant, one major approach is to model the exercise times using an exogenous counting process. In other words, the early exercises are the arrival counts that come at different random times before expiration. The frequency of the early exercises are modulated by an exogenous intensity function or process.

The *intensity-based* approach does not distinguish voluntary and involuntary exercise, and model the contract termination by a single random time, characterized by the first arrival time of an exogenous jump process. In the literature, Jennergren and Naslund (1993) model the exercise time using an exogenous Poisson process, and Carr and Linetsky (2000) propose an intensity-based model for ESO valuation where both job termination and voluntary exercise intensities are functions of the company stock price. In the theoretical study by Szimayer (2004), the employee is allowed to optimally select a voluntary exercise time, while the sudden departure is represented by an exogenous Cox process. In practice, the job termination intensity specification depends on the firm's history and estimation methodology. For empirical studies on the early exercise patterns of ESOs, we refer to Huddart and Lang (1996); Marquardt (2002); Bettis *et al.* (2005).

In Chapter 3, we propose a novel framework that captures all the random exercises of different quantities while also accounting for the ESO holder's job termination risk and its impact on the payoffs of both vested and unvested ESOs. The key difference in our approach is that we consider all options in an ESO grant in our valuation, rather than modeling a single ESO exercise. In essence, this top-down approach offers a flexible setup to model any exercise pattern. The idea is akin to the top-down approach in credit risk (Giesecke and Goldberg, 2011), where the exogenous jump process represents portfolio losses. This work, based on Leung and Zhou (2019), also includes numerical methods for ESO valuation. Specifically, a Fourier transform method and a finite difference method are developed and implemented to solve the associated systems of partial differential equations to obtain the ESO costs to the firm. In addition, we introduce a new valuation method based on maturity randomization that yields analytic formulae for vested and unvested ESO costs. The cost impact of job termination risk, exercise intensity, and various contractual features are also discussed.

Given the long-term risk embedded in ESOs, the holders have strong incentives to reduce risk through hedging. However, ESOs are commonly issued with hedging restrictions. For instance, they are non-transferable and are not traded (and therefore, not priced) in the market. Employees are typically prohibited from short-selling the firm's stock, especially if they are executive officers or 10% owners. These put severe limits on the hedging strategies that an ESO holder can use for protecting from lost payoff.

Hedging strategies can be developed based on various optimization criteria, such as utility maximization, minimum variance and other risk measures. In particular, utility maximization theory has been central to quantifying rational investment decisions and risk-averse valuations of assets at least since the work of von Neumann and Morgenstern in the 1940s. In the Merton (1969) problem of continuous-time portfolio optimization, utility is defined at some time horizon in the future, when investment decisions are assessed in terms of expected utility of wealth. The hedging problems for ESOs also give rise to new meaningful extensions to the traditional portfolio optimization approach.

For hedging ESOs, Huddart (1994), Kulatilaka and Marcus (1994), Detemple and Sundaresan (1999), and Chance and Yang (2005) adopt a utility-based approach to study the discrete-time dynamic hedging strategies under short-sale restrictions. In the presence of short-sale and other trading restrictions, a risk-averse employee may find it optimal to exercise his American-style ESO early even if the underlying stock pays no dividend. This result helps explain the well-known phenomenon that employees tend to exercise their ESOs long before the maturity. Hence, the utility-based approach is capable of capturing the effects of non-tradability and hedging restrictions on the employee's hedging and exercising strategies.

A recent advancement in financial engineering involves the continued development of a methodology called *utility indifference pricing*. This mechanism is a dynamic version of the *certainty equivalent* concept; it accounts for the holder's investment opportunities or partial hedging instruments in addition to the option. The option holder's utility indifference price is defined as the amount of money that he is willing to pay so that his maximal expected utility is the same as that from an investment without the option. Hall and Murphy (2002) use a certainty-equivalence framework to analyze the divergence between the firm's cost of issuing ESOs and the value to employees. Lau and Kwok (2005) investigate the incentive effect of ESOs under a utility maximization framework. In Ingersoll (2006) and Henderson (2005), the methodology of continuous-time utility maximization to dynamically and partially hedge ESOs is studied. This leads to a valuation model for a European ESO that captures the employee's risk aversion.

Since most ESOs are early exercisable, the indifference pricing approach needs to be adapted to value American options. Moreover, the contract features and the employee's job termination risk must also be included to properly capture the employee's timing decisions and value of the options (see Oberman and Zariphopoulou, 2003; Leung and Sircar, 2009a; Carpenter *et al.*, 2010). According to Leung and Sircar (2009a), the ESO cost is reduced as the employee's job termination risk increases. Quite surprisingly, longer vesting period typically leads to a higher ESO cost because it forces the employee to wait longer and prevent pre-mature exercises.

In Chapter 4, we discuss a methodology that derives the value of the early exercisable ESOs to the employee and also the cost to the firm. The major characteristics of ESOs, including vesting, job termination risk, and multiple exercises, are all included. This is achieved through a two-stage procedure. First, we take the employee's perspective and solve for the optimal (partial) hedging and exercise timing problem. In this step, we obtain the employee's optimal exercise strategy, which in turn becomes the input for computing the cost to the firm. Specifically, from the firm's perspective, the ESO cost is computed by risk-neutral expectation assuming the option will be exercised at the utility-maximizing boundary or job termination time, whichever is earlier.

In Chapter 5, we present a new mathematical framework for hedging long-term options, such as ESOs, through (i) dynamic trading of a correlated liquid asset, and (ii) static positions in market-traded options. This is particularly relevant to ESO holders who cannot trade the company stock frequently or sell it short to create a direct viable hedge. Since most market-traded options are short-term contracts relative to the ESOs, it is necessary to rolling the static positions over time till the long-term option expires. For this reason, the proposed strategy is called *sequential static-dynamic* hedging (İlhan and Sircar, 2005; İlhan *et al.*, 2009; Leung, 2012; Leung and Ludkovski, 2012).

The sequential static-dynamic hedging mechanism is applicable to both European and American ESOs. The ESO holder dynamically invests in the market index (e.g. through an index ETF) which is correlated with the company stock. On top of that, market-traded put options are also purchased repeatedly over time. The strategy provides partial hedges, but not all risks can be removed. The valuation and exercise timing of the ESOs still depend on the holder's risk preferences. To that end, we adopt a utility maximization approach to determine the optimal static positions at different times, along with the optimal dynamic trading strategy.

Stock price dynamics are often seen as being dependent on the market conditions. Market regimes may change suddenly and persist for a certain period of time. The unpredictability of the timing of regime changes also means that associated risks are almost impossible to hedge. To capture these crucial properties in pricing options, one major approach is to represent stochastic market regimes by a finite state Markov chain (see, e.g., Guo and Zhang, 2004; Elliot *et al.*, 2005). In these regime switching models, the Markov chain is an exogenous random process and is not tradable. The effect of the Markov chain is also reflected in the stock price dynamics. For example, the stock's expected return and volatility may vary across regimes.

In Chapter 6, we consider the problem of timing to exercise multiple early exercisable ESOs in a regime switching market. In the model, the option holder faces the idiosyncratic risk from the non-tradability of the firm's stock as well as the regime switching risk. These two sources of unhedgeable risks render the market incomplete. Since not all risks can be hedged, the holder's risk preferences play a key role in the valuation and investment decisions. We apply the utility indifference pricing methodology, whereby the optimal hedging and exercising strategies are determined through the associated utility maximization problems. In addition, our approach also accounts for the partial hedge with a correlated liquid asset and the multiple early exercises of American options.

For portfolios involving early exercisable ESOs, and associated utility indifference pricing problems, option payoffs may be realized at random times, which requires the specification of utility at other times, not just at a single terminal time. One way to address this issue is to consider the definition of utility at the time of a random cash flow as analogous to specifying what the investor does with the endowment thereafter. Some examples include Oberman and Zariphopoulou (2003), Leung and Sircar (2009a) for utility indifference pricing of American options, and Sircar and Zariphopoulou (2010), Leung *et al.* (2008), and Jaimungal and Sigloch (2012) for defaultable securities. This approach allows for comparing utilities of wealth at different times. However, as is common in classical utility indifference pricing, the investor's risk preferences at intermediate times and the investment decisions still directly depend on an *a priori* chosen investment horizon and a utility function defined at the terminal time. Investor's inter-temporal risk preferences are inferred backward in time.

This horizon dependence issue can be addressed through the construction of the forward performance criterion (see, e.g., Musiela and Zariphopoulou (2008)). In this approach, the investor's utility is specified at an *initial* time, and his risk preferences at subsequent times evolve *forward* without reference to any specific ultimate time horizon. This results in a stochastic utility process, called the *forward performance process*, which satisfies certain properties so that it evolves consistently forward in time with the random market conditions. Hence, this approach necessarily connects risk preferences with market models without pre-specifying an investment horizon.

In Chapter 7, we develop a valuation methodology based on the forward performance criterion. Specifically, we study the valuation of a long position in an American-style stock option in an incomplete diffusion market model. This leads us to a combined stochastic control and optimal stopping problem. Our main objective is to analyze the optimal trading and exercising strategies that maximize the option holder's forward performance from the dynamic portfolio together with the option payoff upon exercise. We also study the holder's *forward indifference price* for the American option, which is defined by comparing his optimal expected forward performance with and without the option.

1.4. Related Problems

During the 2008 financial crisis, executive compensation, including bonuses and stock options, received much public outcry and criticism. Among the controversies, one question was whether ESOs were effective in aligning the interests of executives and shareholders. This is a fundamentally important issue for ESOs especially given their widespread use in companies across various industries. As studied by Kolb (2012), the incentive effect of executive compensation has critical implications to corporate governance.

From a financial engineering standpoint, this is related to the research problem of optimal contract design. One approach is to examine the combined effects of the contract features such as the vesting period, expiration date, and strike price, along with the less typical provisions such as reload and reset. Alternative compensation vehicles have been proposed. For example, equity-linked compensation (Meulbroek, 2001), performance-vested options, and indexed options (Brisley, 2006; Johnson and Tian, 2000).

To understand the incentive effect of various compensation schemes, a major approach is based on the *principal-agent* theory. This involves mathematical formulation to model the interests of the firm (principal) and the employee (agent) under each compensation scheme. For instance, Bebchuk and Fried (2003) study executive compensation as an agency problem. Cvitanic and Zhang (2007) present an optimal contracting model, where the firm determines the compensation for the employee whose actions can directly affect the firm's output process. Chen and Pelger (2014) examine several stock option schemes to see which one best aligns the interests of the firm and employee when both are risk-averse.

The valuation models in this book cover the most common features of ESOs, but some ESOs come with additional exotic features, such as reload, repricing, knockout, and blackout. There is a host of research on stock options with different payoff structures and non-standard features.

The practice of ESO repricing has decades of history, but became particularly popular during and after the dot-com bust in the early 2000s.[6] There was also resurgence of the practice after the financial crisis in 2009 and energy market meltdown.[7] Repricing an ESO means lowering the

---

[6] According to the Wall Street Journal article by Maremont and Forelle (2006).

[7] See Alix (2016) and McLaughlin and French (2020).

strike price originally assigned to the option, which in turn increases the option value. During a market downturn, some employee stock options may become out of the money, meaning that the company's stock is below the strike price. This motivates some firms to adjust the strike price downward so that the options are in/at-the-money.

In the literature, Acharya *et al.* (2000) argue that ESO repricing is an "important, value-enhancing aspect of compensation contracts, even from an *ex-ante* standpoint." They continue to suggest that "some resetting is almost always optimal." The question is why should firms reward poor performance by repricing the options. For related studies on ESO repricing, we refer to Saly (1994), Callaghan *et al.* (2003), Chen (2004), Zamora (2008), Leung and Kwok (2008), Kalpathy (2009), Yang and Carleton (2011), and Sun and Shin (2014). Alternatives to repricing have also been proposed, such as delayed repricing, advanced repricing, and share swap (see Yang, 2011).

ESO reloading, invented by Frederic W. Cook and Co. in 1987, involves granting additional at-the-money stock options upon exercising the initial ones. Most typically, these are non-transferable non-hedgeable (NTNH) American call options, like most ESOs. With the reloading provision, the ESO holder pays the strike price in stock shares that he/she already owns, rather than paying in cash. Upon exercise, the new options are granted at-the-money with a new expiration date. In the literature, Dybvig and Loewenstein (2015) study the pricing, hedging, and exercise strategy of reload options. Dai and Kwok (2005) consider several variations of the standard ESOs by adding reloading and other features. The valuation of these options involves solving a number of optimal stopping problems and thereby determining the optimal exercise strategy. Johnson and Tian (2000) examine the value and incentive effects of non-traditional ESOs, including those with reload and repricing features.

Another controversial issue with ESOs is backdating. This is a practice of opportunistic granting whereby the firm pretends that an ESO was granted earlier than it really was, at a lower strike price, to enhance the value of the option. In a sample of 620 stock option awards to CEOs of Fortune 500 companies between 1992 and 1994, Yermack (1997) finds that the timing of the ESO grants coincides with favorable movements in company stock prices. For example, CEOs tend receive stock options shortly *before* favorable corporate news, like earnings announcements. Aboody and Kasznik (2000) examine over 2000 CEO option grants and provide evidence to show that the CEOs make opportunistic voluntary disclosure decisions that maximize their stock option compensation. Cicero (2009) finds that executives use private information and backdating to increase the profitability of their stock option exercises. Lie (2005) and Heron and Lie (2009) provide evidence that "most of the abnormal return pattern around option grants is attributable to backdating of option grant dates." In essence, backdating represents a timing option embedded in the ESO grant. Henderson *et al.* (2018) present a utility-based valuation model to quantify and illustrate how backdating increases the value of ESO to risk-averse executives.

Accurate valuation for ESOs and related compensation instruments are critically important for companies. Given the various features and constraints that come with different compensation plans, there are many opportunities for future research. ESO valuation and related models will help not only shareholders but also regulators understand the real costs and impact on corporate governance of these compensation vehicles.

Chapter 2

Risk-Neutral Models with Optimal Exercises

2.1. Introduction

The key to ESO valuation involves modeling the employee's voluntary exercise strategy as well as job termination time, especially since the option is typically terminated prior to the contractual expiration date. Moreover, the possibility of future employment shock can influence the employee's decision to exercise now or later. In fact, the Financial Accounting Standards Board (FASB) guideline also recommends that any reasonable ESO valuation model incorporates "the effects of employees' expected exercise and post-vesting employment termination behavior."[1]

In this chapter, we study a valuation framework that incorporates the common ESO features of vesting period, early exercise and job termination risk, while allowing for different price dynamics with jumps. Specifically, we model the arrival of the employment shock by an exogenous jump process, and formulate the American-style ESO as an optimal stopping problem with possible forced exercise prior to expiration date. Our valuation problem is studied under a class of exponential Lévy price processes, rather than limiting to the geometric Brownian motion (GBM) framework commonly found in the literature (see, e.g., Hull and White, 2004b; Cvitanic et al., 2008; Carpenter et al., 2010). Under different job termination intensity assumptions (constant or stochastic), we analyze the corresponding free boundary problems in terms of an inhomogeneous partial integro-differential variational inequality (PIDVI), and discuss the computational methods to solve for the option value as well as the optimal exercise strategy.

---

[1] See Section A.16, FASB Statement 123R (revised 2004).

Analytically and numerically, we find that with higher job termination risk it is optimal for the holder to voluntarily accelerate ESO exercise. For risk analysis, we also apply our numerical schemes to calculate the probability of cost exceedance and the probability of contract termination under various scenarios.

In contrast to many existing ESO models, we study a versatile valuation framework that is compatible for a wide class of Lévy price processes, including Merton (1976) and Kou (2002) jump diffusions, as well as Variance Gamma (VG) (Madan *et al.*, 1998) and CGMY (Carr *et al.*, 2002) models, in addition to GBM that is commonly found in the literature including those cited above. This allows us to study the combined effect of jumps in stock price and job termination intensity on the ESO value and optimal exercise boundary.

More importantly, our model provides the end-user, i.e. the firm, the flexibility in choosing the appropriate price model (within a general Lévy class) for the underlying stock. Currently, the FASB permits the use of the Black–Scholes formula with the ESO's contractual term replaced by its average life, as well as a number of variations.[2] In this regard, we offer an alternative valuation approach that accounts for both voluntary exercise and job termination risk along with various choices of models for the company stock price.

The ESO valuation problem can be considered as an extension to the pricing of American options under Lévy processes. See Pham (1997), Hirsa and Madan (2004), Bayraktar and Xing (2009), Lord *et al.* (2008), and Lamberton and Mikou (2008), among others. For vested ESOs, the job termination arrival forces the employee to exercise immediately. This leads to an optimal stopping problem with forced exit. In terms of the variational inequality for the option value, this restriction gives rise to an inhomogeneous term that depends on both the option payoff and job termination intensity. When the stock price follows a geometric Brownian motion, we provide the closed-form formulas for both the vested and unvested perpetual ESO costs. The optimal exercise threshold can be determined uniquely from a polynomial equation, and it admits an explicit expression in the case without job termination risk.

In order to compute the ESO value and exercise boundary, we apply the Fourier Stepping Timing (FST) method, whereby the associated

---

[2]See Section A.25, FASB Statement 123R (revised 2004).

inhomogeneous PIDVI is simplified by Fourier transform and the optimal exercise price is determined in each time step. Furthermore, the structure of the inhomogeneous PIDVI varies under different job termination intensity specifications. In particular, if the intensity is affine in the (log) stock price, then the inhomogeneous PIDE for the ESO in the continuation region can be simplified to an inhomogeneous partial differential equation (PDE). In the constant intensity case, we further reduce the associated PIDE into an ODE. These observations lead to several efficient numerical algorithms for valuation. In all these cases, we compare with the numerical results from an implicit–explicit finite difference method for valuing the ESO. To this end, we refer to the finite difference methods for pricing American options under Lévy or jump diffusion models, including Cont and Voltchkova (2003), d'Halluin *et al.* (2003), Hirsa and Madan (2004), and Forsyth *et al.* (2007).

Firms typically expense the granted ESOs according to a fixed schedule, such as quarterly or annually, but the cost of an ESO changes over time depending on the stock price movement. From the firm's perspective, a rise in the ESO value implies a higher expected cost of compensation as compared to the initially reported value. On the other hand, existing ESOs can be either exercised voluntarily by the employee, or terminated due to employment termination. This motivates us to study (i) the probability that the ESO cost will exceed a given level in the future, and (ii) the contract termination probability in Section 2.5. The ESO cost exceedance probability bears similarity to the loss probability used in classical value-at-risk calculation. The contract termination probability sheds light on the likelihood that the firm will have to pay the employee over a future horizon, from a week to a few years. We apply Fourier transform based methods to compute these probabilities under constant job termination intensity, and we show the connection between our approach and that developed by Carr and Madan (1999) in the computation of these probabilities.

2.2. Model Formulation

In the background, we fix a probability space $(\Omega, \mathscr{G}, \mathbb{P})$ satisfying the usual conditions of right continuity and completeness, where $\mathbb{P}$ is the historical probability measure. Let $(X_t)_{t \geq 0}$ be a Lévy process, which admits the well-known Lévy–Itô decomposition (Sato, 1999, p. 119):

$$X_t = \mu t + \sigma B_t + X_t^l + \lim_{\epsilon \searrow 0} X_t^\epsilon, \quad X_0 = 0,$$

where B is a standard Brownian motion under $\mathbb{P}$, and the jump terms are given by

$$X_t^l = \int_{|y| \geq 1, s \in [0,t]} y J(dy, ds), \tag{2.1}$$

$$X_t^\epsilon = \int_{\epsilon \leq |y| < 1, s \in [0,t]} y (J(dy, ds) - \nu(dy)\, ds)$$

$$= \int_{\epsilon \leq |y| < 1, s \in [0,t]} y \tilde{J}(dy, ds). \tag{2.2}$$

The characteristic triplet (μ, σ^2, ν) of X consists of the constant drift μ and volatility σ, along with the Lévy measure ν. In (2.1) and (2.2), the Poisson random measure $J(dy, ds)$ counts the number of jumps of size y occurring at time s, and $\tilde{J}$ is the associated compensator.

The characteristic exponent $\Psi(\omega)$ of X is given by the Lévy–Khintchine formula (Sato, 1999, p. 119):

$$\Psi(\omega) = i\mu\omega - \frac{1}{2}\sigma^2\omega^2 + \int_{\mathbb{R}} (e^{i\omega y} - 1 - iy\omega \mathbf{1}_{\{|y|<1\}})\, \nu(dy), \quad \omega \in \mathbb{C}. \tag{2.3}$$

With this, the characteristic function of X_t is

$$\phi_{X_t}(\omega) = e^{\Psi(\omega)t}.$$

We denote $\mathbb{F}^X = (\mathscr{F}_t^X)_{t \geq 0}$ as the filtration generated by X.

In Table 2.1, we summarize the Lévy densities and characteristic exponents for several well-known Lévy models used in this chapter. In the GBM model (Black and Scholes, 1973), the Lévy density is absent as the stock price has no jumps. The Merton (1976) model features normally distributed jump sizes, while the Kou (2002) model assumes a double exponential distribution for the jump sizes. In contrast, under the Variance Gamma (VG) (Madan *et al.*, 1998) and CGMY models (Carr *et al.*, 2002), the stock price follows a pure jump process with infinite activity.

The company stock price is modeled by an exponential Lévy process

$$S_t = S_0 e^{X_t}, \quad t \geq 0,$$

with constant initial stock price $S_0 > 0$. In addition, we assume positive constant interest rate r and non-negative dividend rate q. For ESO valuation, we work with a risk-neutral pricing measure $\mathbb{Q}$ such that

$$\mathbb{E}^{\mathbb{Q}}\{e^{X_1}\} = e^{r-q} \Leftrightarrow \hat{\Psi}(-i) = r - q,$$

Table 2.1. Lévy densities and characteristic exponents for some well-known Lévy processes.

Model	Lévy density $\nu(dy)$	Characteristic exponent $\Psi(\omega)$
GBM	N/A	$i\mu\omega - \frac{\sigma^2\omega^2}{2}$
Merton	$\frac{\alpha}{\sqrt{2\pi\tilde{\sigma}^2}}e^{-\frac{1}{2}((y-\tilde{\mu})/\tilde{\sigma})^2}$	$i\mu\omega - \frac{\sigma^2\omega^2}{2} + \alpha\left(e^{i\tilde{\mu}\omega - \frac{\tilde{\sigma}^2\omega^2}{2}} - 1\right)$
Kou	$\alpha\big(p\eta_+e^{-y\eta_+}\mathbb{1}_{\{y>0\}}$ $+ (1-p)\eta_-e^{-\|y\|\eta_-}\mathbb{1}_{\{y<0\}}\big)$	$i\mu\omega - \frac{\sigma^2\omega^2}{2} + \alpha\left(\frac{p}{1-i\omega/\eta_+} + \frac{1-p}{1-i\omega/\eta_-} - 1\right)$
VG	$\frac{1}{\kappa\|y\|}e^{b_1y-b_2\|y\|}$	$-\frac{1}{\kappa}\log\left(1 - i\tilde{\mu}\kappa\omega + \frac{\tilde{\sigma}^2\kappa\omega^2}{2}\right)$
CGMY	$\frac{C}{\|y\|^{1+Y}}\big(e^{-G\|y\|}\mathbb{1}_{\{y<0\}}$ $+ e^{-My}\mathbb{1}_{\{y>0\}}\big)$	$C\Gamma(-Y)[(M - i\omega)^Y - M^Y$ $+ (G + i\omega)^Y - G^Y]$

In all these models, μ and σ are the drift and volatility of the Brownian Motion under $\mathbb{P}$. For the Merton and Kou models, α denotes the jump intensity. In the Merton model, $\tilde{\mu}$ and $\tilde{\sigma}^2$ are the mean and variance of the IID normally distributed jumps. In the Kou model, p (respectively $(1-p)$) is the probability of positive (respectively negative) exponential jumps. In the VG model, $b_1 = \tilde{\mu}/\tilde{\sigma}^2$, $b_2 = \sqrt{\tilde{\mu}^2 + 2\tilde{\sigma}^2/\kappa}/\tilde{\sigma}^2$, and in the CGMY model, $C, G, M > 0, Y \leq 2$.

where $\hat{\Psi}$ is given in (2.3) with μ replaced by

$$\hat{\mu} = r - q - \frac{\sigma^2}{2} - \int_{\mathbb{R}}(e^y - 1 - y\mathbf{1}_{\{|y|<1\}})\,\hat{\nu}(dy), \qquad (2.4)$$

and $\hat{\nu}$ is the Lévy measure under $\mathbb{Q}$.

2.2.1. *Payoff structure*

Figure 2.1 illustrates the payoff structure of an ESO with strike K, vesting period of t_v years, and expiration date T. During the vesting period, the ESO is not exercisable and is forfeited if the employee leaves the firm. As soon as the option is *vested* (at or after time t_v), the employee can exercise the option at any time prior to the expiration date T, but will also be forced to exercise immediately upon job termination. We model the employee's job termination time τ^λ by an exponential random variable with rate parameter $\lambda \geq 0$, and assume that τ^λ and X are independent. The case of stochastic job termination will be discussed in Section 2.4.

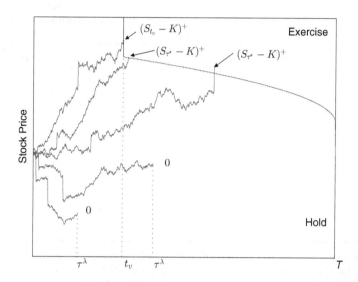

Figure 2.1. ESO payoff structure. From bottom to top: (i) The employee leaves the firm during the vesting period, resulting in forfeiture of the ESO. (ii) The employee is forced to exercise the vested ESO early due to job termination. (iii) The stock price path jumps across the exercise boundary after vesting, so the employee exercises the ESO immediately. (iv) The stock price reaches the exercise boundary (without jump) after vesting, and the option is exercised there. (v) The employee exercises the ESO at the end of vesting. Along each stock price path, the vertical line segments depict jumps in the stock price.

2.2.2. *ESO cost*

The value of a vested ESO at time $t \in [t_v, T]$ is given by

$$C(t,x) = \sup_{\tau \in \mathscr{T}_{t,T}} \mathbb{E}^{\mathbb{Q}}_{t,x} \left\{ e^{-r(\tau \wedge \tau^{\lambda} - t)}(S_0 e^{X_{\tau \wedge \tau^{\lambda}}} - K)^{+} \right\} \qquad (2.5)$$

$$= \sup_{\tau \in \mathscr{T}_{t,T}} \mathbb{E}^{\mathbb{Q}}_{t,x} \left\{ e^{-(r+\lambda)(\tau-t)}(S_0 e^{X_{\tau}} - K)^{+} \right.$$

$$\left. + \int_t^{\tau} e^{-(r+\lambda)(u-t)} \lambda (S_0 e^{X_u} - K)^{+} du \right\}, \qquad (2.6)$$

where $\mathscr{T}_{t,T}$ is the set of $\mathbb{F}^X$ stopping times taking values in $[t, T]$, and $\mathbb{E}^{\mathbb{Q}}_{t,x}\{\cdot\}$ denotes the conditional expectation with $X_t = x$. In other words, after the vesting period, the employee faces an optimal stopping problem similar to that for an American call option, but is subject to forced early exercise due to sudden job termination. From (2.6), we can also interpret the vested ESO as an American call option with a cash flow stream of

$\lambda(S_0 e^{X_t} - K)^+$ up to the exercise time τ^λ. Using the ESO payoff structure, it is straightforward to show that the vested ESO cost $C(t,x)$ is increasing and convex in x for every $t \in [t_v, T)$, and is decreasing in t for every $x \in \mathbb{R}$.

During the vesting period, the ESO is forfeited if the employee leaves the firm. Hence, given the ESO is still alive at time $t \le t_v$, the value of an *unvested* ESO is

$$\tilde{C}(t,x) = \mathbb{E}^{\mathbb{Q}}_{t,x}\left\{e^{-r(t_v-t)}C(t_v, X_{t_v})\mathbf{1}_{\{\tau^\lambda > t_v\}}\right\}$$

$$= \mathbb{E}^{\mathbb{Q}}_{t,x}\left\{e^{-(r+\lambda)(t_v-t)}C(t_v, X_{t_v})\right\}. \tag{2.7}$$

The vesting provision prohibits the employee from exercising the option even if the ESO happens to be in the money during $[0, t_v)$.

The valuation of a vested ESO leads to the analytical and numerical studies of an inhomogeneous partial integro-differential variational inequality (PIDVI). To this end, we first define the infinitesimal generator of X under $\mathbb{Q}$

$$\hat{\mathscr{L}}f(x) = \hat{\mu}f'(x) + \frac{\sigma^2}{2}f''(x)$$

$$+ \int_{\mathbb{R}\setminus\{0\}} \big(f(x+y) - f(x) - yf'(x)\mathbf{1}_{\{|y|<1\}}\big)\hat{\nu}(dy), \tag{2.8}$$

with $\hat{\mu}$ given in (2.4). For the vested ESO cost, job termination risk gives rise to an inhomogeneous term in the PIDVI, namely,

$$\min\{-(\partial_t + \hat{\mathscr{L}})C + (r+\lambda)C - \lambda(S_0 e^x - K)^+, C(t,x) - (S_0 e^x - K)^+\} = 0, \tag{2.9}$$

for $(t,x) \in (t_v, T) \times \mathbb{R}$, with terminal condition

$$C(T,x) = (S_0 e^x - K)^+,$$

for $x \in \mathbb{R}$.

For the unvested ESO cost, we set the terminal condition at time t_v by matching it with the vested ESO cost, namely, $\tilde{C}(t_v, x) = C(t_v, x)$, for $x \in \mathbb{R}$. During the vesting period, the unvested ESO cost satisfies the partial integro-differential equation (PIDE)

$$(\partial_t + \hat{\mathscr{L}})\tilde{C} - (r + \tilde{\lambda})\tilde{C} = 0, \qquad (t,x) \in [0, t_v) \times \mathbb{R}. \tag{2.10}$$

When the vesting period coincides with maturity, the ESO becomes European-style as no early exercise is permitted. Setting $t_v = T$ yields the

European ESO cost

$$\tilde{C}^E(t,x) = \mathbb{E}_{t,x}^{\mathbb{Q}}\left\{e^{-r(T-t)}(S_0 e^{X_T} - K)^+ \mathbf{1}_{\{\tau^{\tilde{\lambda}}>T\}}\right\}, \quad 0 \leq t \leq T.$$

This cost function also satisfies the PIDE (2.10).

2.2.3. *Exercise boundary*

For a vested ESO, the holder's exercise strategy can be described by the optimal exercise boundary $t \mapsto s^*(t)$ that divides the domain $[t_v, T) \times \mathbb{R}$ into the continuation region $\mathscr{C}$ and exercise region $\mathscr{S}$, defined by

$$\mathscr{C} = \{(t,s) \in [t_v, T) \times \mathbb{R}_+, s < s^*(t)\},$$

$$\mathscr{S} = \{(t,s) \in [t_v, T) \times \mathbb{R}_+, s \geq s^*(t)\},$$

where

$$s^*(t) := \sup\{s \geq 0 | C(t,x) > (s-K)^+\}, \quad \text{for } t \in [t_v, T). \tag{2.11}$$

If $s^*(t) < +\infty$, then we have

$$C(t,x) > (s-K)^+, \quad \text{for } s < s^*(t),$$

$$C(t,x) = (s-K)^+, \quad \text{for } s \geq s^*(t),$$

for $s = S_0 e^x \in (s^*(t), +\infty)$, due to the convexity and positivity of $C(t,x)$. Since, for every fixed $x \in \mathbb{R}$, $C(t,x)$ is decreasing in t, the optimal exercise boundary $s^*(t)$ must be decreasing in t in view of (2.11). As for the impact of job termination risk, we have the following result.

Proposition 2.1. *A higher post-vesting job termination intensity decreases the costs of vested and unvested ESOs, and lowers the optimal exercise boundary.*

We provide a proof in Section 2.8.1. A similar result has been established under the GBM model by Leung and Sircar (2009a). We remark that the cost reduction effect of the post-vesting job termination intensity holds with and without dividends. However, with $q = 0$, the job termination does not affect the employee's voluntary exercise timing since it is optimal not to exercise early voluntarily regardless of job termination risk. In this case, the value of an American ESO equals to that of a European ESO, and the variational inequality in (2.9) is simplified to a PIDE. On the other hand, a higher pre-vesting job termination intensity can reduce the unvested ESO cost, but has no impact on the vested ESO value or the post-vesting exercise strategy.

Remark 2.2. Here, the optimal exercise boundary is computed based on the risk-neutral pricing measure. In practice, the ESO holder is likely unable to perfectly hedge the ESO exposure. In addition, the ESO holder may opt to exercise early due to other exogenous factors, such as liquidity risk or need for diversification. To this end, one can develop a reduced form or intensity-based approach by treating the ESO exercise timing as fully exogenous and calibrating to observed exercise behaviors.

2.3. Fourier Transform Method for ESO Valuation

For ESO valuation, we now discuss a numerical approach for solving the PIDVI (2.9) based on Fourier transform. We first state the definition and some basic properties of Fourier transform. For any function $f(x)$, the associated Fourier transform is defined by

$$\mathscr{F}[f](\omega) = \int_{-\infty}^{\infty} f(x)e^{-i\omega x}dx,$$

with angular frequency ω in radians per second. In turn, if we denote by $\hat{f}(\omega)$ the Fourier transform of $f(x)$, then its inverse Fourier transform is

$$\mathscr{F}^{-1}[\hat{f}](x) = \frac{1}{2\pi} \int_{-\infty}^{\infty} \hat{f}(\omega)e^{i\omega x}d\omega.$$

As is well known, the Fourier transform of derivatives satisfies

$$\mathscr{F}[\partial_x^n f](\omega) = i\omega\mathscr{F}[\partial_x^{n-1}f](\omega) = \cdots = (i\omega)^n\mathscr{F}[f](\omega). \tag{2.12}$$

Applying (2.12) to (2.8), we have

$$\mathscr{F}[\hat{\mathscr{L}}f](\omega) = \{i\hat{\mu}\omega - \frac{1}{2}\sigma^2\omega^2 + \int_{\mathbb{R}}(e^{i\omega\hat{\mu}} - 1 - iy\omega 1_{\{|y|<1\}})\hat{\nu}(dy)\}\mathscr{F}[f](\omega)$$

$$= \hat{\Psi}(\omega).\mathscr{F}[f](\omega),$$

where $\hat{\Psi}$ is the characteristic exponent under $\mathbb{Q}$.

In the continuation region, the vested ESO cost $C(t,x)$ satisfies the inhomogeneous PIDE

$$-(\partial_t + \hat{\mathscr{L}})C + (r + \lambda)C - \varphi(x) = 0, \tag{2.13}$$

where

$$\varphi(x) := \lambda(S_0 e^x - K)^+.$$

An application of Fourier transform to (2.13) yields

$$\partial_t \mathscr{F}[C](t,\omega) + \left(\hat{\Psi}(\omega) - r - \lambda\right)\mathscr{F}[C](t,\omega) = -\mathscr{F}[\varphi](\omega). \qquad (2.14)$$

Therefore, the original inhomogeneous PIDE is transformed into an inhomogeneous ODE in (2.14) satisfied by $\mathscr{F}[C](t,\omega)$, a function of time t parameterized by ω. Given the value of $\mathscr{F}[C]$ at any time $t_2 \leq T$, we have at an earlier time t_1 that

$$\mathscr{F}[C](t_1,\omega) = \mathscr{F}[C](t_2,\omega)e^{(\hat{\Psi}(\omega)-r-\lambda)(t_2-t_1)}$$

$$+ \left(\frac{\mathscr{F}[\varphi](\omega)}{\hat{\Psi}(\omega) - r - \lambda}\right)(e^{(\hat{\Psi}(\omega)-r-\lambda)(t_2-t_1)} - 1), \quad t_1 < t_2.$$

By inverse Fourier transform, we recover the vested ESO cost in the continuation region

$$C(t_1,x) = \mathscr{F}^{-1}[\mathscr{F}[C](t_2,\omega)e^{(\hat{\Psi}(\omega)-r-\lambda)(t_2-t_1)}](x)$$

$$+\mathscr{F}^{-1}\left[\left(\frac{\mathscr{F}[\varphi](\omega)}{\hat{\Psi}(\omega) - r - \lambda}\right)(e^{(\hat{\Psi}(\omega)-r-\lambda)(t_2-t_1)} - 1)\right](x).$$

Since the ESO is early exercisable, we need to compare the vested ESO value with the payoff from immediate exercise. Precisely, we partition the time interval $[t_v, T]$ into $t_m, m = M, M-1, \ldots, 1$, then we iterate backward in time with

$$\begin{cases} C(t_{m-1},x) = \mathscr{F}^{-1}\left[\mathscr{F}[C](t_m,\omega)e^{(\hat{\Psi}(\omega)-r-\lambda)(t_m-t_{m-1})}\right.\\ \qquad\qquad\qquad \left. +\frac{\mathscr{F}[\varphi](\omega)}{\hat{\Psi}(\omega) - r - \lambda}(e^{(\hat{\Psi}(\omega)-r-\lambda)(t_m-t_{m-1})} - 1)\right](x),\\ C(t_{m-1},x) = \max\{C(t_{m-1},x), (S_0 e^x - K)^+\}, \end{cases}$$

where $t_M = T$ and $t_0 = t_v$.

For numerical implementation, we discretize the original domain $\Omega = [t_v, T] \times \mathbb{R}$ into a large finite grid: $\{(t_m, x_n) : m = 0, 1, \ldots, M, n = 0, 1, \ldots, N-1\}$, where $t_m = t_v + m\Delta t$, and $x_n = x_{\min} + n\Delta x$, with the increments $\Delta t = (T - t_v)/M$ and $\Delta x = (x_{\max} - x_{\min})/(N - 1)$. As most ESOs are granted at the money, it is natural to set the upper/lower price bounds

$x_{\min} = -x_{\max}$ equidistant from zero. With $x_{\max}$, M, and N fixed, we apply the Nyquist critical frequency $\omega_{\max} = \pi/\Delta x$ and set $\Delta \omega = 2\omega_{\max}/N$.

The continuous Fourier transform is approximated by the discrete Fourier transform (DFT)

$$\mathscr{F}[C](t_m, \omega_n) \approx \sum_{k=0}^{N-1} C(t_m, x_k)e^{-i\omega_n x_k}\Delta x = \alpha_n \sum_{k=0}^{N-1} C(t_m, x_k)e^{\frac{-ink}{N}},$$

(2.15)

with

$$\alpha_n = e^{-i\omega_n x_{\min}}\Delta x.$$

In (2.15), we evaluate the sum $\sum_{k=0}^{N-1} C(t_m, x_k)e^{\frac{-ink}{N}}$ using the Fast Fourier Transform (FFT) algorithm. The corresponding Fourier inversion is conducted by inverse FFT, yielding the vested ESO cost $C(t_m, x_n)$. Note that the coefficient α_n will be cancelled in the process.

After computing the vested ESO values, the unvested ESO cost is given by

$$\tilde{C}(t, x) = \mathscr{F}^{-1}\big[\mathscr{F}[\tilde{C}](t_v, \omega)e^{(\hat{\Psi}(\omega)-r-\tilde{\lambda})(t_v-t)}\big](x), \quad \text{for } t \leq t_v, \quad (2.16)$$

where $\tilde{C}(t_v, x) = C(t_v, x)$. Again, the Fourier and its inversion are implemented via FFT.

2.3.1. *Finite difference method for ESO valuation*

We summarize the finite difference method (FDM) for computing the ESO costs in Tables 2.2 and 2.4. For this purpose, we adapt the FDM algorithm for European options detailed in Cont and Voltchkova (2003) to the current case of early exercisable ESO with job termination risk.

First, we introduce the change of variable $u = T - t$ and denote $F(u, x) = C(T - t, x)$. Then, the PIDE for the vested ESO cost in the continuation region becomes

$$\frac{\partial F}{\partial u} = \hat{\mathscr{L}}F - (r + \lambda(T - u, x))F + \lambda(T - u, x)(S_0 e^x - K)^+,$$

for $(u, x) \in (0, T - t_v) \times \mathbb{R}$, with the initial condition

$$F(0, x) = (S_0 e^x - K)^+, \quad x \in \mathbb{R},$$

where

$$\hat{\mathscr{L}}F = (r-q)\frac{\partial F}{\partial x} + \frac{\sigma^2}{2}\left(\frac{\partial^2 F}{\partial x^2} - \frac{\partial F}{\partial x}\right)$$

$$+ \int_{-\infty}^{\infty} \hat{\nu}(dy)\left(F(u, x+y) - F(u,x) - (e^y-1)\frac{\partial F}{\partial x}\right).$$

To proceed, we split the operator $\hat{\mathscr{L}}$ into two parts, namely,

$$\hat{\mathscr{L}}F = DF + JF,$$

where

$$DF = \frac{\sigma^2}{2}\frac{\partial^2 F}{\partial x^2} - \left(\frac{\sigma^2}{2} - r + q + \beta\right)\frac{\partial F}{\partial x} - \alpha F, \qquad (2.17)$$

and

$$JF = \int_{B_l}^{B_r} \hat{\nu}(dy)F(u, x+y),$$

with

$$\beta = \int_{B_l}^{B_r} \hat{\nu}(dy)(e^y - 1).$$

We define a uniform grid on $[0, T - t_v] \times [-A, A]$ by $\{(u_n, x_i) : u_n = n\Delta t, n = 0, 1, 2, \ldots, M, x_i = -A + i\Delta x, i \in 0, 1, 2 \ldots, N\}$, with $\Delta t = (T - t_v)/M, \Delta x = 2A/N$. In Tables 2.2 and 2.4, we have $M = 4000$ and $N = 8000$. Also, denote F_i^n be the cost at the grid point (u_n, x_i). We use trapezoidal quadrature rule with Δx to approximate the integral terms in (2.17). To do so, we let K_l, K_r be such that $[B_l, B_r] \subset [(K_l - 1/2)\Delta x, (K_r + 1/2)\Delta x]$, and apply the approximations

$$\int_{B_l}^{B_r} \hat{\nu}(dy)F(u, x_i + y) \approx \sum_{j=K_l}^{K_r} \hat{\nu}_j F_{i+j},$$

$$\alpha \approx \sum_{j=K_l}^{K_r} \hat{\nu}_j, \qquad \beta \approx \sum_{j=K_l}^{j=K_r} \hat{\nu}_j(e^{y_j} - 1),$$

with

$$\hat{\nu}_j = \int_{(j-1/2)\Delta x}^{(j+1/2)\Delta x} \hat{\nu}(dy).$$

The space derivatives are approximated by the finite differences

$$\left(\frac{\partial F}{\partial x}\right)_i \approx \frac{F_{i+1} - F_i}{\Delta x}, \qquad \left(\frac{\partial^2 F}{\partial x^2}\right)_i \approx \frac{F_{i+1} - 2c_i + F_{i-1}}{(\Delta x)^2}.$$

Next, we replace DF and JF with their approximations $D_\Delta F$ and $J_\Delta F$, respectively. Lastly, we arrive at the following implicit-explicit time-stepping scheme:

$$\frac{F^{n+1} - F^n}{\Delta t} = D_\Delta F^{n+1} + J_\Delta F^n - \left(r + \lambda(T - (n+1)\Delta t, x)\right) F^{n+1}$$
$$+ \lambda\left(T - (n+1)\Delta t, x\right)(S_0 e^x - K)^+,$$

where

$$(D_\Delta F)_i = \frac{\sigma^2}{2} \frac{F_{i+1} - 2F_i + F_{i-1}}{(\Delta x)^2} - \left(\frac{\sigma^2}{2} - r + q + \beta\right) \frac{F_{i+1} - F_i}{\Delta x} - \alpha F_i,$$

$$(J_\Delta F)_i = \sum_{j=K_l}^{K_r} \hat{\nu}_j F_{i+j}.$$

Due to the early exercise feature, the iteration is coupled with a comparison to the payoff from immediate exercise. After computing the vested ESO cost till the end of the vesting period, similar finite difference method can be applied to solve the PIDE for the unvested ESO cost:

$$\frac{\partial F}{\partial u} = \hat{\mathscr{L}} F - (r + \tilde{\lambda}(T - u, x)) F,$$

for $(u, x) \in (0, t_v) \times \mathbb{R}$.

The above algorithm works for the case when the underlying Lévy process has finite activity, with $\hat{\nu}(\mathbb{R}) = \alpha < +\infty$. In the infinite activity case with $\hat{\nu}(\mathbb{R}) = +\infty$, we can use an auxiliary process $(X_t^\varepsilon)_{t \geq 0}$ with the Lévy triplet $(\hat{\mu}(\varepsilon), \sigma^2 + \sigma(\varepsilon)^2, \hat{\nu} 1_{|x| > \varepsilon})$ to approximate the original process $(X_t)_{t \geq 0}$, where $\sigma(\varepsilon)^2 = \int_{-\varepsilon}^{\varepsilon} y^2 \hat{\nu}(dy)$, and $\hat{\mu}(\varepsilon)$ is again determined by the risk-neutral condition. Therefore, F^ε satisfies

$$\frac{\partial F^\varepsilon}{\partial u} = \hat{\mathscr{L}}^\varepsilon F^\varepsilon - (r + \lambda(T - u, x)) F^\varepsilon + \lambda(T - u, x)(S_0 e^x - K)^+, \quad (2.18)$$

for $(u, x) \in (0, T - t_v) \times \mathbb{R}$ with initial condition $F^\varepsilon(0, x) = (S_0 e^x - K)^+$, $x \in \mathbb{R}$. Here, the operator $\hat{\mathscr{L}}^\varepsilon$ is defined by

$$\hat{\mathscr{L}}^\varepsilon F^\varepsilon = \left(\frac{\sigma^2 + \sigma(\varepsilon)^2}{2}\right) \frac{\partial^2 F^\varepsilon}{\partial x^2} - \left(\frac{\sigma^2 + \sigma(\varepsilon)^2}{2} - r + q + \beta(\varepsilon)\right) \frac{\partial F^\varepsilon}{\partial x}$$

$$- \alpha(\varepsilon) F^\varepsilon(x) + \int_{|y| \geq \varepsilon} \hat{\nu}(dy) F^\varepsilon(x + y),$$

with

$$\beta(\varepsilon) = \int_{|y| \geq \varepsilon} (e^y - 1)\hat{\nu}(dy),$$

$$\alpha(\varepsilon) = \int_{|y| \geq \varepsilon} \hat{\nu}(dy).$$

The PIDE in (2.18) can be solved by the same numerical scheme as in the finite activity case. We apply this finite difference method for comparing with our FST method. For alternative finite difference methods, especially those designed to address specific Lévy processes, such as VG and CGMY, we refer to Hirsa and Madan (2004), Forsyth *et al.* (2007), and references therein.

We now provide some numerical results to illustrate the application of the pricing methods discussed above. In Table 2.2, we summarize the ESO costs for different vesting periods $t_v = 0, 2, 4$. As a numerical check, we compare with the ESO costs computed from a finite difference method (see Section 2.3.1), and observe that the two numerical methods return very close values.

Figure 2.2 illustrates how the optimal exercise boundary changes with respect to job termination intensity λ and stock price jump intensity α. As λ increases from 0.1 to 0.3, the optimal exercise boundary is lowered. As the stock price jump intensity increases, the optimal exercise boundary moves upward. Also, we remark that in all cases the exercise boundary is decreasing in time t.

Table 2.2.   ESO cost comparison.

Model	$t_v = 0$		$t_v = 2$		$t_v = 4$	
	FST	FDM	FST	FDM	FST	FDM
GBM	1.3736	1.3730	1.3822	1.3816	1.2365	1.2360
Merton	1.4820	1.4803	1.4899	1.4887	1.3313	1.3306
Kou	1.4566	1.4558	1.4648	1.4646	1.3091	1.3104
VG	1.5584	1.5595	1.5816	1.5811	1.4131	1.4139
CGMY	1.8409	1.8411	1.8532	1.8535	1.6484	1.6490

For each vesting period ($t_v = 0, 2, 4$), the three columns contain ESO costs computed, respectively, by FSTC, FSTG, and the finite difference method. Common parameters: $S_0 = K = 10, r = 0.05, q = 0.04, \lambda = 0.2, \tilde{\lambda} = 0.1, T = 8$. In the *GBM* model, $\sigma = 0.2$. In the Merton model, $\sigma = 0.2, \alpha = 3, \tilde{\mu} = 0.02, \tilde{\sigma} = 0.045$. In the Kou model, $p = 0.5, \sigma = 0.2, \alpha = 3, \eta_+ = 50, \eta_- = 25$. In the Variance Gamma model, $\tilde{\mu} = -0.22, \tilde{\sigma} = 0.2, \kappa = 0.5$. In the CGMY model, $C = 1.1, G = 10, M = 10, Y = 0.6$. The grid sizes for FST methods are the same, with $x_{\max} = 6, M = 2048, N = 32768$.

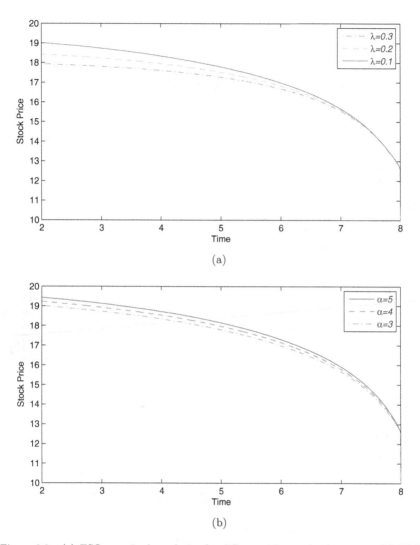

Figure 2.2. (a) ESO exercise boundaries for different job termination rates. (b) ESO exercise boundaries for different stock price jump intensities. This example is based on the Kou model with parameters: $S_0 = K = 10, r = 0.05, p = 0.5, \sigma = 0.2, q = 0.04, \eta_+ = 50, \eta_- = 25, \tilde{\lambda} = 0.1, T = 8$.

The cost impact of job termination intensity and vesting period is demonstrated in Figure 2.3. As suggested by Proposition 2.1, a higher post-vesting job termination intensity reduces the ESO cost. Also, when the post-vesting and pre-vesting job termination rates are the same, the

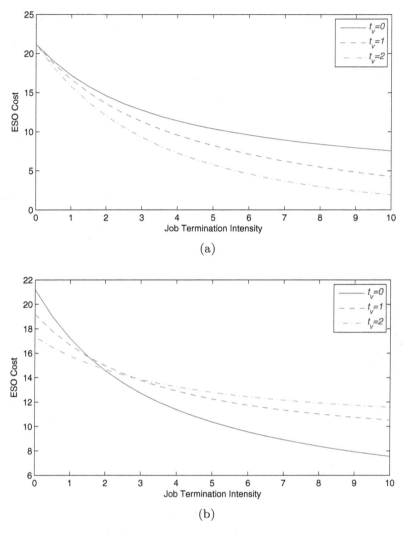

Figure 2.3. (a) The ESO cost decreases as vesting period t_v lengthens or as post-vesting job termination rate λ increases. (b) With $\lambda = 0.2$ and $\tilde{\lambda} = 0.1$, longer vesting can increase the ESO cost. This example is based on the Kou model with parameters: $S_0 = K = 10, r = 0.05, p = 0.5, \sigma = 0.2, q = 0.04, \eta_+ = 50, \eta_- = 25, T = 8$.

ESO cost decreases as vesting period lengthens (see Figure 2.3(a)). However, if the post-vesting job termination rate ($\lambda = 0.2$) is higher than the pre-vesting rate ($\tilde{\lambda} = 0.1$), then it is possible that the ESO can first increase with vesting period.

Remark 2.3. The model proposed by Cvitanic *et al.* (2008) assumes that the ESO holder will voluntarily exercise as soon as the log-normal stock price reaches an upper exogenous barrier. In addition, they also incorporate a vesting period and constant job termination intensity. Our current framework can also be adapted to their model. Precisely, one can numerically solve the PIDE

$$(-\partial_t + \hat{\mathscr{L}})C + (r + \lambda)C - \lambda(S_0 e^x - K)^+ = 0,$$

with the modified boundary condition

$$C(t, x) - C(t, L(t)) = 0,$$

for $(t, x) \in (t_v, T) \times (\log(L(t)), +\infty)$, and terminal condition

$$C(T, x) = (S_0 e^x - K)^+,$$

for $x \in (\log(L(t)), +\infty)$. Here, the function $L(\cdot)$ is a given exponentially decaying barrier. An ESO cost comparison is provided in Table 2.3.

In Table 2.3, the barrier ESO corresponds to Case D in Cvitanic *et al.* (2008), i.e. the optimal exercise boundary is an exponentially decaying curve: $L(t) = Le^{at}$, where $a < 0$. Accordingly, we can see: (1) The ESO cost in Cvitanic *et al.* (2008) is always underestimated if the ESO holder is allowed to exercise the ESO after the vesting period, because the exogenous exercise boundary is not generally the real optimal exercise boundary for the ESO holder. (2) In Cvitanic *et al.* (2008), as L increases, which implies that the ESO holder is unlikely to exercise the ESO according to exogenous exercise boundary, the ESO cost gets closer to the European option value. This case is also discussed in Carr and Linetsky (2000). (3) When $q = 0$,

Table 2.3. ESO cost comparison.

	$q = 0$			$q = 0.04$		
	Barrier	European	American	Barrier	European	American
L=125	22.7792	37.5435	37.5435	15.4209	16.5753	18.2484
L=150	26.8375	37.5435	37.5435	17.4808	16.5753	18.2484
L=9999	37.5450	37.5435	37.5435	16.5751	16.5753	18.2484

Under the GBM model, the *Barrier ESO* assumes exercise at an exogenous decaying boundary, $L(t) = L \cdot \exp(at)$ for $t_v \le t \le T$ with $a = -0.02$, as presented in (Cvitanic *et al.*, 2008, Table 2). In the zero dividend ($q = 0$) case, the *European* and *American* ESO costs coincide, and they dominate *Barrier ESO* cost. Other common parameters: $S_0 = K = 100, r = 0.05, \sigma = 0.2, \lambda = 0.04, \tilde{\lambda} = 0.04, t_v = 3, T = 10$.

the value of European ESO is equal to the value of American ESO, and when $q > 0$, the value of European ESO is less than the value of American ESO. In general, our algorithm can also be modified to adapt other appropriate payoff at job termination. In the special case with zero payoff at job termination, the ESO can be interpreted as being forfeited at the time of departure. Alternatively, this can be considered as an American call option with default risk and zero recovery.

2.4. Stochastic Job Termination Intensity

As an extension to our ESO valuation model, one can randomize the job termination rate by defining

$$\tau^\lambda = \inf \left\{ t \geq 0 : \int_0^t \lambda(s, X_s)\, ds > E \right\},$$

where $\lambda(t, x)$ is a smooth positive deterministic function and $E \sim \exp(1) \perp \mathbb{F}^X$. This Markovian stochastic intensity for job termination allows for dependence between τ^λ and X while preserving tractability by not increasing the dimension of the PIDVI. In related ESO studies, Carr and Linetsky (2000) and Cvitanic *et al.* (2008) also consider this Markovian intensity approach to model job termination and exogenous exercise, though they do not incorporate optimal voluntary exercise. In particular, Carr and Linetsky (2000) consider the job termination intensity of the form:

$$\lambda(t, X_t) = \lambda_f + \lambda_e \mathbf{1}_{\{S_0 e^{X_t} > K\}}.$$

The second term is to model the early exercise due to the holder's exogenous desire for liquidity, and it is constant if the ESO is in-the-money and zero otherwise.

We assume the job termination intensity functions before and after the vesting period to be affine in log-price, denoted respectively, by $\lambda(t, x) = ax + b$ and $\tilde{\lambda}(t, x) = \tilde{a}x + \tilde{b}$, for some constants a, b, $\tilde{a}$, and $\tilde{b}$. Intuitively, the ESO holder's employment is more at risk when the company stock price is low, so one can let a and $\tilde{a}$ be negative. For implementation, one can select parameters and control the grid size so that the intensity remains positive within the truncated log-price interval $[x_{\min}, x_{\max}]$. The affine intensity assumption is utilized in simplifying the associated inhomogeneous PIDE.

The PIDE for the vested ESO cost in the continuation region is

$$(\partial_t + \hat{\mathscr{L}})C - rC = (ax + b)C + \psi(x), \tag{2.19}$$

where $\psi(x) = (ax+b)(S_0 e^x - K)^+$. Differentiating Eq. (2.19) with respect to x, and applying Fourier transform and (2.12), we obtain an inhomogeneous PDE in t and ω, namely,

$$i\omega\big(\partial_t + (\hat{\Psi}(\omega) - r)\mathscr{F}[C](t,\omega)\big) = \mathscr{F}[aC + (ax+b)C_x](t,\omega) - i\omega\mathscr{F}[\psi](\omega), \tag{2.20}$$

with terminal condition

$$\mathscr{F}[C](T,\omega) = \mathscr{F}[(S_0 e^x - K)^+].$$

Using the following well-known property of Fourier transform:

$$\mathscr{F}[xC_x](t,\omega) = -\mathscr{F}[C](t,\omega) - \omega\partial_\omega\mathscr{F}[C](t,\omega),$$

followed by the substitution

$$\mathscr{F}[C](t,\omega) = e^{\frac{-i}{a}\int_{-\infty}^{\omega}(\hat{\Psi}(s)-r-b)ds}H(t,\omega),$$

we simplify (2.20) to obtain a first-order PDE:

$$\partial_t H(t,\omega) + \frac{a}{i}\partial_\omega H(t,\omega) = -e^{\frac{i}{a}\int_{-\infty}^{\omega}(\hat{\Psi}(s)-r-b)ds}\mathscr{F}[\psi](\omega), \tag{2.21}$$

with terminal condition

$$H(T,\omega) = \mathscr{F}[(S_0 e^x - K)^+](\omega)e^{\frac{i}{a}\int_{-\infty}^{\omega}(\hat{\Psi}(s)-r-b)ds}.$$

Finally, solving (2.21) and unraveling the substitution, the Fourier transform of C can be expressed as

$$\mathscr{F}[C(t_1,x)](\omega) = e^{\frac{-i}{a}\int_{-\infty}^{\omega}(\hat{\Psi}(s)-r-b)ds}\left(\mathscr{F}[C(t_2,x)](\omega)e^{\frac{i}{a}\int_{-\infty}^{\omega+\frac{a}{i}\Delta t}(\hat{\Psi}(s)-r-b)ds}\right.$$

$$\left. + \int_0^{\Delta t} g\left(\omega - \frac{a}{i}(s-\Delta t)\right)ds\right), \tag{2.22}$$

where

$$g(\omega) = e^{\frac{i}{a}\int_{-\infty}^{\omega}(\hat{\Psi}(s)-r-b)ds}\mathscr{F}[\psi](\omega), \quad t_v \le t_1 < t_2 \le T, \quad \Delta t = t_2 - t_1.$$

The Fourier transform (2.22) allows us to compute the values of $C(t,x)$ backward in time, starting from expiration date T. The numerical implementation of (2.22) requires computing the integral $\int_0^{\Delta t} g(\omega - \frac{a}{i}(s-\Delta t))ds$. Within each small time step $[t, t + \Delta t]$, we approximate the integral

$\int_0^{\Delta t} g(\omega - \frac{a}{i}(s - \Delta t))ds$ by summing over a further divided time discretization, namely, $\sum_{k=0}^{n'-1} g(\omega + \frac{ak}{in'}\Delta t)\Delta t/n'$. Therefore, the solution for vested ESO cost in the continuation region is given by

$$C(t_1, x) = \mathscr{F}^{-1}\left[e^{\frac{i}{a}\int_\omega^{\omega + \frac{a}{i}\Delta t}(\hat{\Psi}(s)-r-b)ds}\mathscr{F}[C(t_2,x)]\left(\omega + \frac{a}{i}\Delta t\right)\right.$$

$$\left. + \sum_{k=0}^{n'-1} g\left(\omega + \frac{ak}{in'}\Delta t\right)\frac{\Delta t}{n'}e^{\frac{-i}{a}\int_{-\infty}^\omega (\hat{\Psi}(s)-r-b)ds}\right](x),$$

for $t_v \le t_1 < t_2 \le T$, $x \in \mathbb{R}$. Again, within each iteration, we impose the condition

$$C(t_1, x) = \max\{C(t_1, x), (S_0 e^x - K)^+\}$$

to obtain the American option value.

As for the unvested ESO, we have $\tilde{C}(t_v, x) = C(t_v, x)$ at time t_v, and

$$(\partial_t + \mathscr{L})\tilde{C} - (r + (\tilde{a}x + \tilde{b}))\tilde{C} = 0,$$

for $(t, x) \in [0, t_v) \times \mathbb{R}$. At time $t < t_v$, the unvested ESO cost is computed by

$$\tilde{C}(t, x) = \mathscr{F}^{-1}\left[\mathscr{F}[\tilde{C}(t_v,x)]\left(\omega + \frac{\tilde{a}}{i}(t_v - t)\right)e^{\frac{i}{a}\int_\omega^{\omega + \frac{\tilde{a}}{i}(t_v-t)}(\hat{\Psi}(s)-r-\tilde{b})ds}\right](x).$$

Remark 2.4. Suppose the pre-vesting and post-vesting job termination intensities, λ and $\tilde{\lambda}$, are positive bounded functions of x and t. The Fourier transform of the ESO cost satisfies

$$\partial_t \mathscr{F}[C](t, \omega) + (\hat{\Psi}(\omega) - r)\mathscr{F}[C](t, \omega) - \mathscr{F}[\lambda C](t, \omega) = -\mathscr{F}[\xi](\omega),$$

where

$$\xi(t, x) = \lambda(t, x)(S_0 e^x - K)^+.$$

In order to solve this ODE, one can apply an *explicit* scheme to the term $\mathscr{F}[\lambda C](t, \omega)$, and apply *implicit* scheme to the other terms. Therefore, given the value of $C(t_2, x)$ at time $t_2 > t_1$, we compute the value of $C(t_1, x)$ by

$$C(t_1, x) = \mathscr{F}^{-1}\left[\mathscr{F}[C](t_2, \omega)e^{(\hat{\Psi}(\omega)-r)(t_2-t_1)}\right]$$

$$+ \mathscr{F}^{-1}\left[\frac{\mathscr{F}[\xi](\omega) - \mathscr{F}[\lambda C](t_2, \omega)}{\hat{\Psi}(\omega) - r}(e^{(\hat{\Psi}(\omega)-r)(t_2-t_1)} - 1)\right].$$

Table 2.4. ESO cost comparison under affine job termination intensity.

Model	$t_v = 0$			$t_v = 2$			$t_v = 4$		
	FSTA	FSTG	FDM	FSTA	FSTG	FDM	FSTA	FSTG	FDM
GBM	1.3732	1.3733	1.3729	1.1368	1.1369	1.1364	0.8429	0.8428	0.8429
Merton	1.4817	1.4814	1.4800	1.2261	1.2259	1.2260	0.9085	0.9083	0.9082
Kou	1.4565	1.4562	1.4556	1.2054	1.2052	1.2064	0.8934	0.8933	0.8942
VG	1.5670	1.5669	1.5680	1.3073	1.3069	1.3068	0.9765	0.9754	0.9758
CGMY	1.8402	1.8398	1.8402	1.5249	1.5247	1.5245	1.1299	1.1297	1.1296

For each vesting period ($t_v = 0, 2, 4$), the three columns contain ESO costs computed, respectively, by the two FST methods in Section 2.4 and Remark 2.4 and a finite difference method. The job termination intensities are $\lambda(x) = \tilde{\lambda}(x) = -0.02x + 0.2$, while other parameters are the same as in Table 2.2.

With this, we can compute the vested ESO cost by iterating backward in time and comparing with the payoff from immediate exercise. Finally, we remark that this implicit–explicit algorithm is also applicable when the job termination intensity is constant or affine.

In Table 2.4, we compute the ESO cost with affine pre-vesting and post-vesting job termination rates using the FST method in Section 2.4 and that in Remark 2.4, along with the finite difference method. We observe that ESO costs for different vesting periods from these three different methods are very close.

2.5. Risk Analysis for ESOs

Over the life of an ESO, the option value will fluctuate depending on the company stock price movement. From the firm's perspective, an increase in the ESO value implies a higher expected cost of compensation as compared to the initially reported value. For the purposes of risk management and financial reporting, it is important to consider the probability that the ESO cost will exceed a given level.

In addition, the ESO can be terminated early voluntarily or involuntarily prior to the expiration date. This also motivates the study of the contract termination probability, which can be a tool to calibrate the job termination intensity parameter. Such a calibration would provide a crucial input to the ESO valuation model, and permit the pricing to be consistent with the firm's characteristic. Moreover, it is also interesting to examine the impact of job termination risk on the contract termination probability.

Generally speaking, the job termination rate can differ under $\mathbb{P}$ and $\mathbb{Q}$. However, since ESOs are not traded, market prices are unavailable for inferring the $\mathbb{Q}$ intensity. For this reason and notational simplicity, we assume that the historical and risk-neutral job termination rates are identical.

2.5.1. *Cost exceedance probability*

Let us evaluate at the current time t the *cost exceedance probability*, which is the probability that the ESO cost will exceed a given level ℓ on a fixed future date $\tilde{T}$. To this end, we need to consider three scenarios separately.

Case 1: $t < \tilde{T} \leq t_v$. In this case, the time interval $[t, \tilde{T}]$ lies within the vesting period $[0, t_v]$, where the unvested ESO can be forfeited upon job termination. Therefore, the probability that the ESO value will exceed a pre-specified level $\ell > 0$ at time $\tilde{T}$ is given by $\mathbb{P}_{t,x}\{\tilde{C}(\tilde{T}, X_{\tilde{T}}) > \ell\}$, where $\mathbb{P}_{t,x}$ is the historical probability measure with $X_t = x$. Since the ESO becomes worthless if $\tau^{\tilde{\lambda}}$ arrives before $\tilde{T}$, we have

$$\mathbb{P}_{t,x}\{\tilde{C}(\tilde{T}, X_{\tilde{T}}) > \ell\} = \mathbb{P}_{t,x}\{\tilde{C}(\tilde{T}, X_{\tilde{T}}) > \ell, \tau^{\tilde{\lambda}} \geq \tilde{T}\}$$

$$+ \mathbb{P}_{t,x}\{\tilde{C}(\tilde{T}, X_{\tilde{T}}) > \ell, \tau^{\tilde{\lambda}} < \tilde{T}\}$$

$$= \mathbb{P}_{t,x}\{\tilde{C}(\tilde{T}, X_{\tilde{T}}) > \ell \,|\, \tau^{\tilde{\lambda}} \geq \tilde{T}\}\mathbb{P}_{t,x}\{\tau^{\tilde{\lambda}} \geq \tilde{T}\}. \quad (2.23)$$

In (2.23), we notice that

$$\mathbb{P}_{t,x}\{\tau^{\tilde{\lambda}} \geq \tilde{T}\} = e^{-\tilde{\lambda}(\tilde{T}-t)}$$

since $\tau^{\tilde{\lambda}} \sim \exp(\tilde{\lambda})$. Hence, the evaluation of $\mathbb{P}_{t,x}\{\tilde{C}(\tilde{T}, X_{\tilde{T}}) > \ell\}$ amounts to computing the conditional probability

$$\mathbb{P}_{t,x}\{\tilde{C}(\tilde{T}, X_{\tilde{T}}) > \ell \,|\, \tau^{\tilde{\lambda}} \geq \tilde{T}\}.$$

Since $\tilde{C}(\tilde{T}, x)$ is increasing in x, we can find the critical log-price $\bar{x}$ such that $\tilde{C}(\tilde{T}, \bar{x}) = \ell$ and write

$$p(t,x) := \mathbb{P}_{t,x}\{\tilde{C}(\tilde{T}, X_{\tilde{T}}) > \ell \,|\, \tau^{\tilde{\lambda}} \geq \tilde{T}\} = \mathbb{P}_{t,x}\{X_{\tilde{T}} > \bar{x} \,|\, \tau^{\tilde{\lambda}} \geq \tilde{T}\}. \quad (2.24)$$

The probability function $p(t, x)$ satisfies the PIDE problem

$$(\partial_t + \mathscr{L})p = 0, \qquad (t, x) \in [0, \tilde{T}] \times \mathbb{R}, \qquad (2.25)$$

$$p(\tilde{T}, x) = \mathbf{1}_{\{x > \bar{x}\}}, \quad x \in \mathbb{R},$$

where $\mathscr{L}$ is the infinitesimal generator of X under $\mathbb{P}$. We observe that the PIDE (2.25) for $p(t, x)$ is very similar to (2.13) without the inhomogeneous term. Applying the Fourier transform arguments from Section 2.3 yields that

$$p(t, x) = \mathscr{F}^{-1}[\mathscr{F}[\mathbf{1}_{\{x > \bar{x}\}}](\omega)e^{\Psi(\omega)(\tilde{T}-t)}](x), \quad t \leq \tilde{T} \leq t_v. \tag{2.26}$$

The Fourier transform and its inversion in (2.26) can be numerically evaluated by the FFT algorithm. In contrast to the ESO cost, this probability does not involve early exercise and can be computed in one time step.

Remark 2.5. An equivalent way to obtain (2.26) is to adapt the convolution method used by Lord *et al.* (2008). To verify this, we express (2.24) as

$$p(t, x) = \int_{-\infty}^{\infty} \mathbf{1}_{\{z > \bar{x}\}} f_{X_{\tilde{T}} \mid X_t}(z)dz = \int_{-\infty}^{+\infty} \mathbf{1}_{\{x+y > \bar{x}\}} f_{X_{\tilde{T}-t}}(y)dy, \tag{2.27}$$

where $f_{X_{\tilde{T}} \mid X_t}(z)$ of $X_{\tilde{T}}$ is the conditional probability distribution function given $X_t = x$. Then, we express (2.27) in terms of Fourier transform:

$$\begin{aligned}
\mathscr{F}[p](t, \omega) &= \int_{-\infty}^{\infty} e^{-i\omega x} \left(\int_{-\infty}^{+\infty} \mathbf{1}_{\{x+y > \bar{x}\}} f_{X_{\tilde{T}-t}}(y)dy \right) dx \\
&= \int_{-\infty}^{\infty} e^{-i\omega(u-y)} \left(\int_{-\infty}^{+\infty} \mathbf{1}_{\{u > \bar{x}\}} f_{X_{\tilde{T}-t}}(y)dy \right) du \quad (u = x+y) \\
&= \int_{-\infty}^{\infty} e^{-i\omega u} \mathbf{1}_{\{u > \bar{x}\}} du \int_{-\infty}^{+\infty} e^{i\omega y} f_{X_{\tilde{T}-t}}(y)dy \\
&= \mathscr{F}[\mathbf{1}_{\{x > \bar{x}\}}](\omega)e^{\Psi(\omega)(\tilde{T}-t)}.
\end{aligned}$$

Lastly, applying inverse Fourier transform to the last equation yields (2.26), and hence the equivalence.

A slightly different approach is to adapt the Fourier transform method by Carr and Madan (1999). To illustrate, we assume without loss of generality that $X_t = 0$ at a fixed time $t < \tilde{T}$, and define

$$\begin{aligned}
\tilde{p}(t, z) &:= \mathbb{P}_{t,0}\{X_{\tilde{T}} > z \mid \tau^{\hat{\lambda}} \geq \tilde{T}\} \\
&= \int_z^{\infty} f_{X_{\tilde{T}-t}}(y)dy,
\end{aligned} \tag{2.28}$$

where $f_{X_{\tilde{T}-t}}$ is the probability density function of $X_{\tilde{T}-t}$ with $X_0 = 0$. The value z can be considered as the difference between the upper threshold $\bar{x}$ and the current value of X.

Applying Fourier transform to both sides of (2.28), we get

$$\mathscr{F}[\tilde{p}](t,\omega) = \int_{-\infty}^{\infty} e^{-i\omega z} \left(\int_{z}^{\infty} f_{X_{\tilde{T}-t}}(y) dy \right) dz$$

$$= \int_{-\infty}^{\infty} f_{X_{\tilde{T}-t}}(y) \left(\int_{-\infty}^{y} e^{-i\omega z} dz \right) dy.$$

We notice that the inner integral $\int_{-\infty}^{y} e^{-i\omega z} dz = \frac{e^{-i\omega z}}{-i\omega}\Big|_{-\infty}^{y}$ does not converge, so we incorporate a damping factor e^{az}, for $a > 0$, and consider $\tilde{p}_a(t,z) = e^{az}\tilde{p}(t,z)$. Then, the corresponding Fourier transform is given by

$$\mathscr{F}[\tilde{p}_a](t,\omega) = \int_{-\infty}^{\infty} f_{X_{\tilde{T}-t}}(y) \int_{-\infty}^{y} e^{(a-i\omega)z} dz dy$$

$$= \frac{1}{a - i\omega} \phi_{\tilde{T}-t}(-\omega - ia), \qquad (2.29)$$

where $\phi_{\tilde{T}-t}$ is the characteristic function of $X_{\tilde{T}-t}$. In turn, inverse Fourier transform to (2.29) yields

$$\tilde{p}(t,z) = \frac{e^{-az}}{2\pi} \int_{-\infty}^{\infty} \frac{e^{iz\omega} \phi_{\tilde{T}-t}(-\omega - ia)}{a - i\omega} d\omega$$

$$= \frac{e^{-az}}{\pi} \int_{0}^{\infty} \frac{e^{i\omega z} \phi_{\tilde{T}-t}(-\omega - ia)}{a - i\omega} d\omega, \qquad (2.30)$$

where we have used the fact that the Fourier transform of the real function $\tilde{p}(t,z)$ is even in its real part and odd in its imaginary part. Lastly, the integral in (2.30) is approximated by the FFT algorithm. We remark that $\tilde{p}(t,z)$ is independent of the choice of a, and we choose $a \in [1.5, 2.0]$ for numerical implementation.

In Table 2.5, we present the numerical results for the ESO cost exceedance probabilities under different thresholds ℓ. The FST–FST method first computes the ESO cost vector via FST (see (2.16)) which gives the critical value $\bar{x}$ (see (2.24)). In the second step, it applies FST to solve for the exceedance probability as shown in (2.26). The FFT–FST method differs from the FST–FST method in its second step where FFT (see (2.30)) is used to compute the probability. For the GBM, Merton, and Kou models, the reference values are given by closed-form formulas (see Section 2.8.3). The numerical results show that both Fourier transform methods are very accurate.

Table 2.5. Cost exceedance probability in case 1.

Model	$\ell = 1.1\, \tilde{C}(0,0)$ Reference value	FST–FST	FFT–FST	$\ell = 1.2\, \tilde{C}(0,0)$ Reference value	FST–FST	FFT–FST
GBM	0.2534	0.2532	0.2535	0.0868	0.0869	0.0869
Merton	0.2607	0.2608	0.2607	0.0943	0.0942	0.0943
Kou	0.2431	0.2430	0.2431	0.0799	0.0797	0.0798

Here, $t = 0, \tilde{T} = 10/252, t_v = 2, T = 8$ and other parameters are the same as in Table 2.2.

Case 2: $t_v < t < \tilde{T} \leq T$. After the vesting period, the employee intends to exercise at any $\tau^* \leq T$, but may be forced to exercise at τ^λ. The probability of interest is

$$\hat{p}(t,x) := \mathbb{P}_{t,x}\{C(\tilde{\tau}^* \wedge \tau^\lambda, X_{\tilde{\tau}^* \wedge \tau^\lambda}) \geq \ell\},$$

with $\tilde{\tau}^* = \tau^* \wedge \tilde{T}$. To compute this, we first identify the critical log-price $\bar{x}(t)$, such that $C(t, \bar{x}(t)) = \ell$, for $t \in [0, \tilde{T}]$. In turn, we write down the corresponding inhomogeneous PIDE

$$(\partial_t + \mathscr{L})\hat{p} - \lambda\hat{p} + \lambda \mathbf{1}_{\{x \geq \bar{x}(t)\}} = 0, \tag{2.31}$$

for $(t,x) \in (t_v, \tilde{T}) \times \mathbb{R}$. The boundary and terminal conditions depend on the relative positions of the critical log-price $\bar{x}(t)$ and optimal exercise boundary $x^*(t) := \log(s^*(t)/S_0)$. Precisely, if $\bar{x}(t) \leq x^*(t)$, then we set

$$\hat{p}(t,x) = 1, \text{ for } x \geq x^*(t).$$

If $\bar{x}(t) > x^*(t)$, we set

$$\hat{p}(t,x) = 1, \text{ for } x \geq \bar{x}(t),$$

and

$$\hat{p}(t,x) = 0, \text{ for } x^*(t) < \bar{x}(t).$$

As for the terminal condition, if $\bar{x}(\tilde{T}) \leq K$, then we set

$$\hat{p}(\tilde{T}, x) = 1, \text{ for } x \geq K.$$

If $\bar{x}(\tilde{T}) > K$, then we have

$$\hat{p}(t,x) = 1, \text{ for } x \geq \bar{x}(t),$$

and

$$\hat{p}(t, x) = 0, \text{ for } K \leq x < \bar{x}(t).$$

For numerical implementation, we first solve for the ESO values $C(t, x)$, which are then used to determine the critical log-price $\bar{x}(t)$, and the associated optimal exercise boundary $s^*(t)$ that gives $x^*(t)$. With these, we apply Fourier transform implicit–explicit method, as discussed in Section 2.4, to the PIDE problem (2.31). Iterating backward in time, we have for each time step

$$\hat{p}(t_{m-1}, x) = \mathscr{F}^{-1} \left[\mathscr{F}[\hat{p}(t_m, x)](\omega) e^{(\Psi(\omega) - \lambda)(t_m - t_{m-1})} \right.$$
$$\left. + \frac{\mathscr{F}[\mathbf{1}_{\{x \geq \bar{x}(t_{m-1})\}}](\omega)}{\Psi(\omega) - \lambda} \left(e^{(\Psi(\omega) - \lambda)(t_m - t_{m-1})} - 1 \right) \right] (x),$$

for $m = M, \ldots, 1, 0$, along with the boundary conditions. In Figure 2.4, the cost exceedance probability rises as the horizon $\tilde{T}$ lengthens. The probability also increases as the job termination intensity λ decreases.

Case 3: $t \leq t_v < \tilde{T} \leq T$. This scenario is a combination of case 1 and case 2. The ESO is forfeited if $\tau^\lambda < t_v$, as in case 1. However, if that does not happen, then case 2 applies after the vesting. Consequently, we

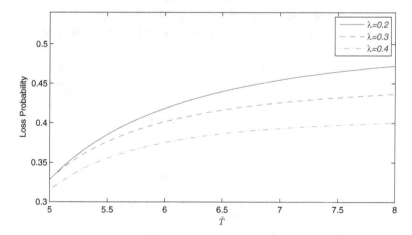

Figure 2.4. ESO cost exceedance probability in case 2 increases with $\tilde{T}$, and decreases with job termination rate λ. This example is based on the Kou model with common parameters: $S_4 = K = 10, r = 0.05, p = 0.5, q = 0.04, \mu = 0.08, \tilde{\lambda} = 0.1, T = 8, t = 4, \sigma = 0.2, \alpha = 3, \eta_+ = 50, \eta_- = 25$.

consider the following probability for ESO cost exceedance

$$\bar{p}(t, x) := \mathbb{E}^{\mathbb{P}}_{t,x}\{\mathbf{1}_{\{\tau^{\tilde{\lambda}} \geq t_v\}}\hat{p}(t_v, X_{t_v})\}, \quad 0 \leq t \leq t_v,$$

if the job termination has not occurred by time t. The corresponding PIDE problem is

$$(\partial_t + \mathscr{L})\bar{p} - \tilde{\lambda}\bar{p} = 0, \qquad (t, x) \in [0, t_v) \times \mathbb{R},$$

$$\bar{p}(t_v, x) = \hat{p}(t_v, x), \qquad x \in \mathbb{R}.$$

The solution via Fourier transform is given by

$$\bar{p}(t_v, x) = \hat{p}(t_v, x),$$

$$\bar{p}(t, x) = \mathscr{F}^{-1}\big[\mathscr{F}[\hat{p}(t_v, x)](\omega)e^{(\Psi(\omega)-\tilde{\lambda})(t_v-t)}\big](x), \quad \text{for } t \leq t_v. \quad (2.32)$$

Here, the probability $\hat{p}(t_v, x)$ from case 2 is used as the input, and then $\bar{p}(t, x)$ can be computed directly without recursion by (2.32) for any time $t \leq t_v$.

2.5.2. *Contract termination probability*

The ESO contract can be terminated either due to job termination before vesting, or voluntary/forced exercise after vesting. We now study the ESO contract termination probability during a given time interval $[t, \tilde{T}]$. Again, we consider three different scenarios.

Case 1: $t < \tilde{T} \leq t_v$. During the vesting period, the contract termination is totally due to job termination before t_v, of which the probability is simply $1 - e^{-\tilde{\lambda}(\tilde{T}-t)}$.

Case 2: $t_v \leq t < \tilde{T} \leq T$. After vesting, contract termination can arise from either involuntary exercise due to job termination, or the holder's voluntary exercise. For calculation purpose, we divide the contract termination probability into two parts according to whether job termination occurs before or after $\tilde{T}$.

First, we consider the scenario where job termination does not occur during $[t, \tilde{T}]$ and the ESO holder voluntarily exercises the ESO. This corresponds to the probability

$$\mathbb{P}_{t,x}\{\tau^* \leq \tilde{T}, \tau^{\lambda} > \tilde{T}\} = \mathbb{P}_{t,x}\{\tau^* \leq \tilde{T}\}e^{-\lambda(\tilde{T}-t)}, \quad (2.33)$$

where τ^* is the holder's optimal exercise time. To evaluate (2.33), we solve for $\hat{h}(t, x) := \mathbb{P}_{t,x}\{\tau^* \leq \tilde{T}\}$ from the PIDE

$$(\partial_t + \mathscr{L})\hat{h} = 0,$$

for $(t, x) \in (t_v, \tilde{T}) \times \mathbb{R}$, with the boundary condition

$$\hat{h}(t, x) = 1, \quad \text{for } x > x^*(t),$$

and terminal condition

$$\hat{h}(\tilde{T}, x) = 1_{\{x \geq x^*(\tilde{T})\}},$$

where

$$x^*(t) := \log(s^*(t)/S_0).$$

For numerical solution, we apply recursively

$$\begin{cases} \hat{h}(t_{m-1}, x) = \mathscr{F}^{-1}[\mathscr{F}[\hat{h}(t_m, x)](\omega)e^{\Psi(\omega)(t_m - t_{m-1})}](x), & x \leq x^*(t), \\ \hat{h}(t_{m-1}, x) = 1, & x > x^*(t). \end{cases}$$

The other scenario is when job termination arrives before $\tilde{T}$. Consequently, the total contract termination probability $h(t, x)$ is the sum

$$h(t, x) := e^{-\lambda(\tilde{T}-t)}\hat{h}(t, x) + 1 - e^{-\lambda(\tilde{T}-t)}. \tag{2.34}$$

From this expression, we observe that the contract termination probability is increasing with job termination intensity λ since the optimal exercise boundary is decreasing with λ, and so is $(1 - \hat{h}(t, x))$.

Alternatively, we look at the employee's voluntary exercise probability

$$h^v(t, x) := \mathbb{P}_{t,x}\{\tau^* < \tau^\lambda \wedge \tilde{T}\}.$$

This probability satisfies the PIDE

$$(\partial_t + \mathscr{L})h^v - \lambda h^v = 0, \tag{2.35}$$

for $(t, x) \in (t_v, \tilde{T}) \times \mathbb{R}$, with the boundary condition

$$h^v(t, x) = 1, \text{ for } x > x^*(t),$$

and terminal condition

$$h^v(\tilde{T}, x) = 1_{\{x \geq x^*(\tilde{T})\}},$$

where

$$x^*(t) := \log(s^*(t)/S_0).$$

The numerical solution is found from backward iteration with

$$
\begin{cases}
h^v(t_{m-1}, x) = \mathscr{F}^{-1}\big[\mathscr{F}[h^v(t_m, x)](\omega)e^{(\Psi(\omega)-\lambda)(t_m-t_{m-1})}\big](x), & x \le x^*(t), \\
h^v(t_{m-1}, x) = 1, & x > x^*(t),
\end{cases}
$$

for $m = M, \ldots, 1, 0$.

Figure 2.5 illustrates the contract termination probability on top of the voluntary exercise probability. From PIDE (2.35), we observe two competing factors governing the effect of job termination intensity λ on the voluntary exercise probability. On the one hand, a higher job termination intensity λ implies a lower optimal exercise boundary, which in turn increases the voluntary exercise probability. On the other hand, a higher job termination intensity will more likely force early exercise before the stock price reaching the holder's optimal exercise boundary. This reduces the voluntary exercise probability. In Figure 2.5(a), we see that voluntary exercise probability is decreasing with post-vesting job termination intensity λ, so in this case the job termination effect outweighs the effect of lowered exercise boundary, and therefore, reduces the probability of voluntary exercise. Also, in Figure 2.5(b), the contract termination probability is increasing with job termination intensity λ, as expected.

Case 3: $t \le t_v < \tilde{T} \le T$. This scenario is a combination of cases 1 and 2 above. The contract termination can occur before or after vesting. During $[t, t_v]$, only job termination can cancel the contract. If there is no job termination before t_v, then the contract termination resembles that in case 2. Therefore, the contract termination probability is the sum

$$
1 - e^{-\tilde{\lambda}(t_v-t)} + \underbrace{\mathbb{E}_{t,x}^{\mathbb{P}}\{h(t_v, X_{t_v})\mathbf{1}_{\{\tau^{\tilde{\lambda}} \ge t_v\}}\}}_{=:\tilde{h}(t,x)},
$$

where $h(t, x)$ is given in (2.34). Hence, $\tilde{h}(t, x)$ satisfies, for $(t, x) \in [0, t_v) \times \mathbb{R}$, the PIDE

$$
(\partial_t + \mathscr{L})\tilde{h} - \tilde{\lambda}\tilde{h} = 0.
$$

At time t_v, we set $\tilde{h}(t_v, x) = h(t_v, x)$, where $h(t_v, x)$ is computed from case 2. Again, the FST method discussed in Section 2.3 can be applied to solve for $\tilde{h}(t, x)$. At any time $t < t_v$, the probability can be computed in one step (without time iteration) via

$$
\tilde{h}(t, x) = \mathscr{F}^{-1}\big[\mathscr{F}[h(t_v, x)](\omega)e^{(\Psi(\omega)-\tilde{\lambda})(t_v-t)}\big](x).
$$

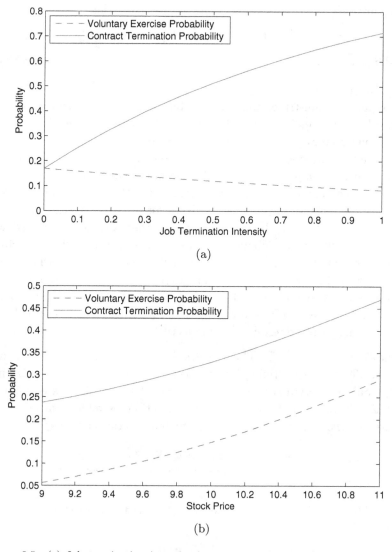

Figure 2.5. (a) Job termination intensity increases contract termination probability, but decreases voluntary exercise probability. (b) Stock price increases both contract termination probability and voluntary exercise probability with $\tilde{\lambda} = 0.1$ and $\lambda = 0.2$. This example is based on the GBM model with common parameters: $S_6 = 10, K = 9, r = 0.05, \sigma = 0.2, q = 0.04, \mu = 0.08, t_v = 2, T = 8, t = 6, \tilde{T} = 7$.

2.6. Perpetual ESO with Closed-Form Solution

We now discuss the valuation of a perpetual ESO under the GBM model. In contrast to the valuation under the general Lévy framework, the perpetual ESO admits a closed-form solution, and thus represents a highly tractable alternative. We first consider a vested perpetual ESO, whose value can be expressed in terms of an optimal stopping problem, namely,

$$V(s) = \sup_{\tau \in \mathscr{T}_{0,\infty}} \mathbb{E}^{\mathbb{Q}} \left\{ e^{-(r+\lambda)\tau}(S_\tau - K)^+ + \int_0^\tau e^{-(r+\lambda)u} \lambda (S_u - K)^- du \mid S_0 = s \right\},$$

where S is the real stock price. The associated variational inequality is

$$\min\{-\hat{\mathscr{L}}V + (r+\lambda)V - \lambda(s-K)^+, \; V(s) - (s-K)^+\} = 0, \quad s \in \mathbb{R}_+.$$
$$(2.36)$$

A similar inhomogeneous variational inequality has been derived and solved for the problem of pricing American puts with maturity randomization (Canadization) introduced by Carr (1998). Indeed, the perpetual ESO can be considered as an American call whose maturity is an exponential random variable. For a mathematical analysis on the Canadization of American options with a Lévy underlying, we refer to Kyprianou and Pistorius (2003). Next, we present the closed-form solution for this ESO valuation problem.

Proposition 2.6. *Under the GBM model, the value of a vested perpetual ESO is given by*

$$V(s) = \begin{cases} Ds^{\gamma_+} & \text{if } s < K, \\ As^{\gamma_+} + Bs^{\gamma_-} + \dfrac{\lambda}{\lambda+q}s - \dfrac{\lambda}{r+\lambda}K & \text{if } K \le s < s^*, \\ s - K & \text{if } s \ge s^*, \end{cases} \quad (2.37)$$

where

$$\gamma_\pm = \frac{(q - r + \frac{\sigma^2}{2}) \pm \sqrt{(q - r + \frac{\sigma^2}{2})^2 + 2(r+\lambda)\sigma^2}}{\sigma^2}, \quad (2.38)$$

$$B = \frac{\lambda(1 - \gamma_+)}{\gamma_-(\gamma_+ - \gamma_-)(\lambda+q)} K^{1-\gamma_-}, \quad (2.39)$$

$$A = \frac{q}{(\lambda+q)\gamma_+}(s^*)^{1-\gamma_+} - \frac{\gamma_-}{\gamma_+}B(s^*)^{\gamma_- - \gamma_+}, \quad (2.40)$$

$$D = A + BK^{\gamma_- - \gamma_+} + \frac{\lambda(r-q)}{(\lambda+q)(\lambda+r)}K^{1-\gamma_+}.$$

The optimal exercise threshold $s^* \in (K, \infty)$ is uniquely determined from

$$B\left(1 - \frac{\gamma_-}{\gamma_+}\right)(s^*)^{\gamma_-} - \left(1 - \frac{1}{\gamma_+}\right)\left(\frac{q}{\lambda + q}\right)s^* + \frac{r}{r + \lambda}K = 0.$$

A number of interesting observations can be drawn from Proposition 2.6. First, in the case without job termination ($\lambda = 0$), we have $B = 0$ and $A = D$. This implies that the perpetual ESO reduces to an ordinary American call with the well-known price formula

$$V(s) = \begin{cases} Ds^{\gamma_+} & \text{if } s < s^*, \\ s - K & \text{if } s \geq s^*, \end{cases}$$

where s^* is the optimal exercise threshold given by

$$s^* = \frac{\gamma_+}{1 - \gamma_+}K. \tag{2.41}$$

This result dates back to Samuelson (1965) and McKean (1965), and is also used in the real option literature (see McDonald and Siegel, 1986; Dixit, 1994, among others).

Furthermore, if both λ and q are zero, then we see from (2.38) and (2.41) that $s^* = \infty$. An infinite exercise threshold means that it is optimal for the option holder to never exercise the option. This result is expected and intuitive since the ESO now resembles an ordinary American call without dividend.

When a vesting period of t_v years is imposed, we compute the ESO cost at time t from the conditional expectation

$$\tilde{V}(t, s) = \mathbb{E}^{\mathbb{Q}}\{e^{-(r+\lambda)(t_v - t)}V(S_{t_v}) \mid S_t = s\}. \tag{2.42}$$

By substituting the vested ESO cost function $V(s)$ into (2.42), and recognizing that $S_{t_v}^a$, for any $a \in \mathbb{R}$, is lognormal, we can directly compute the unvested ESO cost.

Corollary 2.7. *Under the GBM model, the unvested perpetual ESO cost admits the formula*

$$\tilde{V}(t, s) = e^{-(r+\lambda)(t_v - t)}\left\{Ds^{\gamma_+}e^{(m_1 + \frac{\sigma_1^2}{2})}\bar{\Phi}\left(\frac{\gamma_+ \ln(s/K) + m_1 + \sigma_1^2}{\sigma_1}\right)\right.$$

$$+ As^{\gamma_+}e^{(m_1 + \frac{\sigma_1^2}{2})}\left[\Phi\left(\frac{\gamma_+ \ln(s/K) + m_1 + \sigma_1^2}{\sigma_1}\right)\right.$$

$$\left.\left. - \Phi\left(\frac{\gamma_+ \ln(s/s^*) + m_1 + \sigma_1^2}{\sigma_1}\right)\right]\right]$$

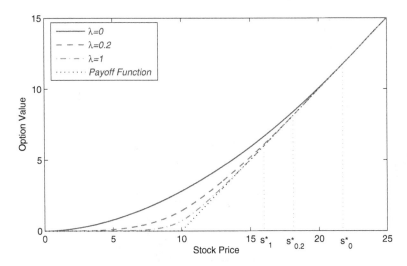

Figure 2.6. As job termination rate increases ($\lambda \in \{0, 0.2, 1\}$), the vested ESO cost decreases and the corresponding optimal exercise threshold is lowered ($s_0^* > s_{0.2}^* > s_1^*$). Parameters: $K = 10, r = 0.05, \sigma = 0.2, q = 0.04$.

$$+ Bs^{\gamma_-} e^{(m_2 + \frac{\sigma_2^2}{2})} \left[\Phi\left(\frac{\gamma_- \ln(s/s^*) + m_2 + \sigma_2^2}{\sigma_2} \right) \right.$$

$$\left. - \Phi\left(\frac{\gamma_- \ln(s/K) + m_2 + \sigma_2^2}{\sigma_2} \right) \right]$$

$$+ s\left(1 + \frac{\lambda}{\lambda + q}\right) e^{(m_3 + \frac{\sigma_3^2}{2})} \Phi\left(\frac{\ln(s/K) + m_3 + \sigma_3^2}{\sigma_3} \right)$$

$$- \left(1 + \frac{\lambda}{r + \lambda}\right) K \Phi\left(\frac{\ln(s/K) + m_3 + \sigma_3^2}{\sigma_3} \right) \Bigg\},$$

where $\bar{\Phi}$ is the standard normal complementary cumulative distribution function and

$$m_1 = \left(r - \frac{\sigma^2}{2}\right)(t_v - t)\,\gamma_+, \quad \sigma_1 = \sigma\sqrt{t_v - t}\,\gamma_+,$$

$$m_2 = \left(r - \frac{\sigma^2}{2}\right)(t_v - t)\,\gamma_-, \quad \sigma_2 = -\sigma\sqrt{t_v - t}\,\gamma_-,$$

$$m_3 = \left(r - \frac{\sigma^2}{2}\right)(t_v - t), \quad \sigma_3 = \sigma\sqrt{t_v - t}.$$

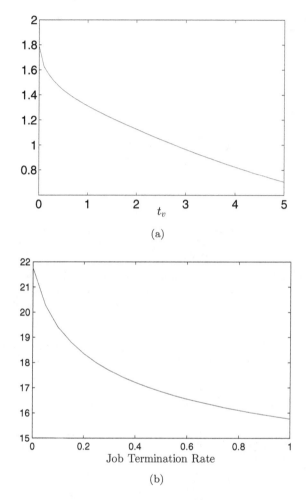

Figure 2.7. The perpetual ESO cost decreases as (a) vesting period increases and (b) as job termination rate increases. Parameters: $S_0 = K = 10, r = 0.05, \sigma = 0.2, q = 0.04, t = 0, t_v = 0$.

In contrast to its vested counterpart, the unvested perpetual ESO cost is time-dependent. In Figure 2.7(a), we observe that the perpetual ESO cost decreases as the vesting period increases. A higher job termination rate not only rapidly decreases the perpetual ESO cost (see Figure 2.6) but also the optimal exercise threshold s^* significantly (see Figure 2.7(b)).

2.7. Conclusion

We have provided the analytical and numerical studies for the valuation and risk analysis of ESOs under Lévy price dynamics. Our results are useful for reporting ESO cost, as mandated by regulators, and for understanding holder's exercise behavior. In particular, we show job termination risk has a direct effect on the ESO holder's exercise timing, which in turn affects the ESO cost as well as contract termination probability.

For future research, modeling exercises and valuation for large ESO portfolios are both practical and challenging. As we have examined the effect of jumps in the company stock price on exercise timing, it would also be useful to investigate the exercise behaviors around earnings announcements and other significant corporate events when large price movements are often observed. Lastly, our valuation framework can also be applied to pricing American options with liquidity, default, or other event risks. This would require an appropriate modification of the payoff at the exogenous termination time.

2.8. Appendix

2.8.1. *Proof of proposition* 2.1

Let $C_1(t, x)$ and $C_2(t, x)$ be the vested ESO cost associated with λ_1 and λ_2, respectively, and assume $\lambda_1 < \lambda_2$. We define an operator $\mathcal{M}$ by

$$\mathcal{M}_i C(t, x) = (\partial_t + \hat{\mathscr{L}})C - (r + \lambda_i)C + \lambda_i (S_0 e^x - K)^+.$$

From the variational inequality (2.9), we see that $\mathcal{M}_i C_i \leq 0$. We choose a point (t, x) in the continuation region of C_2, which means that $\mathcal{M}_2 C_2 = 0$. Since $\lambda_1 < \lambda_2$ and $C_2 > (S_0 e^x - K)^+$, direct substitution shows that $\mathcal{M}_1 C_2 > 0$.

Next, we define the process

$$m(t, X_t) = e^{-(r+\lambda_1)t} C_2(t, X_t) + \int_0^t e^{-(r+\lambda_1)u} \lambda_1 (S_0 e^{X_u} - K)^+ du, \quad t \geq 0.$$

Using the fact that $\mathcal{M}_1 C_2 > 0$ and Optional Sampling Theorem, we deduce that, for any $\tau \in \mathscr{T}_{t,T}$,

$$\mathbb{E}_{t,x}^{\mathbb{Q}}\{m(\tau, X_\tau)\} \geq m(t, x).$$

In particular, we denote τ_1^* and τ_2^* as the optimal stopping times associated with C_1 and C_2, and get

$$
\begin{aligned}
C_2(t,x) &\leq \mathbb{E}_{t,x}^{\mathbb{Q}}\left\{ e^{-(r+\lambda_1)(\tau_2^*-t)} C_2(\tau_2^*, X_{\tau_2^*}) \right. \\
&\left. \quad + \int_t^{\tau_2^*} e^{-(r+\lambda_1)(u-t)} \lambda_1 (S_0 e^{X_u} - K)^+ du \right\} \\
&= \mathbb{E}_{t,x}^{\mathbb{Q}}\left\{ e^{-r(\tau_2^* \wedge \tau^{\lambda_1}-t)}(S_0 e^{X_{\tau_2^* \wedge \tau^{\lambda_1}}} - K)^+ \right\} \leq C_1(t,x).
\end{aligned}
$$

The last inequality follows since τ_2^* is one candidate stopping time for the optimal stopping value function C_1. Hence, we conclude that

$$
C_1(t,x) \geq C_2(t,x) > (S_0 e^x - K)^+.
$$

This implies that any point (t,x) in the continuation region of C_2 must also lies in the continuation region of C_1, which means that the optimal exercise boundary for C_1 dominates that for C_2.

As for the unvested ESO, the job termination intensity reduces its terminal values, and increases the probability of forfeiture (with payoff zero) during the vesting period. As a result, a higher job termination intensity also reduces the unvested ESO cost.

2.8.2. *Proof of proposition 2.6*

We conjecture that it is optimal to exercise the ESO as soon as the stock reaches some level $s^* > K$. Then, we split the stock price domain into three regions: $[s^*, \infty)$, $[K, s^*)$, and $[0, K)$. In region 1, we have $s \geq s^*$ and $V(s) = s - K$. In region 2, the ESO cost solves the inhomogeneous ODE

$$
\frac{\sigma^2 s^2}{2} V''(s) + (r-q)s V'(s) - (r+\lambda)V(s) + \lambda(s-K) = 0. \qquad (2.43)
$$

One can check by substitution that the general solution to (2.43) is given by

$$
V(s) = A s^{\gamma_+} + B s^{\gamma_-} + \frac{\lambda}{\lambda+q} s - \frac{\lambda}{r+\lambda} K,
$$

where γ_- and γ_+ are given in (2.38).

In region 3, since the option is out of the money, we have the ODE

$$
\frac{\sigma^2 s^2}{2} V''(s) + (r-q)s V'(s) - (r+\lambda)V(s) = 0,
$$

whose solution is the form

$$V(s) = Ds^{\gamma_+} + Es^{\gamma_-}.$$

Since $V(s) \to 0$ as $s \to 0$, it follows that $E = 0$.

To solve for the constants A, B, D, along with the critical stock price s^*, we apply continuity and smooth-pasting conditions at $s = K$ and $s = s^*$ to get

$$\lim_{s \uparrow K} V(s) = V(K) \Rightarrow DK^{\gamma_+} = AK^{\gamma_+} + BK^{\gamma_-} + \left(\frac{\lambda}{\lambda + q} - \frac{\lambda}{r + \lambda} \right) K,$$

$$\lim_{s \uparrow K} V'(s) = V'(K) \Rightarrow \gamma_+ DK^{\gamma_+ - 1} = \gamma_+ AK^{\gamma_+ - 1} + \gamma_- BK^{\gamma_- - 1} + \frac{\lambda}{\lambda + q},$$

$$\lim_{s \uparrow s^*} V(s) = V(s^*) \Rightarrow A(s^*)^{\gamma_+} + B(s^*)^{\gamma_-} + \frac{\lambda}{\lambda + q} s^* - \frac{\lambda}{r + \lambda} K$$

$$= s^* - K, \tag{2.44}$$

$$\lim_{s \uparrow s^*} V'(s) = V'(s^*) \Rightarrow \gamma_+ A(s^*)^{\gamma_+ - 1} + \gamma_- B(s^*)^{\gamma_- - 1} + \frac{\lambda}{\lambda + q} = 1.$$

$$\tag{2.45}$$

Solving this system of equations yields (2.39)–(2.40). In particular, we see that $B > 0$ since $\gamma_+ > 1$ and $\gamma_- < 0$.

From (2.44)–(2.45), the threshold s^* satisfies the equation

$$f(s^*) := B \left(1 - \frac{\gamma_-}{\gamma_+} \right) (s^*)^{\gamma_-} - \left(1 - \frac{1}{\gamma_+} \right) \left(\frac{q}{\lambda + q} \right) s^* + \frac{r}{r + \lambda} K = 0.$$

To show this has a unique real solution, we note that f is continuous, and

$$f'(s^*) = \gamma_- B \left(1 - \frac{\gamma_-}{\gamma_+} \right) (s^*)^{\gamma_- - 1} + \left(1 - \frac{1}{\gamma_+} \right) \left(\frac{-q}{\lambda + q} \right) < 0,$$

since $B > 0, \gamma_- < 0$, and $\gamma_+ > 1$. In addition, we have the limits:

$$\lim_{s^* \downarrow 0} = \frac{r}{r + \lambda} > 0 \quad \text{and} \quad \lim_{s^* \uparrow \infty} = -\infty,$$

as well as $f(K) = \frac{K}{\gamma_+} > 0$. Together, this implies that $f(s^*) = 0$ has a unique real root $s^* > K$. Hence, we obtain formula (2.37) for V. By direct substitution, it satisfies the VI (2.36).

2.8.3. Closed-form probabilities

The probability $p(t, x)$ that an ESO cost surpasses a given threshold $\bar{x}$, as defined in (2.24), can be viewed as a European digital option with zero interest rate, computed under $\mathbb{P}$. We summarize the corresponding closed-form formulas under the GBM, Merton, and Kou models (see Table 2.1).

(i) Under the GBM model, the ESO cost exceedance probability is given by

$$p(t, x) = e^{-\tilde{\lambda}(\tilde{T}-t)} \Phi(\tilde{d}), \quad \text{where } \tilde{d} = \frac{x - \bar{x} + \mu(\tilde{T} - t)}{\sigma\sqrt{\tilde{T} - t}},$$

and Φ is the standard normal cumulative distribution function.

(ii) When the company stock price follows the Merton jump diffusion, we have

$$p(t, x) = e^{-\tilde{\lambda}(\tilde{T}-t)} \sum_{j=0}^{+\infty} \frac{e^{-\alpha(\tilde{T}-t)}(\alpha(\tilde{T}-t))^j}{j!} \cdot \Phi\left(\frac{x - \bar{x} + \mu(\tilde{T} - t) + j\tilde{\mu}}{\sqrt{\sigma^2(\tilde{T} - t) + j\tilde{\sigma}^2}}\right).$$

(iii) In the Kou jump diffusion model, the cost exceedance probability is given by

$$\begin{aligned}
p(t, x) = e^{-\tilde{\lambda}v} &\left[\frac{e^{(\sigma\eta_+)^2 v/2}}{\sigma\sqrt{2\pi v}} \sum_{n=1}^{\infty} \pi_n \sum_{k=1}^{n} P_{n,k}(\sigma\sqrt{v}\eta_+)^k \right. \\
&\times I_{k-1}\left(\bar{x} - x - \mu v; -\eta_+, \frac{-1}{\sigma v}, -\sigma\eta_+\sqrt{v}\right) \\
&+ \frac{e^{(\sigma\eta_-)^2 v/2}}{\sigma\sqrt{2\pi v}} \sum_{n=1}^{\infty} \pi_n \sum_{k=1}^{n} Q_{n,k}(\sigma\sqrt{v}\eta_-)^k \\
&\times I_{k-1}\left(\bar{x} - x - \mu v; -\eta_-, \frac{-1}{\sigma v}, -\sigma\eta_-\sqrt{v}\right) \\
&\left. + \pi_0 \Phi\left(\frac{\mu v - \bar{x} + x}{\sigma\sqrt{v}}\right)\right],
\end{aligned}$$

where

$$P_{n,k} = \sum_{i=k}^{n-1} \binom{n-k-1}{i-k}\binom{n}{i}\left(\frac{\eta_+}{\eta_+ + \eta_-}\right)^{i-k}\left(\frac{\eta_-}{\eta_+ + \eta_-}\right)^{n-i}$$

$$p^i(1-p)^{n-i}, \quad 1 \leq k \leq n-1, \ P_{n,n} = p^n,$$

$$Q_{n,k} = \sum_{i=k}^{n-1} \binom{n-k-1}{i-k} \binom{n}{i} \left(\frac{\eta_+}{\eta_+ + \eta_-}\right)^{n-i} \left(\frac{\eta_-}{\eta_+ + \eta_-}\right)^{i-k}$$

$$p^{n-i}(1-p)^i, \quad 1 \le k \le n-1, \quad Q_{n,n} = (1-p)^n,$$

$I_n(c; d, b, \delta)$

$$= \begin{cases} -\dfrac{e^{dc}}{d} \displaystyle\sum_{i=0}^{n} \left(\dfrac{b}{d}\right)^{n-i} Hh_i(bc - \delta) \\ \quad + \left(\dfrac{b}{d}\right)^{n+1} \dfrac{\sqrt{2\pi}}{b} e^{\frac{d\delta}{b} + \frac{\sigma^2}{2b^2}} \Phi\left(-bc + \delta + \dfrac{d}{b}\right) \\ \quad \text{if } b > 0, \, d \ne 0, \\[2mm] -\dfrac{e^{dc}}{d} \displaystyle\sum_{i=0}^{n} \left(\dfrac{b}{d}\right)^{n-i} Hh_i(bc - \delta) \\ \quad + \left(\dfrac{b}{d}\right)^{n+1} \dfrac{\sqrt{2\pi}}{b} e^{\frac{d\delta}{b} + \frac{\sigma^2}{2b^2}} \Phi\left(bc - \delta - \dfrac{d}{b}\right) \\ \quad \text{if } b < 0, \, d < 0, \end{cases}$$

with

$$Hh_n(x) = (n!)^{-1} \int_x^{\infty} (t - x)^n e^{-t^2/2} dt,$$

$$\pi_n = e^{-\alpha v}(\alpha v)^n / n!,$$

$$v = \tilde{T} - t.$$

Chapter 3

Top-Down Valuation Approach

3.1. Introduction

Empirical studies suggest that ESO holders tend to start exercising their options early, often soon after the vesting period, and gradually exercise the remaining options over multiple dates before maturity. Huddart and Lang (1996), Marquardt (2002), and Bettis *et al.* (2005) point out that, for ESOs with 10 years to maturity, the expected time to exercise is 4–5 years. Investigating how ESO exercises are spread out over time, Huddart and Lang (1996) show that the mean fraction of options exercised by a typical employee at one time varied from 0.18 to 0.72. For more empirical studies, we refer to Bettis *et al.* (2001), Armstrong *et al.* (2007), Heron and Lie (2016) and Carpenter *et al.* (2017). These empirical findings motivate us to consider a valuation model that accounts for multiple exercises of various units of options at different times. As noted by Jain and Subramanian (2004), "the incorporation of multiple-date exercise has important economic and account consequences."

In this chapter, we take the firm's perspective to determine the cost of an ESO grant, which commonly involves multiple options with a long maturity. There is also a vesting period, during which option exercise is prohibited and job termination leads to forfeiture of the options. The key component of our proposed valuation framework is an exogenous jump process that models the random exercises over time. Within our framework, the employee's exercise intensity can be constant or stochastic, and the number of options exercised at each time can be specified to be deterministic or random. Since the ESO payoff depends heavily on when the employee leaves the firm, we also include a random job termination time and allow the job termination rate to be different during and after vesting period.

The valuation problem leads to the study of the system of partial differential equations (PDEs) associated with the vested and unvested options. In order to compute the ESO costs, we present two numerical methods to solve the PDEs. We discuss the method of fast Fourier transform (FFT), followed by the finite difference method (FDM). By applying Fourier transform, we simplify the original second-order PDEs to ODEs in the constant intensity case and first-order PDEs in the stochastic intensity case. The ESO costs are recovered via inverse fast Fourier transform. The results from the two methods are illustrated and compared under both deterministic and stochastic exercise intensities. Furthermore, we introduce a new valuation method based on maturity randomization. The key advantage of this method is that it yields analytic formulae, allowing for instant computation.

Using all three numerical methods, we compute the costs and examine the impact of job termination risk, exercise intensity, vesting period, and other features. Among our findings, we illustrate the distributions of exercise times under different model specifications, and also show that the average time of exercises tends to increase nonlinearly with the number of ESOs granted, resulting in a higher per-unit cost. In other words, under the assumption that the ESOs will be exercised gradually, a larger ESO grant has an indirect effect of delaying exercises, and thus leading to higher ESO costs.

In reality, the firm does not know when ESOs will be exercised. Therefore, it is reasonable to model ESO exercises as some exogenous events so that the firm is not assumed to have access to the employee's risk preferences and exercise strategy. This leads to the so-called intensity approach, as studied in the previous chapter, that models ESO exercise by the first arrival time of an exogenous jump process. Although the exercises are exogenous events, the frequency and timing of their exercises can be dependent on the firm's stock and other contract features. Our approach studied herein is essentially an extension of this approach to modeling multiple ESO exercises of random quantity over the life of the options.

The rest of the chapter is organized as follows. In Section 3.2, we present our ESO valuation model. The numerical method is discussed in Section 3.3. In Section 3.4, we discuss the case with stochastic exercise intensity. Then in Section 3.5 we introduce a novel valuation method based on maturity randomization. In Section 3.6, we introduce the notion of implied maturity associated with an ESO grant. Finally, concluding remarks are provided in Section 3.7.

3.2. Valuation Methodology

We begin by describing the ESO payoff structure, and then introduce the stochastic model that captures various sources of randomness. The valuation of both vested and unvested ESOs is presented.

3.2.1. *Payoff structure*

The ESO is an early exercisable call option written on the company stock with a long maturity T ranging from 5 to 10 years. In order to maintain the incentive effect of ESOs, the company typically prohibits the ESO holder (employee) from exercising during a vesting period from the grant date. During the vesting period, which ranges from 1 to 5 years, the holder's departure from the company, voluntarily or forced, will lead to forfeiture of the option, rending it worthless. We denote $[0, t_v)$ as the vesting period, and after the date t_v the ESO is *vested* and free to be exercised until it expires at time T. The ESO payoff at any time τ is $(S_\tau - K)^+ 1_{\{t_v \leq \tau \leq T\}}$, where S_τ is the firm's stock price at time τ and K is the strike price. Upon departure, the employee is supposed to exercise all the remaining options. Figure 3.1 shows all four payoff scenarios associated with an ESO.

3.2.2. *Job termination and exercise process*

The employee's job termination plays a crucial role in the exercise timing and resulting payoff of the ESOs. We model the job termination time during the vesting period by an exponential random variable $\zeta \sim \exp(\alpha)$, with $\alpha \geq 0$. When the ESO becomes vested after t_v, we model the employee's job termination time by another exponential random variable $\xi \sim \exp(\beta)$, with $\beta \geq 0$. We assume that ζ and ξ are mutually independent. This approach of modeling job termination by an exogenous random variable is also used by Jennergren and Naslund (1993), Carpenter (1998), Carr and Linetsky (2000), Hull and White (2004b), Sircar and Xiong (2007), Leung and Sircar (2009b), Carmona *et al.* (2011), and Leung and Wan (2015), among others. In our model, using two different exponential times allows us to account for the varying level of job termination risk during and after the vesting period.

An ESO grant typically contains multiple options. Empirical studies show that employee tends to exercise the options gradually over time, rather than exercising all options at once. This motivates us to model the sequential random timing of exercises. In our proposed model, we consider a grant

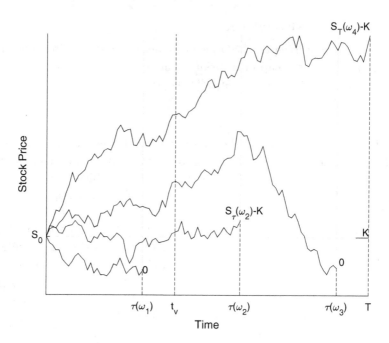

Figure 3.1. ESO payoff structure. From bottom path to top path: (i) The employee leaves the firm during the vesting period, resulting in forfeiture of the ESO and a zero payoff. (ii) The employee exercises the vested ESO before maturity due to desire to liquidate or job termination and receives the payoff $(S_\tau(\omega_2) - K)^+$. (iii) The employee exercises the vested ESO before maturity due to job termination, but receives nothing. (iv) The employee exercises the option at maturity T.

of M units of identical early exercisable ESOs with the same strike price K and expiration date T. These M ESOs are exercisable only after the vesting period $[0, t_v)$. For the vested ESOs, we define the random *exercise process* L_t, for $t_v \le t \le T$, to be the positive jump process representing the number of ESOs exercised over time. As such, L_t is an integer process that takes value on $[0, M]$. The corresponding jump times are denoted by the sequence $(\tau_1, \tau_2, \ldots)$, and the frequency of exercises is governed by the jump intensity process $(\lambda_t)_{t_v \le t \le T}$.

The jump size for the ith jump of L represents the number of ESOs exercised and is described by a discrete random variable δ_i. The exercise process starts at time t_v with $L_{t_v} = 0$. By definition, we have $L_T \le M$. This means that the random jump size at any time t must take value within $[1, M - L_{t-}]$. Also, as soon as L_t reaches the upper bound M, the jump intensity λ_t must be set to be zero thereafter. Given that the employee still holds m options, the probability mass function of the random jump size is

$$p_{m,z} \triangleq \mathbb{P}\{\delta_i = z \mid L_{\tau_i-} = M - m\}.$$

In turn, the expected number of options to be exercised at each exercise time is given by

$$\bar{p}_m \triangleq \sum_{z=1}^{m} z p_{m,z},$$

which again depends on the current number of ESOs held.

The employee may exercise single or multiple units of ESOs over time. On the date of expiration or job termination, any unexercised options must be exercised. Hence, the discounted payoff from the ESOs over $[0, T]$ is a sum of two terms, given by

$$\left(\int_{t_v}^{T \wedge \xi} e^{-rt}(S_t - K)^+ dL_t + e^{-r(T \wedge \xi)}(M - L_{T \wedge \xi})(S_{T \wedge \xi} - K)^+ \right) 1_{\{\zeta \geq t_v\}}.$$

The indicator $1_{\{\zeta \geq t_v\}}$ means that the ESO payoff is zero if the employee leaves the firm during the vesting period.

Example 3.1 (Unit Exercises). Suppose L_t be a non-homogeneous Poisson process $(N_t)_{0 \leq t \leq T}$ with a time-varying jump intensity function $\lambda(t)$, for $0 \leq t \leq T$. At each jump time a single option is exercised. In Figure 3.2, we illustrate three possible scenarios. In scenario (i), the employee exercises six out of 10 options one by one, but must exercise four remaining options upon job termination realized at time $\xi(\omega_1)$. In scenario (ii), the employee exercises all 10 options one by one before maturity. In scenario (iii), the employee has not exercised all the options by maturity, so all remaining options are exercised at time T.

Example 3.2 (Block Exercises). Suppose the employee can exercise one or more options at each exercise time. As an example, we assume a uniform distribution for the number of options to be exercised, so we set $p_{m,z} = m^{-1}$ for $z = 1, \ldots, m$. In Figure 3.3, we illustrate the distributions of the weighted average exercise time $\bar{\tau}$ defined by

$$\bar{\tau} = \frac{\sum_{i=1}^{N} \delta_i * \tau_i}{M}, \tag{3.1}$$

where δ_i is the number of ESOs exercised at the ith exercise time τ_i, and N is the number of distinct exercise times before or at time T. For each

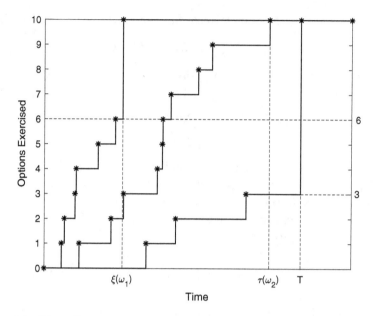

Figure 3.2. Three illustrative sample paths of the process for Poisson exercises of 10 ESOs. From top path to bottom path: (i) The employee first exercises six out of 10 options one by one, but is then forced to exercise four remaining options upon job termination realized at time $\xi(\omega_1)$. (ii) The employee exercises all the options one by one before expiration and job termination. The last option is exercised at $\tau(\omega_2)$ shown in the plot. (iii) The employee exercises three options one by one before maturity and seven remaining options at maturity.

simulated path, we take an average of the distinct exercise times weighted by the number of options exercised at each time. With common parameters $M = 20$, $t_v = 0$, $T = 10$, the histograms of $\bar{\tau}$ correspond to different values of λ and β. With a low job termination rate β and low exercise intensity λ (panel (a) where $\beta = 0$, $\lambda = 0.3$), more options tend to be exercised at maturity. Comparing panel (b) to panel (c), and also panel (b) to panel (d), we see that a higher job termination rate or higher exercise intensity lowers the average exercise time and reduces instances of exercising at maturity. Similar patterns can also be found in empirical studies (Heron and Lie, 2016, Figure 3).

3.2.3. *PDEs for ESO valuation*

To value ESOs, we consider a risk-neutral pricing measure $\mathbb{Q}$ for all stochastic processes and random variables in our model. We model the firm's stock

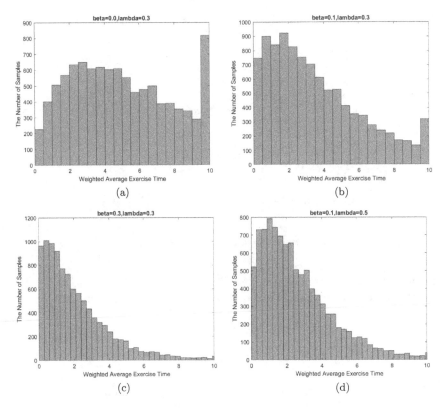

Figure 3.3. Histograms of weighted average exercise times, as defined in (3.1), based on 10,000 simulated exercise processes for 20 vested ESOs with a 10-year maturity. Panels have different rates of job termination β and exercise intensity λ: (a) $\beta = 0$, $\lambda = 0.3$; (b) $\beta = 0.1$, $\lambda = 0.3$; (c) $\beta = 0.3$, $\lambda = 0.3$; (d) $\beta = 0.1$, $\lambda = 0.5$.

price process $(S_t)_{t \geq 0}$ by a geometric Brownian motion

$$dS_t = (r - q)S_t \, dt + \sigma S_t \, dW_t,$$

where the positive constants r, q and σ are the interest rate, dividend rate, and volatility parameter, respectively, and W is a standard Brownian motion under $\mathbb{Q}$, independent of the exponentially-distributed job termination times ζ and ξ. Our default assumption for the employee's exercise intensity is that it is a deterministic function of time, denoted by $\lambda(t)$. We will discuss the case with a stochastic exercise intensity in Section 3.4.

At any time $t \in [t_v, T]$, the ESO is vested. The vested ESO cost functions $C^{(m)}(t, s)$, for $m = 1, 2, \ldots, M$, where m is the number of options currently held, are given by the risk-neutral expectation of discounted future

ESO payoffs provided that the employee has not left the firm.

$$C^{(m)}(t,s) = \mathbb{E}\left\{ \int_t^{T\wedge\xi} e^{-r(u-t)}(S_u - K)^+ dL_u \right.$$

$$\left. + e^{-r(T\wedge\xi-t)}(M - L_{T\wedge\xi})(S_{T\wedge\xi} - K)^+ \mid S_t = s, L_t = M - m \right\}$$

$$= \mathbb{E}\left\{ \int_t^T e^{-(r+\beta)(u-t)}(S_u - K)^+ dL_u + e^{-(r+\beta)(T-t)} \right.$$

$$(M - L_T)(S_T - K)^+ + \int_t^T \beta e^{-(r+\beta)(v-t)}(M - L_v)$$

$$\left. (S_v - K)^+ dv \mid S_t = s, L_t = M - m \right\},$$

for $m = 1, 2, \ldots, M$, and $(t,s) \in [t_v, T] \times \mathbb{R}_+$.

Next, we define the infinitesimal generator associated with the stock price process S by

$$\mathcal{L}\cdot = (r - q)s\partial_s \cdot + \frac{\sigma^2 s^2}{2}\partial_{ss}\cdot.$$

We determine the vested ESO costs by solving the following system of PDEs.

$$-(r + \lambda(t) + \beta)C^{(m)} + C_t^{(m)} + \mathcal{L}C^{(m)}$$

$$+\lambda(t)\sum_{z=1}^{m-1} p_{m,z}C^{(m-z)} + (\lambda(t)\bar{p}_m + m\beta)(s - K)^+ = 0, \quad (3.2)$$

for $(t,s) \in [t_v, T] \times \mathbb{R}_+$ and $m = 1, 2, \ldots, M$. Here, $\bar{p}_m$ is the expected number of options exercised and $p_{m,z}$ is the probability of exercising z options with m options left. The terminal condition is $C^{(m)}(T,s) = m(s - K)^+$ for $s \in \mathbb{R}_+$.

During the vesting period $[0, t_v)$, the ESO is unvested and is subject to forfeiture if the employee leaves the firm. We denote the cost of m units of unvested ESO by $\tilde{C}^{(m)}(t,s)$. Since holding an unvested ESO effectively entitles the holder to obtain a vested ESO at time t_v provided the holder is still with the firm. If the ESO holder leaves the firm at any time $t \in [0, t_v)$, the unvested ESO cost is zero. Otherwise, given that $\zeta > t$, the (pre-departure) unvested ESO cost is

$$\tilde{C}^{(m)}(t, s) = \mathbb{E}\{e^{-r(t_v - t)}C^{(m)}(t_v, S_{t_v})\mathbf{1}_{\{\varsigma \geq t_v\}}|S_t = s\}$$

$$= \mathbb{E}\{e^{-(r+\alpha)(t_v - t)}C^{(m)}(t_v, S_{t_v})|S_t = s\}.$$

To determine the unvested ESO cost, we solve the PDE problem

$$-(r + \alpha)\tilde{C}^{(m)} + \tilde{C}_t^{(m)} + \mathscr{L}\tilde{C}^{(m)} = 0, \quad \text{for } (t, s) \in [0, t_v) \times \mathbb{R}_+,$$
$$\tilde{C}^{(m)}(t_v, s) = C^{(m)}(t_v, s), \quad \text{for } s \in \mathbb{R}^+. \tag{3.3}$$

Here, $C^{(m)}(t_v, s)$ is the vested ESO cost evaluated at time t_v.

3.3. Numerical Methods and Implementation

In this section, we present two numerical methods to solve the PDE (3.2). We first discuss the application of fast Fourier transform (FFT) to ESO valuation, followed by the finite difference method (FDM). The results from the two methods are compared in Section 3.3.3.

3.3.1. *Fast Fourier transform*

We first consider the vested ESO ($t \in [t_v, T]$). Assume x such that $s = Ke^x$, and define the function

$$f^{(m)}(t, x) = C^{(m)}(t, Ke^x), \quad (t, x) \in [t_v, T] \times \mathbb{R},$$

for each $m = 1, \ldots, M$. The PDE for $f^{(m)}(t, x)$ is given by

$$-(r + \lambda(t) + \beta)f^{(m)} + f_t^{(m)} + \widetilde{\mathscr{L}}f^{(m)}$$

$$+\lambda(t)\sum_{z=1}^{m-1}p_{m,z}f^{(m-z)} + (\lambda(t)\bar{p}_m + m\beta)(Ke^x - K)^+ = 0, \tag{3.4}$$

where

$$\widetilde{\mathscr{L}}\cdot = \left(r - q - \frac{\sigma^2}{2}\right)\partial_x \cdot + \frac{\sigma^2}{2}\partial_{xx}\cdot. \tag{3.5}$$

The terminal condition is $f^{(m)}(T, x) = m(Ke^x - K)^+$, for $x \in \mathbb{R}$.

The Fourier transform of $f^{(m)}(t, x)$ is defined by

$$\mathscr{F}[f^{(m)}](t, \omega) = \int_{-\infty}^{\infty} f^{(m)}(t, x)e^{-i\omega x}dx,$$

for $m = 1, \ldots, M$, with frequency $\omega \in \mathbb{C}$. Applying Fourier transform to the PDE (3.4), we obtain an ODE for $\mathscr{F}[f^{(m)}](t, \omega)$, a function of time t parameterized by ω, for each $m = 1, \ldots, M$. Precisely, we have

$$\frac{d}{dt}\mathscr{F}[f^{(m)}](t, \omega) = h(t, \omega)\mathscr{F}[f^{(m)}](t, \omega) + \psi^{(m)}(t, \omega),$$

where

$$h(t, \omega) = r + \lambda(t) + \beta - i\omega\left(r - q - \frac{\sigma^2}{2}\right) + \omega^2\frac{\sigma^2}{2},$$

$$\psi^{(m)}(t, \omega) = -\lambda(t)\sum_{z=1}^{m-1} p_{m,z}\mathscr{F}[f^{(m-z)}](t, \omega) - (\lambda(t)\bar{p}_m + m\beta)\,\varphi(\omega), \quad (3.6)$$

$$\varphi(\omega) = \mathscr{F}[(Ke^x - K)^+](\omega),$$

with the terminal condition $\mathscr{F}[f^{(m)}](T, \omega) = m\varphi(\omega)$. Solving the ODE, we obtain

$$\mathscr{F}[f^{(m)}](t, \omega) = me^{-\int_t^T h(s,\omega)ds}\varphi(\omega) - \int_t^T e^{-\int_t^u h(s,\omega)ds}\psi^{(m)}(u, \omega)du.$$

$$(3.7)$$

In particular, when $m = 1$, we have

$$\mathscr{F}[f^{(1)}](t, \omega) = e^{-\int_t^T h(s,\omega)ds}\varphi(\omega) + \int_t^T e^{-\int_t^u h(s,\omega)ds}(\lambda(u) + \beta)\varphi(\omega)du.$$

$$(3.8)$$

Since the ESO payoff function $(Ke^x - K)^+$ is not integrable over the real axis, $\varphi(\omega)$ contains singularities over $\mathbb{R}$. To address this, we let $\omega = \omega_R + i\omega_I$, where $\omega_R, \omega_I \in \mathbb{R}$ denote the real part and the imaginary part of ω, respectively. Therefore, the Fourier transform in (3.6) can be rewritten as

$$\varphi(\omega) = \int_{-\infty}^{\infty} e^{-i\omega_R x + \omega_I x}(Ke^x - K)^+dx,$$

which is well-defined on the space $(\omega_R, \omega_I) \in \mathbb{R} \times (-\infty, -1)$. Applying this to (3.8), we deduce that $\mathscr{F}[f^{(m)}](t, \omega)$ in (3.7) is also well-defined for $(t, \omega_R, \omega_I) \in [0, T] \times \mathbb{R} \times (-\infty, -1)$. Next, by fixing any $\omega_I < -1$, we recover the ESO cost function through inverse Fourier transform:

$$f^{(m)}(t,x) = \frac{1}{2\pi} \int_{-\infty}^{\infty} e^{i\omega_R x - \omega_I x} \mathscr{F}[f^{(m)}](t, \omega_R + i\omega_I) d\omega_R,$$

for every $m = 1, \ldots, M$, $(t, x) \in (t_v, T) \times \mathbb{R}$.

Remark 3.3. If λ is a constant, then the Fourier transform in (3.7) can be simplified as

$$\mathscr{F}[f^{(m)}](t, \omega) = \sum_{k=0}^{m-1} F_k^{(m)}(\omega)(T-t)^k e^{-(T-t)h(\omega)} + F^{(m)}(\omega),$$

where

$$F^{(m)}(\omega) = \frac{1}{h(\omega)}\left(\lambda \sum_{z=1}^{m-1} p_{m,z} F^{(m-z)}(\omega) + (\lambda \bar{p}_m + m\beta)\varphi(\omega)\right), \tag{3.9}$$

$$F_k^{(m)}(\omega) = \frac{\lambda}{k} \sum_{z=1}^{m-k} p_{m,z} F_{k-1}^{(m-z)}(\omega), \quad k = 1, 2, \ldots, m-1,$$

$$F_0^{(m)}(\omega) = \mathscr{F}[f^{(m)}](T, \omega) - \frac{1}{h(\omega)}\left(\lambda \sum_{z=1}^{m-1} p_{m,z} F^{(m-z)}(\omega) + (\lambda \bar{p}_m + m\beta)\varphi(\omega)\right),$$

$$h(\omega) = r + \lambda + \beta - i\omega\left(r - q - \frac{\sigma^2}{2}\right) + \omega^2 \frac{\sigma^2}{2}. \tag{3.10}$$

In (3.9) and (3.10), $\varphi(\omega)$ is defined in (3.6).

For numerical implementation, we apply the Fourier space time-stepping method (FST) introduced by Jackson *et al.* (2008). We work with a finite domain $[t_v, T] \times [x_{\min}, x_{\max}]$ with uniform discretization of lengths $\delta t = (T - t_v)/N_t$ and $\delta x = (x_{\max} - x_{\min})/(N_x - 1)$ in the time–space dimensions. We set $\delta t = 0.01$, $x_{\min} = -10$, $x_{\max} = 10$ and $N_x = 2^{12}$. As such, singularities of $\varphi(\omega)$ will be pushed off the real axis. Theoretically, it will produce same numerical result for any choice of ω_I. Accordingly, we set $\omega_I = 0$ and discrete the finite frequency space $[\omega_{\min}, \omega_{\max}]$ with uniform grid size of $\delta\omega$, where we apply the Nyquist critical frequency that $\omega_{\max} = \pi/\delta x$ and $\delta\omega = 2\omega_{\max}/N_x$. For $j = 0, \ldots, N_t$, and $k = 0, \ldots, N_x - 1$, we denote

$t_j = t_v + j\delta t$, $x_k = x_{\min} + k\delta x$, and

$$\omega_k = \begin{cases} k\delta\omega, & 0 \le k \le N_x/2, \\ k\delta\omega - 2\omega_{\max}, & N_x/2 + 1 \le k \le N_x - 1]. \end{cases}$$

Then, we numerically compute the discrete Fourier transform

$$\mathscr{F}[f](t_j, \omega_k) \approx \sum_{n=0}^{N_x-1} f(t_j, x_n)e^{-i\omega_k x_n}\delta x$$

$$= \phi_k \sum_{n=0}^{N_x-1} f(t_j, x_n)e^{-i2\pi kn/N_x}, \qquad (3.11)$$

with $\phi_k = e^{-i\omega_k x_{\min}}\delta x$. In (3.11), we evaluate the sum $\sum_{n=0}^{N_x-1} f(t_j, x_n)$ $e^{-i2\pi kn/N_x}$ by applying the standard fast Fourier transform (FFT) algorithm. The corresponding Fourier inversion is conducted by inverse FFT, yielding the vested ESO cost $f(t_j, x_n)$. Note that the coefficient ϕ_k will be canceled in the process.

In the literature, Leung and Wan (2015) apply FST to compute the cost of an American-style ESO when the company stock is driven by a Levy process. This FST method has been applied more broadly by Jackson *et al.* (2008) to solve partial-integro differential equations (PIDEs) that arise in options pricing problems.

As for the unvested ESO, we define the associated cost function

$$\tilde{f}^{(m)}(t, x) = \tilde{C}^{(m)}(t, Ke^x),$$

for each $m = 1, \ldots, M$. From (3.3), we derive the PDE for $\tilde{f}^{(m)}(t, x)$

$$-(r + \alpha)\tilde{f}^{(m)} + \tilde{f}_t^{(m)} + \widetilde{\mathscr{L}}\tilde{f}^{(m)} = 0, \qquad (3.12)$$

for $(t, x) \in [0, t_v) \times \mathbb{R}$, with the terminal condition $\tilde{f}^{(m)}(t_v, x) = f^{(m)}(t_v, x)$, for $x \in \mathbb{R}$. As we can see, once the vested ESO cost is computed, it determines the terminal condition for the unvested ESO problem.

Applying Fourier transform to (3.12), we can derive the ODE for $\mathscr{F}[\tilde{f}^{(m)}](t, \omega)$,

$$\frac{d}{dt}\mathscr{F}[\tilde{f}^{(m)}](t, \omega) = \tilde{h}(\omega)\mathscr{F}[\tilde{f}^{(m)}](t, \omega),$$

where

$$\tilde{h}(\omega) = r + \alpha - i\omega\left(r - q - \frac{\sigma^2}{2}\right) + \omega^2\frac{\sigma^2}{2},$$

for $(t,\omega) \in [0,t_v) \times \mathbb{R}$, with the terminal condition $\mathscr{F}[\tilde{f}^{(m)}](t_v,\omega) = \mathscr{F}[f^{(m)}](t_v,\omega)$. We solve the ODE to get

$$\mathscr{F}[\tilde{f}^{(m)}](t,\omega) = e^{-\tilde{h}(\omega)(t_v-t)}\mathscr{F}[\tilde{f}^{(m)}](t_v,\omega).$$

In turn, by fixing $\omega_I < -1$, the imaginary part of ω, we apply inverse Fourier transform to recover the unvested ESO cost:

$$\tilde{C}^{(m)}(t, Ke^x) = \tilde{f}^{(m)}(t,x) = \frac{1}{2\pi}\int_{-\infty}^{\infty} e^{i\omega_R x - \omega_I x}\mathscr{F}[\tilde{f}^{(m)}](t,\omega_R + i\omega_I)d\omega_R,$$

for $(t,x) \in [0,t_v) \times \mathbb{R}$, where ω_R denotes the real part of ω. Again, in numerical implementation, we can let $\omega_I = 0$ and numerically compute the Fourier transform by FFT. Then, we use inverse FFT to recover the cost function.

3.3.2. *Finite difference method*

For comparison, we also compute the ESO costs using a finite difference method. Specifically, we apply the Crank–Nicolson method on a uniform grid. Here we provide an outline with focus on the boundary conditions for our application. For more details, we refer to Wilmott *et al.* (1995), among other references.

As for grid settings, we restrict the domain $[t_v, T] \times \mathbb{R}_+$ to a finite domain $\mathscr{D} = \{(t,s)|t_v \le t \le T, 0 \le s \le S_*\}$, where S_* must be relatively very large such that if the current stock price $S_t = S_*$, then the stock price will be larger than the strike price K over $[t, T]$ with great probability.

To determine the boundary condition at $s = S_*$, we introduce a new function

$$\begin{aligned}
\bar{C}^{(m)}(t,s) = \mathbb{E}\Bigg\{ &\int_t^T e^{-(r+\beta)(u-t)}(S_u - K)dL_u \\
&+ e^{-(r+\beta)(T-t)}(M - L_T)(S_T - K) \\
&+ \int_t^T \beta e^{-(r+\beta)(v-t)}(M - L_v)(S_v - K)dv \,\Big|\, S_t = s, \\
&L_t = M - m\Bigg\},
\end{aligned}$$

for $m = 1, \ldots, M$. When $s = S_*$, we see that $C^{(m)}(t, s) \approx \bar{C}^{(m)}(t, s)$. Thus, we can set the boundary condition at $s = S_*$ to be $C^{(m)}(t, S_*) = \bar{C}^{(m)}(t, S_*)$. By the Feynman–Kac formula, $\bar{C}^{(m)}(t, s)$ satisfies the PDE

$$-(r + \lambda(t) + \beta)\bar{C}^{(m)} + \bar{C}_t^{(m)} + \mathscr{L}\bar{C}^{(m)}$$

$$+\lambda(t) \sum_{z=1}^{m-1} p_{m,z}\bar{C}^{(m-z)} + (\lambda(t)\bar{p}_m + m\beta)(s - K) = 0,$$

for $m = 1, \ldots, M$, and $(t, s) \in (t_v, T) \times \mathbb{R}_+$, with terminal condition

$$\bar{C}^{(m)}(T, s) = m(s - K), \quad s \in \mathbb{R}_+.$$

Then, $\bar{C}^{(m)}(t, s)$ has the ansatz solution

$$\bar{C}^{(m)}(t, s) = A_m(t)s - B_m(t)K,$$

where $A_m(t)$ and $B_m(t)$ satisfy the pair of ODEs respectively,

$$-(q + \lambda(t) + \beta)A_m + A'_m + \lambda(t) \sum_{z=1}^{m-1} p_{m,z}A_{m-z} + (\lambda(t)\bar{p}_m + m\beta) = 0,$$

$$-(r + \lambda(t) + \beta)B_m + B'_m + \lambda(t) \sum_{z=1}^{m-1} p_{m,z}B_{m-z} + (\lambda(t)\bar{p}_m + m\beta) = 0,$$

$$\text{(3.13)}$$

with the terminal condition

$$B_m(T) = A_m(T) = m, \quad \text{for } m = 1, \ldots, M.$$

We can solve the ODEs (3.13) analytically, or numerically solve it using the backward Euler method.

Next, we discrete the domain $\mathscr{D}$ with uniform grid size of $\delta t = (T - t_v)/M_0$ and $\delta S = S_*/N_0$. Then, we apply $C_{i,j}^{(m)}$ to denote discrete approximations of $C^{(m)}(t_i, s_j)$ where $t_i = t_v + i\delta t$ and $s_j = j\delta S$. The Crank–Nicolson method is applied to solve the PDEs satisfied by $C^{(m)}$, for $m = 1, \ldots, M$. Working backward in time, we obtain the vested ESO costs at time t_v, which become the terminal condition values for the unvested ESO valuation problem. For the unvested ESO cost, we restrict the domain

$[0, t_v] \times \mathbb{R}_+$ to the finite domain $\tilde{\mathscr{D}} = \{(t, s) | 0 \leq t \leq t_v, 0 \leq s \leq S_*\}$, where S_* is relatively very large such that

$$\tilde{C}^{(m)}(t, S_*) = \mathbb{E}\{e^{-(r+\alpha)(t_v-t)} C^{(m)}(t_v, S_{t_v}) | S_t = S_*\}$$
$$\approx \mathbb{E}\{e^{-(r+\alpha)(t_v-t)}(A_m(T-t_v)S_{t_v} - B_m(T-t_v)K) | S_t = S_*\}$$
$$= e^{-(q+\alpha)(t_v-t)} A_m(T-t_v)S_* - e^{-(r+\alpha)(t_v-t)} B_m(T-t_v)K.$$

We again apply the Crank–Nicolson method to solve the PDEs satisfied by $\tilde{C}^{(m)}(t, s)$, for $m = 1, \ldots, M$.

3.3.3. *Numerical examples*

Using both FFT and FDM, we compute different ESO costs by varying the vesting period t_v, job termination rate α and β, as well as exercise intensity λ. In Table 3.1, we present the ESO costs and compare the two numerical methods. It is well known that the call option value is increasing with respect to its maturity. In a similar spirit if the employee tends to exercise the ESO earlier, then a smaller ESO cost is expected.

As we can see in Table 3.1, the ESO cost decreases as exercise intensity λ increases, or as job termination rate α or β increases, holding other things constant. On the other hand, the effect of vesting period is not monotone. In a scenario with a high job termination α during the vesting period, the employee is very likely to leave the firm while the options are unvested,

Table 3.1. Vested and unvested ESO costs under different exercise intensities λ and different job termination rates α and β, computed using FFT and FDM for comparison. Common parameters: $S_0 = K = 10$, $r = 5\%$, $q = 1.5\%$, $\sigma = 20\%$, $p_{m,z} = 1/m$, $M = 5$ and $T = 10$. In FDM: $S_* = 30$, $\delta S = 0.1$, $\delta t = 0.1$. In FFT: $N_x = 2^{12}$, $x_{\min} = -10$ and $x_{\max} = 10$.

Parameters		$t_v = 0$		$t_v = 2$		$t_v = 4$	
		FDM	FFT	FDM	FFT	FDM	FFT
$\alpha = 0.1, \beta = 0$	$\lambda = 1$	5.4729	5.4753	7.8399	7.8405	8.2845	8.2849
	$\lambda = 2$	3.7067	3.7101	6.9164	6.9170	7.7054	7.7058
$\alpha = 0.1, \beta = 1$	$\lambda = 1$	3.2483	3.2522	6.7063	6.7069	7.5746	7.5750
	$\lambda = 2$	2.7024	2.7069	6.4655	6.4661	7.4253	7.4257
$\alpha = 0, \beta = 0.1$	$\lambda = 1$	5.0603	5.0629	9.3022	9.3031	12.1510	12.1517
	$\lambda = 2$	3.5595	3.5630	8.3622	8.3631	11.4298	11.4306
$\alpha = 1, \beta = 0.1$	$\lambda = 1$	5.0603	5.0629	1.2579	1.2590	0.2219	0.2226
	$\lambda = 2$	3.5595	3.5630	1.1310	1.1318	0.2087	0.2094

Table 3.2.   Unvested ESO costs under different exercise intensities λ and different job termination rates α and β, computed using FFT and FDM for comparison. Common parameters: $S_0 = 10$, $r = 5\%$, $q = 1.5\%$, $\sigma = 20\%$, $p_{m,z} = 1/m$, $M = 5$, $t_v = 2$ and $T = 10$. In FDM: $S_* = 30$, $\delta S = 0.1$, $\delta t = 0.1$. In FFT: $N_x = 2^{12}$, $x_{\min} = -10$ and $x_{\max} = 10$.

Parameters		$K = 9$		$K = 10$		$K = 11$	
		FDM	FFT	FDM	FFT	FDM	FFT
$\alpha = 0.1, \beta = 0$	$\lambda = 1$	9.9408	9.9410	7.8399	7.8405	6.1206	6.1209
	$\lambda = 2$	9.0949	9.0952	6.9164	6.9170	5.1698	5.1701
$\alpha = 0.1, \beta = 1$	$\lambda = 1$	8.9021	8.9024	6.7063	6.7069	4.9560	4.9563
	$\lambda = 2$	8.6810	8.6813	6.4655	6.4661	4.7115	4.7117
$\alpha = 0, \beta = 0.1$	$\lambda = 1$	11.8915	11.8920	9.3022	9.3031	7.1929	7.1934
	$\lambda = 2$	11.0301	11.0306	8.3622	8.3631	6.2272	6.2277
$\alpha = 1, \beta = 0.1$	$\lambda = 1$	1.6079	1.6094	1.2579	1.2590	0.9731	0.9735
	$\lambda = 2$	1.4916	1.4928	1.1310	1.1318	0.8428	0.8428

leading to a zero payoff. Consequently, the ESO cost is decreasing with respect to t_v. This corresponds to the case with $\alpha = 1$ in Table 3.1.

However, if α is small, then the employee is unlikely to leave the firm and lose the options during the vesting period. Therefore, a longer vesting period would effectively make the employee hold the options for a longer period of time, delaying the exercise. As a result, the ESO cost is increasing with respect to t_v, which is shown in other cases in Table 3.2.

In Figure 3.4, we plot the ESO cost as a function of the exercise intensity λ for $T = 5$, 8 and 10. It shows that the ESO is decreasing and convex with respect to λ. An employee with a high exercise intensity tends to exercise the ESOs earlier than those with a lower exercise intensity. Since the call option value increases with maturity, exercising the ESO earlier will result in a lower cost. As the exercise intensity increases from zero, the ESO cost tends to decrease faster than when the exercise intensity is higher. Moreover, Figure 3.4 also shows that as λ increases, the ESO costs associated with different maturities $T = 5$, 8 and 10 get close to each other. The intuition is that when λ is large, the options will be exercised very early and the maturity will not have a significant impact on the option values.

On the bottom panel of Figure 3.4, we plot the option value as a function of stock price S_0 with exercise intensity $\lambda = 0$, 1 or 5. It shows that, as λ increases from 0 to 1, the option value decreases rapidly. When the exercise intensity is very high, i.e. $\lambda = 5$ in the figure, there is a high chance of immediate exercise, so the ESO value is seen to be very close to the ESO payoff $(S_0 - K)^+$.

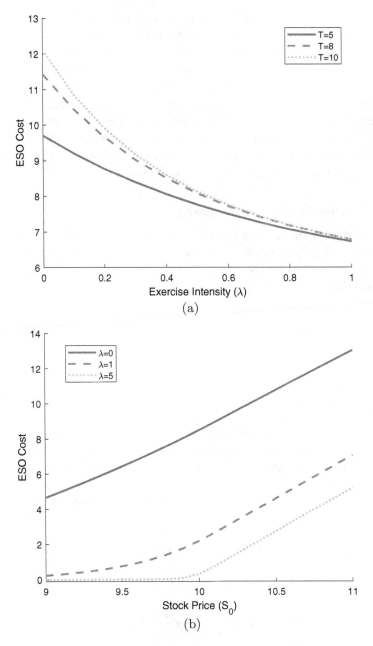

Figure 3.4. (a) ESO cost as a function of employee exercise intensity λ when the maturity $T = 5, 8$ or 10. (b) ESO cost as a function of initial stock price S_0 with $\lambda = 0, 1$, or 5. Parameters: $K = 10$, $r = 5\%$, $q = 1.5\%$, $\sigma = 20\%$, $p_{m,z} = 1/m$, $M = 5$, $T = 10$, $t_v = 0$ and $\beta = 0.1$. In FFT: $N_x = 2^{12}$, $x_{\min} = -10$, $x_{\max} = 10$.

Next, we consider the effect of the total number of ESOs granted. Intuitively we expect the total cost to increase as the number of options M increases, but the effect is far from linear. In Figure 3.5, we see that the average per-unit cost and average time to exercise are increasing as M increases. In other words, under the assumption that the ESOs will be exercised gradually, a larger ESO grant has an indirect effect of delaying exercises, and thus leading to higher ESO costs. The increasing trends hold for different exercise intensities, but the rate of increase diminishes significantly for large M. Also, the higher the exercise intensity, the lower the per-unit cost and shorter averaged time to exercise.

3.4. Stochastic Exercise Intensity

Now we discuss the stochastic exercise intensity, an extension to the previous model, that $\lambda_t = \lambda(t, S_t)$, which is the function not only depends on the time t also depends on the stock price S_t. Accordingly, the corresponding vested ESO cost $C^{(m)}(t, s)$ will satisfy

$$-(r + \lambda(t, s) + \beta)C^{(m)} + C_t^{(m)} + \mathscr{L}C^{(m)} + \lambda(t, s) \sum_{z=1}^{m-1} p_{m,z} C^{(m-z)}$$

$$+ (\lambda(t, s)\bar{p}_m + m\beta)(s - K)^+ = 0, \tag{3.14}$$

for $m = 1, \ldots, M$, and $(t, s) \in [t_v, T] \times \mathbb{R}_+$, with terminal condition $C^{(m)}(T, s) = m(s - K)^+$, for $s \in \mathbb{R}_+$.

Since we only discuss the stochastic exercise intensity and the employee will not exercise the option during the vesting period, the PDE for unvested ESO will remain unchanged. Next, we will discuss how to numerically solve (3.14) by FFT.

For applying Fourier transform, we use the same notation as in Section 3.3.1 that

$$f^{(m)}(t, x) = C^{(m)}(t, Ke^x),$$

for $m = 1, \ldots, M$, $(t, x) \in [t_v, T] \times \mathbb{R}$, and

$$\mathscr{F}[f^{(m)}](t, \omega) = \int_{-\infty}^{\infty} f^{(m)}(t, x)e^{-i\omega x} dx, \tag{3.15}$$

for $m = 1, \ldots, M$. In this section, we assume that $\lambda(t, x) = A(t) - B(t)x$, for some positive time-dependent functions $A(t)$ and $B(t)$. For implementation, we assume $B(t)$ be relative small, such that $\lambda(t, x)$ stay positive in

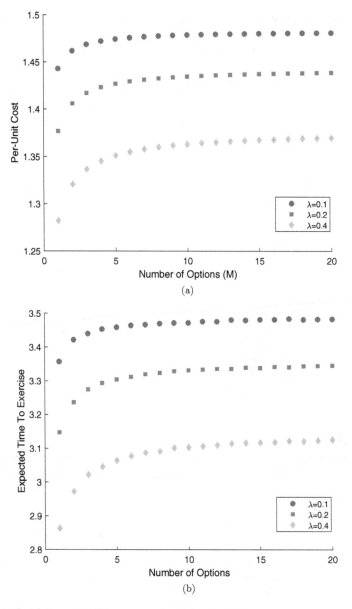

Figure 3.5. (a) Per-unit ESO cost as a function of number of options granted M with different exercise intensities λ. (b) With $M = 20$ options under different exercise intensities λ, we calculate the average exercise times by Monte-Carlo simulation with 10^8 simulated paths of exercise process. Common parameters: $S_0 = K = 10$, $r = 5\%$, $q = 1.5\%$, $\sigma = 20\%$, $p_{m,z} = 1/m$, $T = 10$, $t_v = 1$, $\beta = 0.5$ and $\alpha = 0.1$. In FFT: $N_x = 2^{12}$, $x_{\min} = -10$, $x_{\max} = 10$.

the truncated space $(t_v, T) \times [-x_{\max}, x_{\max}]$. Then, $f^{(m)}(t, x)$ satisfies

$$-(r + A(t) - B(t)x + \beta)f^{(m)} + f_t^{(m)} + \widetilde{\mathscr{L}}f^{(m)}$$

$$+(A(t) - B(t)x) \sum_{z=1}^{m-1} p_{m,z} f^{(m-z)}$$

$$+((A(t) - B(t)x)\bar{p}_m + m\beta)(Ke^x - K)^+ = 0, \qquad (3.16)$$

where $\widetilde{\mathscr{L}}$ is defined in (3.5). The terminal condition is $f^{(m)}(T, x) = m(Ke^x - K)^+$, for $x \in [-x_{\max}, x_{\max}]$.

Using (3.15) and the property of Fourier transform that $\mathscr{F}[xf](t, \omega) = i\partial_\omega \mathscr{F}[f](t, \omega)$, we transform PDE (3.16) into

$$\frac{\partial}{\partial t}\mathscr{F}[f^{(m)}](t, \omega) + iB(t)\frac{\partial}{\partial \omega}\mathscr{F}[f^{(m)}](t, \omega)$$

$$-h(t, \omega)\mathscr{F}[f^{(m)}](t, \omega) + \psi^{(m)}(t, \omega) = 0, \qquad (3.17)$$

where

$$h(t, \omega) = -\left(r - q - \frac{\sigma^2}{2}\right)i\omega + \frac{\sigma^2\omega^2}{2} + r + A(t) + \beta,$$

$$\psi^{(m)}(t, \omega) = \sum_{z=1}^{m-1} p_{m,z}\mathscr{F}[\lambda f^{(m-z)}](t, \omega)$$

$$+ \mathscr{F}[(\lambda\bar{p}_m + m\beta)(Ke^x - K)^+](t, \omega),$$

for $(t, \omega) \in [t_v, T) \times \mathbb{R}$.

Observe that (3.17) is a first-order PDE with terminal condition that $\mathscr{F}[f^{(m)}](T, \omega) = m\varphi(\omega)$ (see (3.6)). Therefore, we apply the method of characteristics and get

$$\mathscr{F}[f^{(m)}](t, \omega) = e^{-\int_t^T h\left(s, \omega - i\int_s^t B(u)du\right)ds} \mathscr{F}[f^{(m)}]\left(T, \omega + i\int_t^T B(u)du\right)$$

$$+ \int_t^T g^{(m)}(\tau, \omega; t)d\tau, \qquad (3.18)$$

where

$$g^{(m)}(\tau, \omega; t) = e^{-\int_t^\tau h\left(s, \omega - i\int_s^t B(u)du\right)ds}\psi^{(m)}\left(\tau, \omega + i\int_t^\tau B(u)du\right).$$

$$(3.19)$$

For numerical implementation, we can use the similar method mentioned in Section 3.3.1. We can make the approximation

$$\int_t^T g^{(m)}(\tau, \omega; t) d\tau$$

$$\approx \left(\frac{1}{2} g^{(m)}(t, \omega; t) + \frac{1}{2} g^{(m)}(T, \omega; t) + \sum_{i=1}^{i=N-1} g^{(m)}(t + i\delta t, \omega; t) \right) \delta t,$$

where $\delta t = (T - t)/N$. The integral $\int B(u)du$ in (3.18) and (3.19) can be approximated similarly or computed explicitly depending on the choice of $B(t)$.

Table 3.3 presents the ESO costs in the cases of constant exercise intensity $\lambda = 0.2$ and stochastic intensity with $\lambda(s) = 0.2 - 0.02 \log(s/K)$ under different vesting periods and job termination rates. The stochastic intensity specified here can be larger or smaller than the constant level 0.2 depending on whether the current stock price s is higher or lower than the strike price K. For each case, we compute the ESO cost using both FFT and FDM. For the latter, we apply the Crank–Nicolson method on a uniform grid and adopt Neumann condition at the boundary $s = S_*$ (see

Table 3.3. ESO costs with constant intensity $\lambda = 0.2$ and stochastic exercise intensity $\lambda(s) = 0.2 - 0.02 * \log(s/K)$ with different job termination rates α and β and vesting period t_v, computed using FFT and FDM for comparison. Common parameters: $S_0 = K = 10$, $r = 5\%$, $q = 1.5\%$, $\sigma = 20\%$, $p_{m,z} = 1/m$, $M = 5$, $T = 10$. In FDM: $S_* = 30$, $\delta S = 0.1$, $\delta t = 0.1$. In FFT: $N_x = 2^{12}$, $X_{\min} = -10$ and $X_{\max} = 10$.

Parameters		$t_v = 1$		$t_v = 2$		$t_v = 4$	
		FDM	FFT	FDM	FFT	FDM	FFT
λ							
$\beta = 0$	$\alpha = 0$	12.8052	12.8065	13.7122	13.7134	15.0953	15.0967
	$\alpha = 0.1$	11.5867	11.5878	11.2266	11.2276	10.1187	10.1196
$\beta = 0.5$	$\alpha = 0$	7.8849	7.8859	9.6380	9.6388	12.4022	12.4029
	$\alpha = 0.1$	7.1347	7.1355	7.8910	7.8916	8.3135	8.3139
$\lambda(s)$							
$\beta = 0$	$\alpha = 0$	12.8310	12.8379	13.7364	13.7445	15.1130	15.1235
	$\alpha = 0.1$	11.6099	11.6163	11.2464	11.2531	10.1305	10.1376
$\beta = 0.5$	$\alpha = 0$	7.8895	7.8887	9.6428	9.6423	12.4068	12.4076
	$\alpha = 0.1$	7.1387	7.1381	7.8948	7.8946	8.3165	8.3172

Section 3.3.2). As we can see, the costs from the two methods are practically the same. As the vesting period lengthens, from $t_v = 1$ to $t_v = 4$, the ESO cost tends to increase under different exercise intensities and job termination rates. When the job termination rate β is zero, the ESO costs with stochastic intensity appear to be higher, but this effect is greatly reduced as the job termination rate increases. This is intuitive since a high job termination rate means that most ESOs will be exercised or forfeited at the departure time, rather than exercised according to an exercise process over the life of the options.

3.5. Maturity Randomization

In this section, we propose an alternative valuation method based on maturity randomization. It is an analytical method that yields an approximation to the original ESO valuation problem discussed in Section 3.2.3. The core idea of this method is to randomize the ESO's finite maturity by an exponential random variable $\tau \sim \exp(\kappa)$, with $\kappa = 1/T$ where T here is original constant maturity. Such a choice of parameter means that $\mathbb{E}[\tau] = T$; that is, the ESO is expected to expire at time T. For instance, if the maturity of the ESOs is 10 years, then the randomized maturity is modeled by $\tau \sim \exp(0.1)$. Such a maturity randomization allows us to derive an explicit approximation for ESO cost.

3.5.1. *Vested ESO*

First we consider the ESO cost at the end of the vesting period. Provided that the employee remains at the firm by time t_v, the vested ESO has a remaining maturity of length $T - t_v$. Therefore, for the exponentially distributed maturity $\tau \sim \exp(\kappa)$, one may set $\kappa = 1/(T - t_v)$. At time t_v, the vested ESO cost function $C^{(m)}(s)$ is given by

$$
\begin{aligned}
C^{(m)}(s) = \mathbb{E}\Bigg\{ &\int_{t_v}^{\tau \wedge \xi} e^{-r(u-t_v)}(S_u - K)^+ dL_u \\
&+ e^{-r(\tau \wedge \xi - t_v)}(M - L_{\tau \wedge \xi})(S_{\tau \wedge \xi} - K)^+ \mid S_{t_v} = s, \\
&L_{t_v} = M - m, \tau \wedge \xi \geq t_v \Bigg\} \\
= \mathbb{E}\Bigg\{ &\int_{t_v}^{\infty} e^{-(r+\kappa+\beta)(u-t_v)}(S_u - K)^+ dL_u
\end{aligned}
$$

$$+ \int_{t_v}^{\infty} (\kappa + \beta) e^{-(r+\kappa+\beta)(u-t_v)} (M - L_u)(S_u - K)^+ du \mid S_{t_v} = s,$$

$$L_{t_v} = M - m \Bigg\}$$

$$= \mathbb{E} \Bigg\{ \int_0^{\infty} e^{-(r+\kappa+\beta)u} (S_u - K)^+ dL_u$$

$$+ \int_0^{\infty} (\kappa + \beta) e^{-(r+\kappa+\beta)u} (M - L_u)(S_u - K)^+ du \mid S_0 = s,$$

$$L_0 = M - m \Bigg\}, \tag{3.20}$$

for $m = 1, \ldots, M$. From (3.20), we derive the associated ODE for $C^{(m)}(s)$. For the convenience, we denote

$$a_0 = -(r + \lambda + \beta + \kappa), \quad a_1 = r - q, \quad a_2 = \frac{\sigma^2}{2}, \quad g_m = \lambda \bar{p}_m + m(\beta + \kappa).$$

Then, we obtain a system of second-order linear ODEs:

$$a_0 C^{(m)} + a_1 s \frac{d}{ds} C^{(m)} + a_2 s^2 \frac{d^2}{ds^2} C^{(m)}$$

$$+ \lambda \sum_{z=1}^{m-1} p_{m,z} C^{(m-z)} + g_m (s - K)^+ = 0, \tag{3.21}$$

for $m = 1, \ldots, M$, and $s \in \mathbb{R}_+$, with the boundary condition $C^{(m)}(0) = 0$.

Proposition 3.4. *The solution to the ODE system* (3.21) *is*

$$C^{(m)}(s) = \begin{cases} A_m s + B_m K + \displaystyle\sum_{n=0}^{m-1} E_{m,n} \left[\ln \left(\frac{s}{K} \right) \right]^n \left(\frac{s}{K} \right)^{\gamma-\theta} & \text{if } s > K, \\[2em] \displaystyle\sum_{n=0}^{m-1} F_{m,n} \left[\ln \left(\frac{s}{K} \right) \right]^n \left(\frac{s}{K} \right)^{\gamma+\theta} & \text{if } 0 \le s \le K, \end{cases} \tag{3.22}$$

for $m = 1, \ldots, M$, where

$$A_m = \frac{1}{a_1 + a_0}\left(-\lambda\sum_{z=1}^{m-1} p_{m,z}A_{m-z} - g_m\right),$$

$$B_m = \frac{1}{a_0}\left(-\lambda\sum_{z=1}^{m-1} p_{m,z}B_{m-z} + g_m\right),$$

$$E_{1,0} = -\frac{(A_1 + B_1)K(\gamma + \theta) - A_1 K}{2\theta},$$

$$F_{1,0} = -\frac{(A_1 + B_1)K(\gamma - \theta) - A_1 K}{2\theta},$$

$$E_{m,m-1} = -\frac{\lambda p_{m,1}E_{m-1,m-2}}{(m-1)[a_1 + 2a_2(\gamma - \theta) - a_2]}, \quad \text{for } m \geq 2,$$

$$F_{m,m-1} = -\frac{\lambda p_{m,1}F_{m-1,m-2}}{(m-1)[a_1 + 2a_2(\gamma + \theta) - a_2]}, \quad \text{for } m \geq 2,$$

$$E_{m,n} = -\frac{\lambda\sum_{z=1}^{m-n} p_{m,z}E_{m-z,n-1} + (n+1)na_2 E_{m,n+1}}{n[a_1 + 2a_2(\gamma - \theta) - a_2]},$$

$$\text{for } 1 \leq n \leq m - 2,$$

$$F_{m,n} = -\frac{\lambda\sum_{z=1}^{m-n} p_{m,z}F_{m-z,n-1} + (n+1)na_2 F_{m,n+1}}{n[a_1 + 2a_2(\gamma + \theta) - a_2]},$$

$$\text{for } 1 \leq n \leq m - 2,$$

$$E_{m,0} = -\frac{(A_m + B_m)K(\gamma + \theta) - A_m K + F_{m,1} - E_{m,1}}{2\theta}, \quad \text{for } m \geq 2,$$

$$F_{m,0} = -\frac{(A_m + B_m)K(\gamma - \theta) - A_m K + F_{m,1} - E_{m,1}}{2\theta}, \quad \text{for } m \geq 2,$$

and

$$\gamma = \frac{1}{2} - \frac{r - q}{\sigma^2}, \quad \theta = \sqrt{\gamma^2 + \frac{2(r + \lambda + \beta + \kappa)}{\sigma^2}}.$$

Proof. We begin by considering the case that the employee only holds a single option. With $M = 1$, the general solution to ODE (3.21) is given by

$$C^{(1)}(s) = \begin{cases} A_1 s + B_1 K + E_{1,0}\left(\dfrac{s}{K}\right)^{\gamma - \theta} + \tilde{E}_{1,0}\left(\dfrac{s}{K}\right)^{\gamma + \theta} & \text{if } s > K, \\[2ex] F_{1,0}\left(\dfrac{s}{K}\right)^{\gamma + \theta} + \tilde{F}_{1,0}\left(\dfrac{s}{K}\right)^{\gamma - \theta} & \text{if } 0 \leq s \leq K, \end{cases}$$

where

$$A_1 = -\frac{g_1}{a_1 + a_0}, \quad B_1 = \frac{g_1}{a_0}.$$

By imposing that $C^{(1)}(s)$ and $\frac{d}{ds}C^{(1)}(s)$ to be continuous at the strike price K, we consider $C^{(1)}(s)$ at $s = K$ and obtain

$$\begin{bmatrix} 1 & 1 \\ \gamma - \theta & \gamma + \theta \end{bmatrix} \begin{bmatrix} E_{1,0} - \tilde{F}_{1,0} \\ \tilde{E}_{1,0} - F_{1,0} \end{bmatrix} = -K \begin{bmatrix} A_1 + B_1 \\ A_1 \end{bmatrix}$$

$$\Rightarrow \begin{bmatrix} E_{1,0} - \tilde{F}_{1,0} \\ \tilde{E}_{1,0} - F_{1,0} \end{bmatrix} = -\frac{K}{2\theta} \begin{bmatrix} (\gamma + \theta)(A_1 + B_1) - A_1 \\ -(\gamma - \theta)(A_1 + B_1) + A_1 \end{bmatrix}.$$

In addition, since $\gamma - \theta < 0$, we will have $\tilde{F}_{1,0} = 0$ to guarantee that $C^{(1)}(0) = 0$. And, when $\kappa \to \infty$, the maturity $\tau \to 0$, $\mathbb{P}$-a.s., which will lead to $C^{(1)}(s) \to (s - K)^+$. Therefore, we have $\tilde{E}_{1,0} = 0$. As a result, we obtain the remaining non-zero coefficients:

$$\begin{bmatrix} E_{1,0} \\ F_{1,0} \end{bmatrix} = -\frac{K}{2\theta} \begin{bmatrix} (\gamma + \theta)(A_1 + B_1) - A_1 \\ (\gamma - \theta)(A_1 + B_1) - A_1 \end{bmatrix}.$$

For $M \geq 2$, the general solution to ODE (3.21) is

$$C^{(m)}(s) = \begin{cases} A_m s + B_m K + \sum_{n=0}^{m-1} E_{m,n} \left[\ln\left(\frac{s}{K}\right)\right]^n \left(\frac{s}{K}\right)^{\gamma - \theta} & \text{if } s > K, \\[2em] \sum_{n=0}^{m-1} F_{m,n} \left[\ln\left(\frac{s}{K}\right)\right]^n \left(\frac{s}{K}\right)^{\gamma + \theta} & \text{if } 0 \leq s \leq K. \end{cases}$$

$$(3.23)$$

Applying ODE (3.21), we obtain the relationship between the coefficients of $C^{(m)}(s)$ and the coefficients of $C^{(n)}(s)$, for $n \leq m - 1$, as follows:

$$A_m = \frac{1}{a_1 + a_0}\left(-\lambda \sum_{z=1}^{m-1} p_{m,z} A_{m-z} - g_m\right),$$

$$B_m = \frac{1}{a_0}\left(-\lambda \sum_{z=1}^{m-1} p_{m,z} B_{m-z} + g_m\right),$$

$$E_{m,m-1} = -\frac{\lambda p_{m,1} E_{m-1,m-2}}{(m-1)[a_1 + 2a_2(\gamma - \theta) - a_2]},$$

$$F_{m,m-1} = -\frac{\lambda p_{m,1} F_{m-1,m-2}}{(m-1)[a_1 + 2a_2(\gamma + \theta) - a_2]},$$

$$E_{m,n} = -\frac{\lambda \sum_{z=1}^{m-n} p_{m,z} E_{m-z,n-1} + (n+1)na_2 E_{m,n+1}}{n[a_1 + 2a_2(\gamma - \theta) - a_2]},$$

$$\text{for } 1 \leq n \leq m-2,$$

$$F_{m,n} = -\frac{\lambda \sum_{z=1}^{m-n} p_{m,z} F_{m-z,n-1} + (n+1)na_2 F_{m,n+1}}{n[a_1 + 2a_2(\gamma + \theta) - a_2]},$$

$$\text{for } 1 \leq n \leq m-2,$$

for $m = 2, \ldots, M$.

In addition, the continuity of $C^{(m)}(s)$ and $\frac{d}{ds} C^{(m)}(s)$ around strike price K yields that

$$(A_m + B_m)K + E_{m,0} = F_{m,0},$$

$$A_m + (\gamma - \theta)\frac{E_{m,0}}{K} + \frac{E_{m,1}}{K} = (\gamma + \theta)\frac{F_{m,0}}{K} + \frac{F_{m,1}}{K}.$$

Rearranging, we obtain the remaining coefficients for the solution:

$$E_{m,0} = -\frac{(A_m + B_m)K(\gamma + \theta) - A_m K + F_{m,1} - E_{m,1}}{2\theta},$$

$$F_{m,0} = -\frac{(A_m + B_m)K(\gamma - \theta) - A_m K + F_{m,1} - E_{m,1}}{2\theta}. \qquad \square$$

3.5.2. Unvested ESO

For the unvested ESO, we can model the vesting time t_v by the exponential random variable $\tau_v \sim \exp(\tilde{\kappa})$, where $\tilde{\kappa} = 1/t_v$. Then, the unvested ESO cost at time 0 is given by

$$\tilde{C}^{(m)}(s) = \mathbb{E}\left\{ e^{-(r+\alpha)\tau_v} C^{(m)}(S_{\tau_v}) \middle| S_0 = s \right\}$$

$$= \mathbb{E}\left\{ \int_0^\infty \tilde{\kappa} e^{-(r+\alpha+\tilde{\kappa})u} C^{(m)}(S_u) du \middle| S_0 = s \right\}.$$

Then we will derive the ODE for $\tilde{C}^{(m)}(s)$:

$$-(r+\alpha+\tilde{\kappa})\tilde{C}^{(m)} + (r-q)s\frac{d}{ds}\tilde{C}^{(m)} + \frac{\sigma^2 s^2}{2}\frac{d^2}{ds^2}\tilde{C}^{(m)}$$

$$+\tilde{\kappa}C^{(m)} = 0 \quad \text{for } s \in \mathbb{R}_+,$$

$$\tilde{C}^{(m)}(0) = 0.$$

Assuming $\lambda + \beta + \kappa \neq \alpha + \tilde{\kappa}$, we could derive the solution for $\tilde{C}^{(m)}$ from the solution for $C^{(m)}$ in (3.23), which is

$$
\tilde{C}^{(m)}(s) = \begin{cases} \tilde{A}_m s + \tilde{B}_m K + \sum_{n=0}^{m-1} \tilde{E}_{m,n} \\ \quad \times \left[\ln\left(\frac{s}{K}\right) \right]^n \left(\frac{s}{K}\right)^{\gamma-\theta} + \tilde{E}_m \left(\frac{s}{K}\right)^{\tilde{\gamma}-\tilde{\theta}} & \text{if } s > K, \\[2em] \sum_{n=0}^{m-1} \tilde{F}_{m,n} \left[\ln\left(\frac{s}{K}\right) \right]^n \left(\frac{s}{K}\right)^{\gamma+\theta} + \tilde{F}_m \left(\frac{s}{K}\right)^{\tilde{\gamma}+\tilde{\theta}} & \text{if } 0 \leq s \leq K, \end{cases}
$$

where

$$
\tilde{\gamma} = \gamma = \frac{1}{2} - \frac{r-q}{\sigma^2},
$$

$$
\tilde{\theta} = \sqrt{\tilde{\gamma}^2 + \frac{2(r+\alpha+\tilde{\kappa})}{\sigma^2}},
$$

$$
\tilde{A}_m = \frac{\tilde{\kappa} A_m}{q + \alpha + \tilde{\kappa}},
$$

$$
\tilde{B}_m = \frac{\tilde{\kappa} B_m}{r + \alpha + \tilde{\kappa}},
$$

and

$$
\tilde{E}_{m,m-1} = -\frac{\tilde{\kappa} E_{m,m-1}}{R},
$$

$$
\tilde{F}_{m,m-1} = -\frac{\tilde{\kappa} F_{m,m-1}}{R},
$$

$$
\tilde{E}_{m,m-2} = -\frac{\tilde{\kappa} E_{m,m-2} + (m-1) P_1 \tilde{E}_{m,m-1}}{R},
$$

$$
\tilde{F}_{m,m-2} = -\frac{\tilde{\kappa} F_{m,m-2} + (m-1) Q_1 \tilde{F}_{m,m-1}}{R},
$$

$$
\tilde{E}_m = \frac{(\tilde{\gamma} + \tilde{\theta}) P - Q}{2\tilde{\theta}},
$$

$$
\tilde{F}_m = \frac{(\tilde{\gamma} - \tilde{\theta}) P - Q}{2\tilde{\theta}},
$$

$$
\tilde{E}_{m,n} = -\frac{2\tilde{\kappa} E_{m,n} + 2(n+1) P_1 \tilde{E}_{m,n+1} + \sigma^2 (n+2)(n+1) \tilde{E}_{m,n+2}}{2R},
$$

$$
\tilde{F}_{m,n} = -\frac{2\tilde{\kappa} F_{m,n} + 2(n+1) Q_1 \tilde{F}_{m,n+1} + \sigma^2 (n+2)(n+1) \tilde{F}_{m,n+2}}{2R},
$$

for $0 \leq n \leq m - 3$, with

$$R = \lambda + \beta + \kappa - \alpha - \tilde{\kappa},$$

$$P_1 = r - q + \frac{\sigma^2(2\gamma - 2\theta - 1)}{2},$$

$$Q_1 = r - q + \frac{\sigma^2(2\gamma + 2\theta - 1)}{2},$$

$$P = \tilde{F}_{m,0} - \tilde{E}_{m,0} - K\tilde{A}_m - K\tilde{B}_m,$$

$$Q = (\gamma + \theta)\tilde{F}_{m,0} - (\gamma - \theta)\tilde{E}_{m,0} - K\tilde{A}_m + \tilde{F}_{m,1} - \tilde{E}_{m,1}.$$

Alternatively, one can use FDM or FFT to calculate the unvested ESO cost without applying maturity randomization for the second time.

In Figure 3.6, we show the cost of an unvested ESO, computed by our maturity randomization method, as a function of the initial stock price S_0,

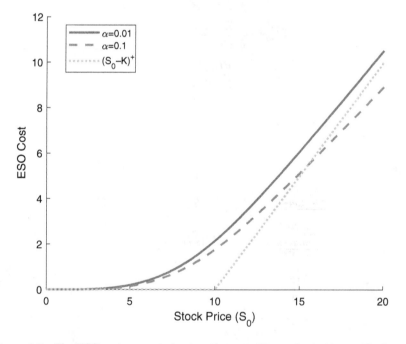

Figure 3.6. The ESO cost computed using the maturity randomization method, and plotted as a function of stock price S_0 with two different job termination rates $\alpha = 0.01, 0.1$, along with the ESO payoff function $(S_0 - K)^+$ for comparison. Parameters: $T = 10$, $t_v = 2$, $\kappa = 0.125$, $\tilde{\kappa} = 0.5$, $r = 5\%$, $q = 1.5\%$, $\sigma = 20\%$, $\lambda = 0.1$ and $\beta = 0.1$.

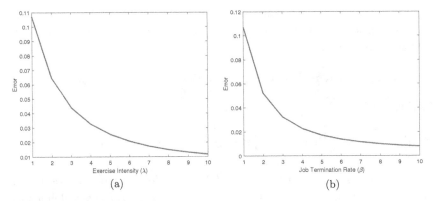

Figure 3.7. Plots of the errors of maturity randomization method as a function of (a) exercise intensity λ and (b) job termination rate β. Parameters: $\beta = 1$ (in (a)), $\lambda = 1$ (in (b)), $S_0 = K = 10$, $T = 10$, $t_v = 0$, $\kappa = 0.1$, $\tilde{\kappa} = 0$, $r = 5\%$, $q = 1.5\%$, $\sigma = 20\%$, $p_{m,z} = 1/m$ and $M = 5$.

along with the ESO payoff. As expected, the ESO cost is increasing convex in S_0. Comparing the costs corresponding to two different job termination rates $\alpha \in \{0.01, 0.1\}$ during the vesting period, we see that a higher job termination rate reduces the ESO value. This is intuitive as the employee has a higher chance of leaving the firm during the vesting period and in turn losing the option entirely.

The maturity randomization method delivers an analytical approximation that allows for instant computation. In Figure 3.7, we examine errors of this method. As we can see, as the exercise intensity λ or post vesting job termination rate β increases the valuation error decreases exponentially to less than a penny for each option. This shows that the maturity randomization method can be very accurate and effective for ESO valuation.

3.6. Implied Maturity

Given that ESOs are very likely to be exercised prior to expiration, the total cost of an ESO grant is determined by how long the employee holds the options. For each grant of M options, the exercise times are different and they depend on the valuation model and associated parameters. Therefore, we introduce the notion of implied maturity to give an intuitive measure of the effective maturity implied by any given valuation model.

Like the well-known concept of implied volatility, we use the Black–Scholes option pricing formula. The price of a vanilla European call with strike K and maturity T is given by

$$C_{BS}(t, S_t; T) = e^{-q(T-t)} S_t \Phi(d_1) - e^{-r(T-t)} K \Phi(d_2),$$

where

$$d_1 = \frac{1}{\sigma\sqrt{T-t}} \left[\ln\left(\frac{S_t}{K}\right) + \left(r + \frac{\sigma^2}{2}\right)(T-t) \right], \quad d_2 = d_1 - \sigma\sqrt{T-t}.$$

Next, recall the ESO cost function $C^{(m)}(t, s)$ under the top-down valuation model in Section 3.2. Then, the *implied maturity* for m ESOs is defined to be the maturity parameter $\tilde{T}$ such that

$$C_{BS}(S_0, \tilde{T}) = \max\left\{ \frac{C^{(m)}(0, S_0)}{m}, (S_0 - K)^+ \right\} \tag{3.24}$$

holds, with all other parameters held constant. To define the implied maturity under another model only requires replacing the corresponding cost function on the right-hand side in (3.24). We summarize the numerically computed implied maturities under different settings in Tables 3.4 and 3.5.

Table 3.4. Implied maturities for vested and unvested ESO costs under different exercise intensities λ and different job termination rates α and β, computed using FFT and FDM for comparison. Common parameters: $S_0 = K = 10$, $r = 5\%$, $q = 1.5\%$, $\sigma = 20\%$, $p_{m,z} = 1/m$, $M = 5$ and $T = 10$. In FDM: $S_* = 30$, $\delta S = 0.1$, $\delta t = 0.1$. In FFT: $N_x = 2^{12}$, $x_{\min} = -10$ and $x_{\max} = 10$.

Parameters		$t_v = 0$		$t_v = 2$		$t_v = 4$	
		FDM	FFT	FDM	FFT	FDM	FFT
$\alpha = 0.1, \beta = 0$	$\lambda = 1$	1.2771	1.2782	2.3956	2.3959	2.6392	2.6394
	$\lambda = 2$	0.6416	0.6426	1.9236	1.9239	2.3240	2.3241
$\alpha = 0.1, \beta = 1$	$\lambda = 1$	0.5065	0.5076	1.8226	1.8229	2.2553	2.2555
	$\lambda = 2$	0.3634	0.3645	1.7097	1.7100	2.1780	2.1783
$\alpha = 0, \beta = 0.1$	$\lambda = 1$	1.1129	1.1140	3.2383	3.2389	5.2532	5.2538
	$\lambda = 2$	0.5967	0.5978	2.6829	2.6835	4.6917	4.6923
$\alpha = 1, \beta = 0.1$	$\lambda = 1$	1.1129	1.1140	0.0880	0.0881	0.0030	0.0030
	$\lambda = 2$	0.5967	0.5978	0.0719	0.0719	0.0027	0.0027

Table 3.5. Implied maturities for unvested ESO costs under different exercise intensities λ and different job termination rates α and β, computed using FFT and FDM for comparison. Common parameters: $S_0 = 10$, $r = 5\%$, $q = 1.5\%$, $\sigma = 20\%$, $p_{m,z} = 1/m$, $M = 5$, $t_v = 2$ and $T = 10$. In FDM: $S_* = 30$, $\delta S = 0.1$, $\delta t = 0.1$. In FFT: $N_x = 2^{12}$, $x_{min} = -10$ and $x_{max} = 10$.

Parameters		$K = 9$		$K = 10$		$K = 11$	
		FDM	FFT	FDM	FFT	FDM	FFT
$\alpha = 0.1, \beta = 0$	$\lambda = 1$	2.0515	2.0516	2.3956	2.3959	2.6279	2.6281
	$\lambda = 2$	1.6113	1.6114	1.9236	1.9239	2.1224	2.1226
$\alpha = 0.1, \beta = 1$	$\lambda = 1$	1.5168	1.5170	1.8226	1.8229	2.0145	2.0147
	$\lambda = 2$	1.4114	1.4115	1.7097	1.7100	1.8935	1.8937
$\alpha = 0, \beta = 0.1$	$\lambda = 1$	3.2369	3.2372	3.2383	3.2389	3.2491	3.2494
	$\lambda = 2$	2.6830	2.6833	2.6829	2.6835	2.6873	2.6876
$\alpha = 1, \beta = 0.1$	$\lambda = 1$	0.0001	0.0001	0.0880	0.0881	0.3822	0.3823
	$\lambda = 2$	0.0001	0.0001	0.0719	0.0719	0.3405	0.3405

Through the lens of implied maturity, we can see that the model and parameter effects in terms of how long the employee will hold the option under the Black–Scholes model. For example, if the exercise intensity λ increases, then the ESOs are more likely to be exercised early, resulting in a lower cost. Since the call option value is increasing in maturity, the implied maturity is expected to decrease as exercise intensity increases. The plots in Figure 3.8 confirm this intuition. Moreover, under high exercise intensity all ESOs will be exercised very early and the contract maturity will play a lesser role on the ESO cost and thus implied maturity. Indeed, Figure 3.8 shows that implied maturities associated with different contract maturities $T = 5, 8$ and 10 get closer as λ increases.

Next, we consider the effect of the total number of ESOs granted. Since the ESOs will be exercised gradually, a larger ESO grant has an indirect effect of delaying exercises and thus intuitively should increase the implied maturity. In Figure 3.9, we see that the implied maturity is indeed increasing as the number of options M increases, but the rate of increase diminishes significantly for large M and the implied maturity stays below the contract maturity T.

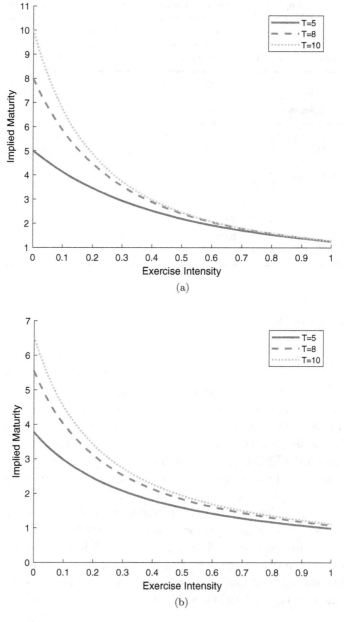

Figure 3.8. Implied maturity as a function of employee exercise intensity λ when the maturity $T = 5, 8$ or 10 year, computed using (a) FFT, or (b) maturity randomization. Parameters: $S_0 = K = 10$, $r = 5\%$, $q = 1.5\%$, $\sigma = 20\%$, $p_{m,z} = 1/m$, $M = 5$, $t_v = 0$ and $\beta = 0.1$. In FFT: $N_x = 2^{12}$, $x_{\min} = -10$, $x_{\max} = 10$.

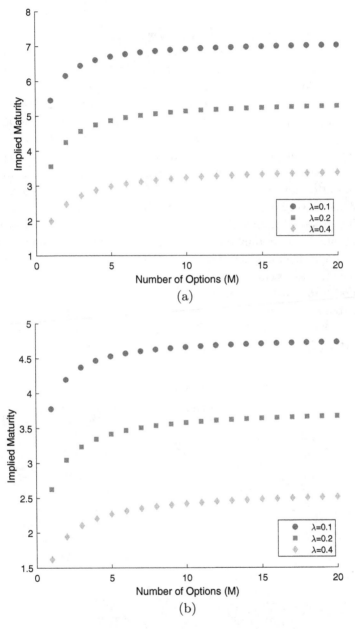

Figure 3.9. Implied maturity as a function of number of options granted M with different exercise intensities λ, computed using (a) FFT, or (b) maturity randomization. Common parameters: $S_0 = K = 10$, $r = 5\%$, $q = 1.5\%$, $\sigma = 20\%$, $p_{m,z} = 1/m$, $T = 10$, $t_v = 0$ and $\beta = 0.5$. In FFT: $N_x = 2^{12}$, $x_{\min} = -10$, $x_{\max} = 10$.

3.7. Conclusion

We have studied a new valuation framework that allows the ESO holder to spread out the exercises of different quantities over time, rather than assuming that all options will be exercised at the same time. The holder's multiple random exercises are modeled by an exogenous jump process. The distribution of multiple-date exercises is consistent with empirical evidence. Additional features included are job termination risk during and after the vesting period. For cost computation, we apply a fast Fourier transform method and finite difference method to solve the associated systems of PDEs. Moreover, we provide an alternative method based on maturity randomization for approximating the ESO cost. Its analytic formulas for vested and unvested ESO costs allow for instant computation.

The proposed numerical method is not only applicable to expensing ESO grants as required by regulators, but also useful for understanding the combined effects of exercise intensity and job termination risk on the ESO cost. For future research, there are a number of directions related to our proposed framework. For many companies, risk estimation for large ESO pool is both practically important and challenging. Another related issue concerns the incentive effect and optimal design of ESOs so that the firm can better align the employee's interest over a longer period of time.

Chapter 4

Utility-Based Valuation Methodology

4.1. Introduction

The ESO early exercise phenomenon, as discussed in previous chapters, indicates that no-arbitrage theory is inadequate for determining the exercise policy for ESOs. In particular, in the case of an American call written on a non-dividend paying underlying stock, no-arbitrage pricing models conclude that the holder should never exercise early.

To account for the employee's early exercise, the Financial Accounting Standards Board (FASB) proposes an expensing approach by adjusting the Black–Scholes (B–S) model. In particular, it recommends substituting the option expiration date with the expected time to exercise. Although this expensing method is very simple and convenient, it is far from accurate. Several studies, including Jennergren and Naslund (1993), Hemmer *et al.* (1994), and Huddart and Lang (1996), conclude that this adjusted B–S model fails to capture the employee's exercise behavior and overstates the cost of the ESOs to the firm.

In this chapter, we propose an ESO valuation model that captures the early exercise phenomenon and account for the associated cost effect. First, we illustrate that early exercises are optimal for a risk-averse employee with sale and hedging restrictions. Then, we show that the possibility of job termination induces the employee to adopt a more conservative exercising strategy, indirectly leading to early exercises. Moreover, job termination prior to maturity directly leads to early exercises by forcing the employee to exercise the ESO.

Our valuation model, in its simplest form, consists of two steps. First, we consider a risk-averse ESO holder who is subject to employment termination and constrained from selling the option or shorting the company stock, but is allowed to trade a partially correlated asset, such as the market index. The holder tries to decide when to exercise the ESO so that his expected utility of wealth is maximized. As a result, the holder obtains an exercise boundary. In technical terms, the ESO holder faces a stochastic control problem with optimal stopping. This problem is then formulated as a free boundary problem, from which we obtain the holder's exercise boundary. Next, the firm will use this boundary to find the cost of issuing this ESO. From the firm's perspective, the cost of this ESO is given by the no-arbitrage price of a barrier-type call option subject to early exercise due to job termination, where the barrier is the employee's optimal exercise boundary.

In our model, the employee's optimal exercise boundary differs from that in no-arbitrage pricing theory because the latter assumes the availability of a perfect hedge and the risk-neutrality of the holder. By no-arbitrage pricing theory, the holder's optimal exercise boundary is the one that maximizes the expected discounted payoff of the option. For this reason, we call it the *price-maximizing* boundary. To the contrary, the risk-averse employee in our model, who is constrained from selling the option and shorting the company stock, has no perfect hedge. The employee's exercise boundary is the one that maximizes the expected utility of holding the ESO, so we also call it the *utility-maximizing* boundary.

By incorporating job termination risk, we obtain a nonlinear free boundary problem of reaction–diffusion type for the employee's investment problem. Reaction–diffusion equations arise in utility problems in incomplete markets, for example, in portfolio choice with recursive utility (Tiu, 2004), and indifference pricing with interacting Itô and point processes (Becherer, 2004; Becherer and Schweizer, 2005), and indifference pricing in credit risk (Sircar and Zariphopoulou, 2010). In this chapter, we study the existence of solution and the properties of the free boundary for this problem.

We also include the case in which the employee is granted multiple ESOs and partial exercises are allowed. In the traditional no-arbitrage pricing theory for American options, the holder's exercise boundary for one American call is identical to that for multiple American calls. In other words, the holder always exercises all the options at the same time. However, it is well documented that ESO holders tend to gradually exercise fractions of their options through maturity. See, for instance, Huddart and Lang (1996).

Several authors have used the utility-based framework to explain the optimality of partial exercises of American options in incomplete markets.

For perpetual American options with zero interest rate, Grasselli and Henderson (2009) provide an analytic formula for the employee's exercise thresholds. For American-style ESOs with finite maturity, Jain and Subramanian (2004), Grasselli (2005) and Rogers and Scheinkman (2007) numerically determine the employee's optimal exercise policy, but in the absence of sudden job termination risk. All these authors show that partial exercises could be optimal for the option holder under certain constraints. In this chapter, we incorporate vesting and job termination risk, and provide a characterization for the optimal exercise time and a numerical scheme for the employee's optimal exercise boundaries. In particular, when a vesting period is imposed, the cost of ESOs with multiple exercise rights and the cost with simultaneous exercise constraint are almost the same.

We have a parametric model for ESO valuation which, given reasonable data, can be calibrated. This is a straightforward test of validity that may be used to select between various models. In addition to evaluating the behavioral assumptions described by the utility formulation, one can also design empirical tests to address questions relevant to ESO valuation. For this purpose, empirical data of ESO exercises that are well-segmented based on employees' attributes, including age, position, and the time and cause of job termination, are highly desirable.

The rest of the chapter is organized as follows. In Section 4.2, we formulate our valuation model for a single ESO. In Section 4.3, we analyze the employee's ESO exercise strategy and show that job termination risk induces the employee to adopt a more conservative exercising strategy. In Section 4.4, we compute the ESO cost with and without vesting. In Section 4.5, we extend our model to the case with multiple exercises and discuss their effects on the employee's exercising strategy and the ESO cost. Finally in Section 3.6, we investigate the existence and uniqueness of solution to the nonlinear free boundary problem associated with the ESO exercise timing.

4.2. The ESO Valuation Model

In this section, we present our valuation model for a single employee stock option. The case with multiple options is discussed in Section 4.5. To start our formulation, we consider a market with a riskless bank account that pays interest at constant rate r, and two risky assets, namely, the company stock, and a market index. The employee can only trade the bank account and the market index, but not the company stock. The latter is modeled as a diffusion process that satisfies

$$dY_u = (\nu - q)Y_u \, du + \eta Y_u \, dW_u, \quad u \geq t,$$

with $Y_t = y > 0$. The coefficients ν, q and η are constant. Here, ν and η are the stock's expected return and volatility, respectively. We also assume that the stock pays a constant proportional dividend q continuously over time.

The market index is another lognormal process that is partially correlated with the company stock

$$dS_u = \mu S_u \, du + \sigma S_u \, dB_u, \quad u \geq t,$$

with $S_t = S > 0$. The constant parameters μ and σ are, respectively, the market index's expected return and volatility. The two Brownian motions B and W are defined on a probability space $(\Omega, \mathscr{F}, (\mathscr{F}_u), \mathbb{P})$, where $\mathscr{F}_u$ is the augmented σ-algebra generated by $\{W_s, B_s; 0 \leq s \leq u\}$, and their instantaneous correlation is $\rho \in (-1, 1)$. The employee can use S to partially hedge away some of the risk in their portfolio, with some remaining idiosyncratic risk. In reality, the employee can trade more than one asset. If so, the aggregate of the traded assets is proxied by the index S.

The employee stock option in this chapter is an American call option, on the company stock with maturity T (typically 10 years, see Marquardt, 2002), with strike K and a vesting period $t_v \leq T$ (typically 2 to 4 years). At the exercise time, the firm sells a new stock issue to the employee at the price K. Following the arguments in Hull and White (2004b) and FASB statement 123R, we work under the assumption that the possible dilution effect is anticipated by the market and already reflected in the stock price immediately after the ESO grant.

Due to vesting, the employee cannot exercise the option before t_v. If the employee leaves the firm during the vesting period, then the option becomes worthless. If the employee's departure happens after the vesting period, then he must exercise the ESO if it is in-the-money. As the vesting period increases to maturity, the ESO becomes a European call — the holder can exercise the ESO only at maturity.

The modeling of job termination is a delicate and important issue that has a crucial impact on ESO valuation, as we demonstrate in Figure 4.6. The fact that the horizon of the valuation problem is typically much shorter than the contractual term of the ESO has even been recognized in the FASB proposal, in which it recommends that the ESO maturity be shortened according to the job termination risk. On the one hand, it would be nice to develop and estimate a detailed model to account for the causes of job termination that separate voluntary and involuntary exits, and the classification of employees, for example, by age. In particular, external opportunities that tempt the employee to depart and exercise the ESO early might be considered. On the other hand, data are scarce and likely not well-segmented according to the identity of employee, or even the cause of job termination. Therefore, the literature has adopted reduced-form modeling that bypasses direct modeling of an individual employee's personal employment choices and potential inducement from external offers. Models that involve more complex information, including the fortellability of the employee's voluntary exit, are topics for future development as more comprehensive empirical data become available.

In our model, the employee's (voluntary or involuntary) employment termination time, denoted by τ^λ, is represented by an exponential random variable with parameter λ that is independent of the Brownian motions W and B. In Remark 4.13, we address how to adapt our formulation to more complex τ^λ. The rate of job termination λ can be estimated from the firm's historical data. For instance, one can take the inverse of the average time to job termination. We illustrate the payoff structure of the ESO in Figure 4.1.

4.2.1. *The employee's investment problem*

Since the employee cannot sell the ESO, or form a perfect hedge, it is important to consider his risk aversion. To this end, we represent his risk preference with the exponential utility function

$$U(x) = -e^{-\gamma x},$$

with a positive constant absolute risk-aversion coefficient $\gamma > 0$.

To solve the employee's investment problem, it is sufficient to consider the case with zero vesting. When vesting increases from zero, it effectively lifts the employee's *pre-vesting* exercise boundary to infinity, but leaves his *post-vesting* exercise policy unaffected. Now suppose, at time $t \in [0, T]$, the employee is endowed with an ESO and some positive wealth. The employee's investment problem is to decide *when* to exercise the option. We define $\mathcal{T}_{t,T}$ as the set of stopping times with respect to the filtration $(\mathcal{F}_u)$, taking values in $[t, T]$. Throughout the *entire period* $[t, T]$, the employee is assumed to trade dynamically in the bank account and the market index. A trading strategy $\{\theta_u; t \le u \le T\}$ is the cash amount invested in the market index S, and it is deemed admissible if it is $\mathcal{F}_u$-progressively measurable and satisfies the integrability condition $\mathbb{E}\{\int_t^T \theta_u^2 \, du\} < \infty$. The set of admissible strategies over the period $[t, T]$ is denoted by $\mathcal{Z}_{t,T}$. For $u \ge t$,

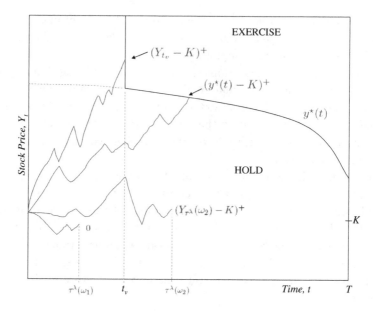

Figure 4.1. **ESO payoff structure.** The bottom path represents the scenario where the employee leaves the firm during the vesting period, resulting in forfeiture of the ESO. In the next path above, the employee is forced to exercise the ESO early due to job termination. The second from the top path hits the optimal exercise boundary $y^\star(t)$ after vesting, so the employee exercises the ESO there. The top one represents that the employee exercises the ESO immediately at the end of vesting.

the employee's trading wealth evolves according to

$$dX_u^\theta = [\theta_u(\mu - r) + rX_u]\, du + \theta_u \sigma\, dB_u, \quad X_t = x. \tag{4.1}$$

Upon the exercise of the option, either voluntarily or forced due to job termination, the employee will add the contract proceeds to his portfolio, and continue to optimally invest in the bank account and market index up to the maturity date T. Therefore, from the exercise time till the expiration date, the employee, who no longer holds an ESO, faces the classical Merton problem of optimal investment. According to Merton (1969), if an investor has x dollars at time $t \leq T$ and invests dynamically in the bank account and the market index until time T, then his maximal expected utility is given by

$$M(t, x) = \sup_{\mathcal{L}_{t,T}} \mathbb{E}\{-e^{-\gamma X_T} \mid X_t = x\}$$

$$= -e^{-\gamma x e^{r(T-t)}} e^{-\frac{(\mu-r)^2}{2\sigma^2}(T-t)}. \tag{4.2}$$

To interpret this, we can think of the first part $-e^{-\gamma x e^{r(T-t)}}$ as the utility from merely saving the proceeds in the bank account. The factor $e^{-\frac{(\mu-r)^2}{2\sigma^2}(T-t)}$ increases the utility (which is negative) due to the fact that the employee can invest in the market index, in addition to the bank account. Observe that, for any fixed x, M is decreasing with t.

We formulate the ESO holder's investment problem as a stochastic utility maximization with optimal stopping. We shall use the following short-hands for conditional expectations:

$$\mathbb{E}_{t,y}\{\cdot\} = \mathbb{E}\{\cdot \,|\, Y_t = y\}, \quad \mathbb{E}_{t,x,y}\{\cdot\} = \mathbb{E}\{\cdot \,|\, X_t = x, Y_t = y\}.$$

The employee's value function at time $t \in [0,T]$, given that he has not departed the firm and that his wealth $X_t = x$ and company stock price $Y_t = y$, is

$$V(t,x,y) = \sup_{\tau \in \mathscr{T}_{t,T}} \sup_{\mathscr{L}_{t,\tau}} \mathbb{E}_{t,x,y}\{M(\hat{\tau}, X_{\hat{\tau}} + (Y_{\hat{\tau}} - K)^+)\}$$

$$= \sup_{\tau \in \mathscr{T}_{t,T}} \sup_{\mathscr{L}_{t,\tau}} \mathbb{E}_{t,x,y}\{-e^{-\gamma(X_{\hat{\tau}}+(Y_{\hat{\tau}}-K)^+)e^{r(T-\hat{\tau})}} e^{-\frac{(\mu-r)^2}{2\sigma^2}(T-\hat{\tau})}\},$$

$$(4.3)$$

where $\hat{\tau} = \tau \wedge \tau^\lambda$. Observe that we are explicitly optimizing the expected utility over all stopping times, and over all trading strategies θ before τ. The *post-exercise* trading is implicitly optimized by the solution to the Merton problem M. Both of the expectations in (4.2) and (4.3) are taken under the historical measure, $\mathbb{P}$. By standard arguments from the theory of optimal stopping, the employee's optimal exercise time is given by

$$\tau^* := \inf\{t \le u \le T : V(u, X_u, Y_u) = M(u, X_u + (Y_u - K)^+)\}.$$

4.2.2. *ESO cost to the firm*

It turns out that the employee's optimal exercise time and the corresponding exercise boundary can be obtained by solving a free boundary problem. This will be discussed in the next section. Meanwhile, let us explain how to use the employee's exercise boundary to determine the ESO cost to the firm. In accordance with the FASB rules,[1] we assume that the company stock

---

[1] In paragraph A13 of FASB 123R, it specifically requires the use of "techniques that are used to establish trade prices for derivative instruments," and approves the use of risk-neutral models. Even if a firm does not hedge its ESOs, it should calculate and report the cost generated from such models.

evolves according to the following diffusion process under the risk-neutral measure $\mathbb{Q}$:

$$dY_u = (r - q)Y_u \, du + \eta Y_u \, dW_u^{\mathbb{Q}}, \quad u \geq t; \quad Y_t = y,$$

where $W^{\mathbb{Q}}$ is a $\mathbb{Q}$-Brownian motion, which is also independent of the job termination time τ^λ. As in Carr and Linetsky (2000), we assume that job termination rate is identical under both measures $\mathbb{P}$ and $\mathbb{Q}$; that is, the job termination risk is unpriced. By no-arbitrage arguments, the firm's granting cost is given by the no-arbitrage price of a barrier-type call option subject to early exercise due to job termination. The barrier is the employee's optimal exercise boundary. It is possible that the employee will leave the firm before the vesting period ends, or job termination arrives before the stock reaches the optimal boundary. In the first case, the ESO is forfeited. In the latter case, the employee is forced to exercise the option immediately. We must consider both cases in order to accurately determine the ESO value to the firm.

We first consider the cost of an *vested* ESO. Suppose the vesting period is t_v years. At time $t \geq t_v$, given that the stock price Y_t is y and the ESO is still alive, the cost of the ESO is given by

$$
\begin{aligned}
C(t, y) &= \mathbb{E}_{t,y}^{\mathbb{Q}} \{ e^{-r(\tau^* \wedge \tau^\lambda - t)} (Y_{\tau^* \wedge \tau^\lambda} - K)^+ \} \\
&= \mathbb{E}_{t,y}^{\mathbb{Q}} \Big\{ e^{-(r+\lambda)(\tau^* - t)} (Y_{\tau^*} - K)^+ \\
&\quad + \int_t^{\tau^*} e^{-(r+\lambda)(u-t)} \lambda (Y_u - K)^+ du \Big\}.
\end{aligned}
\tag{4.4}
$$

Next, we consider the unvested ESO. Let $\tilde{C}(t, y)$ be the cost of the unvested ESO at time $t \leq t_v$ given that it is still alive and the stock price $Y_t = y$. It is given by

$$\tilde{C}(t, y) = \mathbb{E}_{t,y}^{\mathbb{Q}} \{ e^{-r(t_v - t)} C(t_v, Y_{t_v}) \mathbf{1}_{\{\tau^\lambda > t_v\}} \}. \tag{4.5}$$

In Section 4.4, we will present the partial differential equations (PDEs) for $C(t, y)$ and $\tilde{C}(t, y)$.

4.3. The Employee's Exercise Policy

We proceed to determine the employee's post-vesting optimal exercise boundary, and provide a characterization for it. Afterward, we will investigate how various parameters influence the employee's exercising strategy.

4.3.1. *The free boundary problem of reaction–diffusion type*

The employee's optimal exercise boundary is not known *ex ante*; it has to be inferred from the solution to the free boundary problem associated with the value function V. Let us introduce the following differential operators:

$$\mathscr{L} = \frac{\eta^2 y^2}{2}\frac{\partial^2}{\partial y^2} + \rho\theta\sigma\eta y\frac{\partial^2}{\partial x \partial y} + \frac{\theta^2\sigma^2}{2}\frac{\partial^2}{\partial x^2} + (\nu-q)y\frac{\partial}{\partial y} + [\theta(\mu-r)+rx]\frac{\partial}{\partial x},$$

which is the infinitesimal generator of (X,Y), and

$$\tilde{\mathscr{L}} = \frac{\eta^2 y^2}{2}\frac{\partial^2}{\partial y^2} + \left(\nu-q-\rho\frac{\mu-r}{\sigma}\eta\right)y\frac{\partial}{\partial y},$$

which is the infinitesimal generator of Y under the minimal entropy martingale measure (defined later in (4.12)). Also, we define the utility rewarded for immediate exercise

$$\Lambda(t,x,y) = M(t,x+(y-K)^+)$$

$$= -e^{-\gamma(x+(y-K)^+)e^{r(T-t)}}\, e^{-\frac{(\mu-r)^2}{2\sigma^2}(T-t)}.$$

By dynamic programming principle, the value function V is conjectured to solve the following complementarity problem:

$$\lambda(\Lambda - V) + V_t + \sup_\theta \mathscr{L}V \le 0,$$

$$V \ge \Lambda, \tag{4.6}$$

$$\left(\lambda(\Lambda - V) + V_t + \sup_\theta \mathscr{L}V\right)\cdot(\Lambda - V) = 0,$$

for $(t,x,y) \in [0,T] \times \mathbb{R} \times (0,+\infty)$. The boundary conditions are

$$V(T,x,y) = -e^{-\gamma(x+(y-K)^+)},$$

$$V(t,x,0) = -e^{-\gamma x e^{r(T-t)}}\, e^{-\frac{(\mu-r)^2}{2\sigma^2}(T-t)}. \tag{4.7}$$

This free boundary problem can be simplified by a separation of variables and power transformation

$$V(t,x,y) = M(t,x)\cdot H(t,y)^{\frac{1}{(1-\rho^2)}}. \tag{4.8}$$

This is possible due to the exponential utility function (see Oberman and Zariphopoulou (2003) for a similar transformation).

Then, the free boundary problem for H is of *reaction–diffusion* type.

$$H_t + \tilde{\mathscr{L}} H - (1 - \rho^2)\lambda H + (1 - \rho^2)\lambda b(t, y) H^{-\hat{\rho}} \geq 0, \qquad (4.9)$$

$$H(t, y) \leq \kappa(t, y),$$

$$(H_t + \tilde{\mathscr{L}} H - (1 - \rho^2)\lambda H + (1 - \rho^2)\lambda b(t, y) H^{-\hat{\rho}}) \cdot (\kappa(t, y) - H(t, y)) = 0,$$

for $(t, y) \in [0, T] \times (0, +\infty)$, where

$$\hat{\rho} = \frac{\rho^2}{1 - \rho^2}, \quad b(t, y) = e^{-\gamma(y-K)^+ e^{r(T-t)}}, \quad \text{and}$$

$$\kappa(t, y) = e^{-\gamma(1-\rho^2)(y-K)^+ e^{r(T-t)}}.$$

The boundary conditions are

$$H(T, y) = e^{-\gamma(1-\rho^2)(y-K)^+},$$
$$H(t, 0) = 1. \qquad (4.10)$$

Observe that if $\lambda = 0$, the reaction–diffusion term will disappear, and the problem will become linear. This problem for H implies that the employee's optimal exercise time is independent of X and S. Therefore, we define the employee's optimal exercise boundary as the function $y^\star : [0, T] \mapsto \mathbb{R}_+$, where $y^\star(t)$ is the critical stock price at time t, i.e.

$$y^\star(t) = \inf\{y \geq 0 : H(t, y) = \kappa(t, y)\}.$$

In practice, we numerically solve this free boundary problem to obtain the employee's exercise boundary $y^\star$. Then, the employee's optimal exercise time is the first time that the company stock reaches $y^\star$, i.e.

$$\tau^\star = \inf\{t \leq u \leq T : Y_u = y^\star(u)\}.$$

The function H has the following probabilistic representation:

$$H(t, y) = \inf_{\tau \in \mathscr{T}_{t,T}} \tilde{\mathbb{E}}_{t,y} \left\{ e^{-(1-\rho^2)\lambda(\tau-t)} \kappa(\tau, Y_\tau) \right.$$
$$\left. + \int_t^\tau e^{-(1-\rho^2)\lambda(u-t)} (1 - \rho^2)\lambda b(u, Y_u) H(u, Y_u)^{-\hat{\rho}} \, du \right\}. \qquad (4.11)$$

The expectation is taken under the measure $\tilde{\mathbb{P}}$ defined by

$$\tilde{\mathbb{P}}(A) = \mathbb{E}\left\{ \exp\left(-\frac{\mu - r}{\sigma} B_T - \frac{1}{2}\frac{(\mu - r)^2}{\sigma^2} T \right) 1_A \right\}, \qquad A \in \mathscr{F}_T. \qquad (4.12)$$

The measure $\tilde{\mathbb{P}}$ is a martingale measure that has the minimal entropy relative to $\mathbb{P}$ (see Fritelli, 2000). This measure arises frequently in indifference pricing theory. For instance, Musiela and Zariphopoulou (2004a) use it to express the writer's value function for a European call option. We will use this probabilistic representation to prove the existence of a unique solution to the free boundary problem for H in the appendix.

4.3.2. *Characterization of the employee's exercise boundary*

The function H, defined in (4.8), turns out to be related to the employee's indifference price for the ESO, which will allow us to characterize the employee's optimal exercise time. We are primarily interested in the *cost* of an ESO to the firm, not the employee's indifference price. Nevertheless, the indifference price is a useful concept in analyzing the employee's exercise behavior.

Definition 4.1. The ESO holder's indifference price of an ESO (without vesting) is defined as the function $p \equiv p(t, x, y)$ such that

$$M(t, x) = V(t, x - p, y). \tag{4.13}$$

As we shall see, due to the exponential utility function, the indifference price is in fact a function of only t and y. Using (4.13) and the transformation (4.8), one can deduce the following fact.

Proposition 4.2. *The employee's indifference price for the ESO, denoted by p, satisfies*

$$p(t, y) = -\frac{1}{\gamma(1 - \rho^2)e^{r(T-t)}} \log H(t, y), \tag{4.14}$$

or equivalently,

$$V(t, x, y) = M(t, x) \cdot e^{-\gamma p(t,y)e^{r(T-t)}}. \tag{4.15}$$

With this, we can write the original free boundary problem (4.6)–(4.7) in terms of p:

$$p_t + \mathscr{L}p - rp - \frac{1}{2}\gamma(1 - \rho^2)\eta^2 y^2 e^{r(T-t)}p_y^2 + \frac{\lambda}{\gamma}(1 - b(t, y)e^{\gamma p e^{r(T-t)}}) \leq 0,$$

$$p \geq (y - K)^+,$$

$$\left(p_t + \mathscr{L}p - rp - \frac{1}{2}\gamma(1 - \rho^2)\eta^2 y^2 e^{r(T-t)}p_y^2 + \frac{\lambda}{\gamma}(1 - b(t, y)e^{\gamma p e^{r(T-t)}})\right)$$
$$\cdot ((y - K)^+ - p) = 0,$$

for $(t, y) \in [0, T] \times (0, +\infty)$. The boundary conditions are

$$p(T, y) = (y - K)^+,$$
$$p(t, 0) = 0.$$

Finally, we use equation (4.13) or (4.15) to express the employee's optimal exercise time τ^* in terms of p:

$$\tau^* := \inf \{t \le u \le T : V(u, X_u, Y_u) = \Lambda(u, X_u, Y_u)\}$$

$$= \inf \{t \le u \le T : M(u, X_u + p(u, Y_u)) = M(u, X_u + (Y_u - K)^+)\}$$

$$= \inf \{t \le u \le T : p(u, Y_u) = (Y_u - K)^+\}. \tag{4.16}$$

This provides a nice interpretation for the ESO holder's optimal exercising strategy: the holder will exercise the ESO as soon as his indifference price reaches (from above) the ESO payoff. For other utility functions, this interpretation still holds although the indifference price and the optimal exercise time may depend on wealth.

According to the standard no-arbitrage pricing theory, the price-maximizing boundary for an American call on a dividend-paying stock is monotonically decreasing with time. To understand this, we recall that the boundary represents the stock price where the value of an American call equals the payoff from immediate exercise. Note that the value of an American call, for a fixed stock level, is decreasing over time, and the payoff from immediate exercise is time-independent. Therefore, the critical stock price decreases over time. However, in our model, the utility-maximizing boundary is not always monotonically decreasing with time. The reason is that the utility rewarded for exercising the ESO, instead of being time-independent, is decreasing over time. Since both the value function and the reward from immediate exercise decreases over time, it is possible that the critical stock price is increasing for a certain period of time (see Figures 4.2–4.4). In the special case of zero interest rate and no job termination risk, we can prove that the exercise boundary is non-increasing with time.

Proposition 4.3. *Assume $\lambda = r = 0$. The utility-maximizing boundary is non-increasing with time.*

Proof. First, observe that H is non-decreasing with time. Indeed, setting $\lambda = r = 0$ in equation (4.11), we get

$$H(t,y) = \inf_{\tau \in \mathscr{T}_{t,T}} \tilde{\mathbb{E}}_{t,y}\{e^{-\gamma(1-\rho^2)(Y_\tau - K)^+}\}$$

$$= \inf_{\tau \in \mathscr{T}_{0,T-t}} \tilde{\mathbb{E}}_{0,y}\{e^{-\gamma(1-\rho^2)(Y_\tau - K)^+}\},$$

where we have use the time-homogeneity of Y for the second equality. For any $s \leq t$, we have $\mathscr{T}_{0,T-t} \subseteq \mathscr{T}_{0,T-s}$, so $H(s,y) \leq H(t,y)$. Next, fix any $y > 0$ and let $s \leq t$. If the employee should exercise at (s,y), that is, $H(s,y) = e^{-\gamma(1-\rho^2)(y-K)^+}$, then we want to show that the same is true at (t,y). But this is clear from the chain of inequalities

$$e^{-\gamma(1-\rho^2)(y-K)^+} = H(s,y) \leq H(t,y) \leq e^{-\gamma(1-\rho^2)(y-K)^+}.$$

Hence, the employee should also exercise at (t,y). $\qquad\square$

4.3.3. *Effects of parameters on the employee's exercise policy*

Let us first study the effect of job termination risk. Figure 4.2(a) shows that higher job termination risk leads to a lower exercise boundary. In other words, the risk of job termination induces the employee to adopt a more conservative exercising strategy.

Proposition 4.4. *Let λ_1, λ_2 be the job termination rates such that $\lambda_2 \geq \lambda_1$. Then, the utility-maximizing boundary associated with λ_1 dominates that with λ_2.*

Proof. First, the indifference price satisfies the variational inequality:

$$\min\left\{-p_t - \tilde{\mathscr{L}}p + rp + \frac{1}{2}\gamma(1-\rho^2)\eta^2 y^2 e^{r(T-t)}p_y^2 \right.$$

$$\left. + \frac{\lambda}{\gamma}(b(t,y)e^{\gamma p e^{r(T-t)}} - 1), p - (y-K)^+\right\} = 0. \qquad (4.17)$$

Let $p_1(t,y)$ and $p_2(t,y)$ be the indifference prices associated with λ_1 and λ_2, respectively. Since the coefficient of λ is non-negative, the left-hand side is non-decreasing with λ. Then, substituting $p_2(t,y)$ into the variational inequality for $p_1(t,y)$ will render the left-hand side less than or equal to zero.

Therefore, $p_2(t, y)$ is a subsolution to the variational inequality for $p_1(t, y)$, so $p_2(t, y) \leq p_1(t, y)$. We conclude from (4.16) that the optimal exercise time corresponding to λ_1 is longer than or equal to that corresponding to λ_2, which implies that the utility-maximizing boundary corresponding to λ_1 dominates that corresponding to λ_2. □

Empirical studies on ESOs by Hemmer *et al.* (1996), Huddart and Lang (1996), and Marquardt (2002) show that most ESO holders exercise well before the options expire. Our model allows us to rationalize this phenomenon. First, Figure 4.2 illustrates that early exercise is optimal for a risk-averse employee. Also, by Proposition 4.4, the risk of job termination induces the employee to lower his exercise boundary, leading to even earlier exercise. In other words, even if the job termination does not happen before maturity, the employee still lowers his exercise boundary due to the *risk* of job termination. Lastly, when job termination actually happens prior to maturity, then the employee is forced to give up or exercise the ESO. All these contribute to the early exercise phenomenon.

In our numerical example depicted in Figure 4.2(b), the employee's exercise boundary shifts downward as risk aversion increases. Heuristically, a higher risk aversion implies a greater tendency to lock in sure profit now, rather than waiting for a higher but uncertain return in the future. This means that a more risk-averse holder would exercise the option at a lower critical price. Therefore, we have the following proposition.

Proposition 4.5. *The indifference price is non-increasing with risk aversion. The utility-maximizing boundary of a less risk-averse ESO holder dominates that of a more risk-averse ESO holder.*

Proof. We consider the variational inequality in the previous proposition. The p_y^2 term is non-decreasing with γ. Differentiating the nonlinear term with respect to γ, we get

$$\frac{\lambda}{\gamma^2} \{1 + \phi(t, y)e^{\phi(t,y)} - e^{\phi(t,y)}\} \geq 0,$$

with $\phi(t, y) := \gamma(p(t, y) - (y - K)^+)e^{r(T-t)} \geq 0$. Hence, the nonlinear term is also non-decreasing with γ. By comparison principle, this implies the indifference price p is non-increasing with γ. The second assertion follows from the characterization of the optimal exercise time (see (4.16)). □

In the ESO valuation models proposed by Hull and White (2004b), and Cvitanic *et al.* (2008), the employee's exercise boundary is exogenously specified and does not change with the dividend rate, drift, and volatility of the company stock. Empirical studies have shown that these parameters influence the employee's exercise behavior. For example, Bettis *et al.* (2005) point out that ESOs are exercised earlier in firms with higher dividend yields. This is reasonable because a higher dividend rate entices the employee to own the company stock share and receive the dividend. In our model, the employee's exercise policy is consistent with this empirical result. We summarize our results in the following propositions, and illustrate them in Figures 4.3 and 4.4.

Proposition 4.6. *The ESO holder's utility-maximizing boundary shifts upward as the dividend rate q decreases, or as the firm's average growth rate ν increases.*

Proof. Again, we consider the variational inequality (4.17), and notice that q and ν only appears in the term $-(\nu - q - \rho\frac{\mu-r}{\sigma}\eta)y p_y$. One can deduce from (4.3) that the value function V is non-decreasing with y, so by equation (5.10) p is also non-decreasing with y, so $p_y \geq 0$. Therefore, the term $-(\nu - q - \rho\frac{\mu-r}{\sigma}\eta)y p_y$ is non-decreasing with q and non-increasing with ν. By comparison principle, we conclude that the indifference price is non-increasing with q and non-decreasing with ν. Then, the proposition follows from (4.16). □

Remark 4.7. Standard option pricing theory shows that an American call value increases with respect to volatility. By examining the variational inequality (4.17), we notice that the indifference price p is not monotonically increasing with respect to η. Therefore, we expect non-monotonicity of the utility-maximizing boundary with respect to η. We illustrate this in Figure 4.4(b). As volatility rises, the exercise boundary tends to fall first and then rise slightly. This is also observed by Grasselli and Henderson (2009) and Carpenter (2005).

Now suppose the employee can choose between two hedging instruments with correlations being, respectively, ρ and $-\rho$, and both have the same positive Sharpe ratio. Then, which one should the employee use to hedge? Heuristically, if the employee hedges with the ESO with a positively (respectively, negatively) correlated asset with a positive Sharpe ratio, then he needs to short (respectively, long) the asset. But a short position is less favorable than a long position to a risk-averse investor, so the negatively correlated asset should be preferred.

Proposition 4.8. *Assume* $\alpha := \frac{\mu - r}{\sigma} > 0$. *Fix any number* $\rho \in (0, 1)$. *Denote by* p_+ *and* p_- *the indifference prices corresponding to* ρ *and* $-\rho$, *respectively. Then, we have* $p_- \geq p_+$. *Moreover, the utility-maximizing boundary corresponding to* $-\rho$ *dominates that corresponding to* ρ.

Proof. We consider the variational inequality (4.17). Since $\alpha > 0$ and $p_y \geq 0$, the p_y term is non-decreasing in ρ. Therefore, p_+ is a subsolution to the variational inequality for p_-, so $p_+ \leq p_-$. The last statement in the proposition follows from (4.16) and that $p_- \geq p_+$.   □

Remark 4.9. Following from the preceding proof, if $\alpha < 0$, then the opposite happens. In the case of zero Sharpe ratio ($\alpha = 0$), we have $p_+ = p_-$, and the two exercise boundaries coincide. If $\alpha = \rho = 0$, then the employee does not trade in the market index. In this special case, the employee will exercise early even if the firm's stock pays no dividends (see Huddart, 1994; Villeneuve, 1999).

When the hedging instrument has a positive Sharpe ratio, the employee would prefer a negative correlation than a positive one. As the correlation becomes even more negative, the employee can hedge more risk away. Consequently, the employee's indifference price increases and he tends to wait longer before exercise. As a result, the utility-maximizing boundary should move upward. This is illustrated in Figure 4.4(a), and proved in the following proposition.

Proposition 4.10. *Assume* $\alpha := \frac{\mu - r}{\sigma} > 0$. *Then, the indifference price is non-increasing with respect to* ρ, *for* $\rho \leq 0$. *Moreover, the utility-maximizing boundary moves upward with as* ρ *decreases from 0 to* -1.

Proof. From variational inequality (4.17), we collect the terms with ρ and define $g(\rho, y, p_y) := \alpha \rho \eta y p_y - \frac{1}{2} \gamma \eta^2 y^2 e^{r(T-t)} p_y^2 \rho^2$. The function g is quadratic in ρ and is non-decreasing for $\rho \leq \frac{\alpha}{\gamma \eta y p_y e^{r(T-t)}}$. Since $\frac{\alpha}{\gamma \eta y p_y e^{r(T-t)}}$ is positive, when $\rho \leq 0$, the left-side of the above variational inequality is non-decreasing with ρ. Then, by comparison principle, more negative correlation leads to higher indifference price. The last assertion follows from (4.16). □

4.3.4. *Numerical solution*

To obtain the employee's exercise boundaries, we numerically solve (4.9)–(4.10). Our numerical method utilizes the backward Euler finite-difference stencil on a uniform grid. The constraint $H \leq \kappa$ is enforced by the projected successive-over-relaxation (PSOR) algorithm, which iteratively solves the implicit time-stepping equations, while preserving the constraint between iterations. Similar numerical schemes can be found in Wilmott *et al.* (1995).

For computational implementation, we restrict the domain $[0, T] \times \mathbb{R}_+$ to a finite domain $\mathscr{D} = \{(t, y) : 0 \leq t \leq T, 0 \leq y \leq R\}$, where R is sufficiently large to preserve the accuracy of the numerical solutions. Then, we introduce a uniform grid on $\mathscr{D}$ with nodes $\{(t_k, y_j) : k = 0, 1, \ldots, N;$ $j = 0, 1, \ldots, M\}$, with $\Delta t = T/N$, and $\Delta y = R/M$ being the grid spacings. Next, we apply discrete approximations $H_j^k \approx H(t_k, y_j)$ where $t_k = k\Delta t$, and $y_j = j\Delta y$.

We discretize the PDI (4.9). We approximate the y-derivatives by central differences

$$\frac{\partial H}{\partial y}(t_k, y_j) \approx \frac{H_{j+1}^k - H_{j-1}^k}{2\Delta y}, \quad \frac{\partial^2 H}{\partial y^2}(t_k, y_j) \approx \frac{H_{j+1}^k - 2H_j^k + H_{j-1}^k}{\Delta y^2},$$

and the t-derivative by the backward Euler scheme

$$\frac{\partial H}{\partial t}(t_k, y_j) \approx \frac{H_j^{k+1} - H_j^k}{\Delta t}.$$

Furthermore, we use the explicit approximation for the reaction–diffusion term

$$-\lambda(1 - \rho^2)H + \lambda(1 - \rho^2)b(t, y)H^{-\hat{\rho}} \approx -\lambda(1 - \rho^2)H_j^{k+1} + f_j^{k+1}(H_j^{k+1})^{-\hat{\rho}},$$

where $f_j^{k+1} = \lambda(1 - \rho^2)b(t_{k+1}, y_j)$. We refer interested readers to Glowinski (1984) for a detailed account on numerical methods for nonlinear variational inequalities. With these approximations, we solve the discretized version of (4.9)–(4.10) backward in time using PSOR algorithm, and locate the free boundary at t_k, $y^\star(t_k)$, by comparing the values of H_j^k and $\kappa(t_k, y_j)$. The numerically-estimated free boundaries are shown in Figures 4.2–4.4.

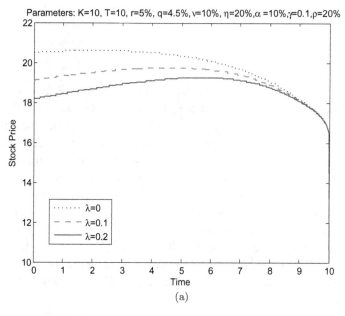

(a)

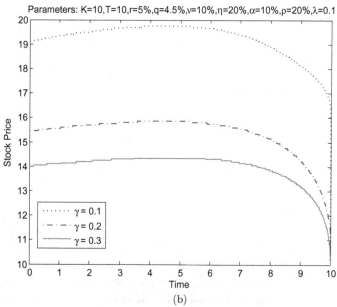

(b)

Figure 4.2. **Effects of job termination risk and risk aversion**: (a) Higher job termination risk lowers the exercise boundary. (b) As risk aversion γ increases, the employee's exercise boundary moves downward.

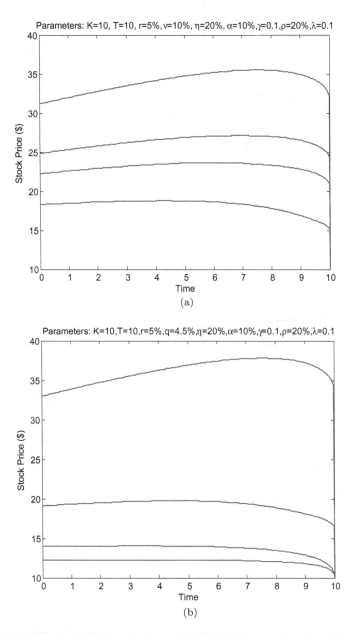

Figure 4.3. Effects of dividend rate and drift: (a) The employee's exercise boundary exists even when the dividend rate is zero. It shifts downward as dividend rate, q, increases (from top to bottom, $q = 0\%, 2\%, 3\%, 5\%$). (b) The employee's exercise boundary is also monotone with respect to the stock's drift (from top to bottom, $\nu = 15\%, 10\%, 5\%, 0\%$).

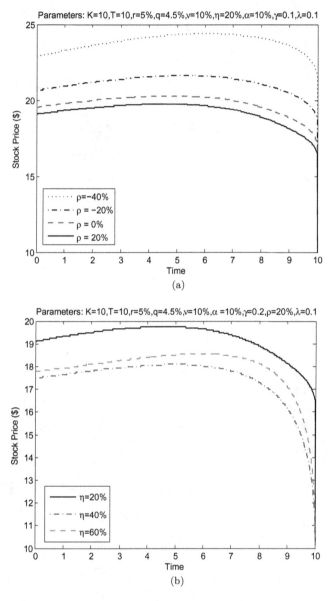

Figure 4.4. **Effects of correlations and volatilities**: (a) When the market index (partial spanning asset) has a positive Sharpe ratio of 10%, the ESO holder's exercise boundary moves upward as the correlation becomes more negative. (b) The employee's exercise boundary moves downward when stock volatility increases from 20% to 40%. When the volatility is raised to 60%, it moves upwards again. This shows that the employee's exercise boundary is not monotone with respect to the stock volatility.

4.4. Analysis of the ESO Cost

With reference to the definitions in (4.4) and (4.5), we now present the PDE formulations for the costs of a vested and an unvested ESO. Suppose the firm imposes a vesting period of t_v years, and denote $y^\star(t)$ as the employee's exercise boundary. The holder does not exercise in the regions $\mathscr{C} = \{(t, y) : t_v \leq t < T, 0 \leq y < y^\star(t)\}$ and $\mathscr{V} = \{(t, y) : 0 \leq t < t_v, 0 \leq y\}$. The cost of an unvested ESO, $C(t, y)$, satisfies the *inhomogeneous* PDE

$$C_t + \frac{\eta^2}{2}y^2 C_{yy} + (r - q)y C_y - (r + \lambda)C + \lambda(y - K)^+ = 0, \qquad (4.18)$$

for $(t, y) \in \mathscr{C}$, and the boundary conditions

$$C(t, 0) = 0, \quad t_v \leq t \leq T,$$

$$C(t, y^\star(t)) = (y^\star(t) - K)^+, \quad t_v \leq t < T,$$

$$C(T, y) = (y - K)^+, \quad 0 \leq y \leq y^\star(T).$$

The inhomogeneous term, $\lambda(y - K)^+$ captures the effect that the ESO may be exercised due to job termination with a probability λdt over an infinitesimal period dt.[2] Next, the cost of an unvested ESO, $\tilde{C}(t, y)$, satisfies the *homogeneous* PDE

$$\tilde{C}_t + \frac{\eta^2}{2}y^2 \tilde{C}_{yy} + (r - q)y \tilde{C}_y - (r + \lambda)\tilde{C} = 0,$$

for $(t, y) \in \mathscr{V}$, and the boundary conditions

$$\tilde{C}(t, 0) = 0, \quad 0 \leq t \leq t_v,$$

$$\tilde{C}(t_v, y) = C(t_v, y), \quad y \geq 0.$$

Given the boundary curve $y^\star(t)$, we solve these two PDE problems numerically using the implicit finite-difference methods computed in Section 4.3.4.

In the following subsections, we study the effects of risk aversion, vesting, and job termination risk on the cost of an ESO, and compare our results with other models.

---

[2]See, for example, Carr and Linetsky (2000), for a similar application.

4.4.1. *Effects of vesting, risk aversion,*
and job termination risk

We first analyze the effects of vesting and risk aversion in the absence of job termination risk. Recall that the risk-averse holder's optimal exercise boundary in general does not maximize the expected discounted payoff of the ESO. From the firm's perspective, the employee's risk-averse attitude means that the ESO costs less than the no-arbitrage price of the corresponding American call. If the risk aversion is small, then the ESO cost would be between the values of an American call and a European call on the company stock with the same strike and maturity. However, as the employee becomes more risk-averse, his utility-maximizing boundary shifts downward, getting further away from the price-maximizing boundary. Consequently, the cost of the ESO decreases as risk aversion increases. If the ESO holder is sufficiently risk-averse, the cost of the ESO to the firm could be even lower than a European call on the company stock with the same strike and maturity.

If the firm imposes vesting on the ESO, then any exercise before the end of the vesting period is prevented. Effectively, the pre-vesting part of the employee's utility-maximizing boundary is lifted to infinity. Since vesting imposes discipline on the employee which restrains the employee's risk-averse behavior, it could increase the expected discounted payoff, implying a higher cost to the firm (see Figure 4.5). We can prove this for the case of no dividend and no job termination risk.

Proposition 4.11. *If $\lambda = q = 0$, then the ESO cost is non-decreasing with respect to the length of the vesting period. Moreover, this cost is dominated by the Black–Scholes price of the European call option written on company stock with the same strike and maturity.*

Proof. Let $0 < a < b < T$. Denote by $\tau_a^\star$ and $\tau_b^\star$ the employee's exercise time when the vesting periods are a and b years, respectively. Then, we have $\tau_a^\star \leq \tau_b^\star \leq T$. Since the discounted payoff process $\{e^{-rs}(Y_s - K)^+\}_{s \geq 0}$ is a $\mathbb{Q}$-submartingale (see Karatzas and Shreve, 1998), it follows from Optional Stopping Theorem that

$$\mathbb{E}_{t,y}^{\mathbb{Q}}\{e^{-r(\tau_a^\star - t)}(Y_{\tau_a^\star} - K)^+\} \leq \mathbb{E}_{t,y}^{\mathbb{Q}}\{e^{-r(\tau_b^\star - t)}(Y_{\tau_b^\star} - K)^+\}$$

$$\leq \mathbb{E}_{t,y}^{\mathbb{Q}}\{e^{-r(T - t)}(Y_T - K)^+\}.$$

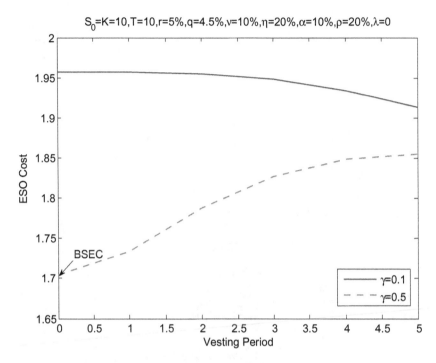

Figure 4.5. **Effect of vesting**: The marker "BSEC" represents the no-arbitrage price of a European call with the same strike and maturity as the ESO. In the absence of job termination risk, the cost of an ESO held by a very risk-averse employee increases (from close to BSEC) with respect to vesting. In the low risk-aversion case, the cost decreases with vesting but stays above BSEC.

From this, we can conclude that the granting cost is non-decreasing with vesting, and is dominated by the price of the corresponding European call.   □

The consideration of the employee's risk aversion gives us an important insight to the cost structure of ESOs to the firm — vesting may involve additional cost. While the firm may be able to maintain the incentive effect of the ESOs and impose discipline on ESO exercises, they may also have to pay for these benefits. This is not reflected by ESO valuation models that assume risk-neutrality of the employee. If the employee were to hedge perfectly and thus were risk-neutral, then the ESO cost would certainly decrease with vesting.

When the risk of job termination is present, the employee adopts a more conservative exercising strategy. Moreover, it potentially shortens the life

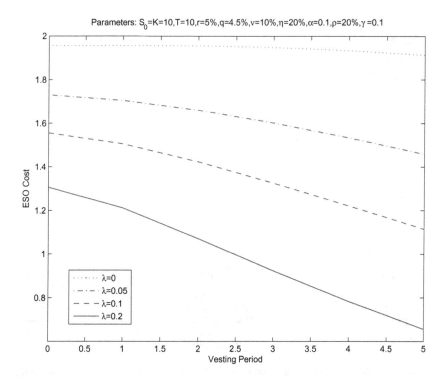

Figure 4.6. **Effect of job termination risk**: The ESO cost decreases significantly as the job termination risk rises. Furthermore, the cost decreases as vesting period lengthens due to the increasing likelihood of forfeiture.

of an ESO, resulting in either forfeiture of the option or early suboptimal exercise. Therefore, in general, higher job termination risk should reduce the ESO cost (see Figure 4.6). The next proposition proves this for the case of zero dividend rate. On the other hand, as the vesting period lengthens, the employee becomes more likely to depart before vesting ends. As illustrated in Figure 4.6, vesting significantly reduces the ESO cost to the firm.

Proposition 4.12. *Assume $q = 0$. A higher job termination risk decreases the cost of both vested and unvested ESOs.*

Proof. We first consider the value of a vested ESO. Define the operator $\mathscr{L}_1$ such that

$$\mathscr{L}_1 C(t,y) = C_t + (r-q)yC_y + \frac{\eta^2}{2}y^2 C_{yy} - (r+\lambda)C + \lambda(y-K)^+.$$

Let λ_1, λ_2 be the job termination rates such that $\lambda_2 \geq \lambda_1 \geq 0$. Let $C_i(t, y)$ and $\tau_i^\star$ be the cost of a vested ESO and optimal exercise time corresponding to λ_i, for $i = 1, 2$. By the PDE (4.18), we have $\mathscr{L}_1 C_1 = 0$. Due to the $\mathbb{Q}$-submartingale property of the process $\{e^{-rs}(Y_s - K)^+\}_{s \geq 0}$, we have $C_i(t, y) \geq (y - K)^+$. Consequently, direct substitution shows that $\mathscr{L}_1 C_2 \geq 0$.

Next, we apply Itô's formula to the function

$$V(t, Y_t) = e^{(r+\lambda_1)t} C_2(t, Y_t) + \int_0^t e^{-(r+\lambda_1)s} \lambda_1 (Y_s - K)^+ \, ds.$$

Then, due to $\mathscr{L}_1 C_2 \geq 0$ and the Optional Sampling Theorem, the following condition holds for any $\tau \geq t$:

$$\mathbb{E}_{t,y}^{\mathbb{Q}}\{V(\tau, Y_\tau)\} \geq V(t, y).$$

In particular, we take $\tau = \tau_2^\star \leq \tau_1^\star$, then we get

$$C_2(t, y) \leq \mathbb{E}_{t,y}^{\mathbb{Q}} \left\{ e^{-(r+\lambda_1)(\tau_2^\star - t)} C_2(\tau_2^\star, Y_{\tau_2^\star}) \right.$$

$$\left. + \int_t^{\tau_2^\star} e^{-(r+\lambda_1)(s-t)} \lambda_1 (Y_s - K)^+ \, ds \right\}$$

$$= \mathbb{E}_{t,y}^{\mathbb{Q}}\{e^{-r(\tau_2^\star \wedge \tau^{\lambda_1} - t)} (Y_{\tau_2^\star \wedge \tau^{\lambda_1}} - K)^+\}$$

$$\leq \mathbb{E}_{t,y}^{\mathbb{Q}}\{e^{-r(\tau_1^\star \wedge \tau^{\lambda_1} - t)} (Y_{\tau_1^\star \wedge \tau^{\lambda_1}} - K)^+\} = C_1(t, y).$$

Hence, the job termination risk reduces the cost of a vested ESO. As for unvested ESOs, we notice that the job termination risk reduces the terminal values of an unvested ESO and increases the probability of forfeiture during the vesting period. Therefore, the job termination risk reduces the value of an unvested ESO. $\qquad \square$

4.4.2. *Comparison with other models*

We compare our model with the ones proposed by Grasselli and Henderson (2009) and Grasselli (2005). In Grasselli and Henderson (2009), the interest rate is assumed to be zero. As shown in Figure 4.7, interest rate has a significant bearing on the ESO cost to the firm, so the assumption of zero interest rate is not benign for valuation of ESOs which are long-dated, as is usual. Moreover, the Grasselli and Henderson (2009) model also assumes that the ESO is perpetual. Consequently, the employee's exercise boundary

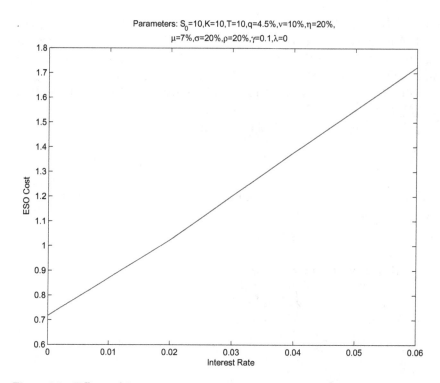

Figure 4.7. **Effect of interest rate**: As interest rate increases from 0% to 6%, the cost of the ESO increases by more than 100%.

is flat and tends to be very high (see Figure 4.8). In fact, her model concludes that the ESO holder will never exercise in the case of $\frac{\nu-q}{\eta} \geq \frac{\mu}{\sigma}\rho + \frac{\eta}{2}$ (which is equivalent to the drift of $\log Y_t$, with $r = 0$, being non-negative under the minimal entropy martingale measure).

Taking into account positive interest rate and finite maturity, but not job termination risk, Grasselli (2005) obtains a lower cost. Our model incorporates the risk of job termination and vesting, which further reduce the ESO cost. Table 4.1 shows the different ESO costs under the parameter values given in Figure 4.8. The first entry is the Black–Scholes price of a 10-year European option, which in this case of no dividend is equal to the American price. The next two entries are from Grasselli and Henderson (2009) and Grasselli (2005) models specialized to just one option. The last two entries add job termination risk and then vesting.

We observe that risk aversion lowers the cost by about 8% in the perpetual approximation, or by about 30% when we retain finite maturity,

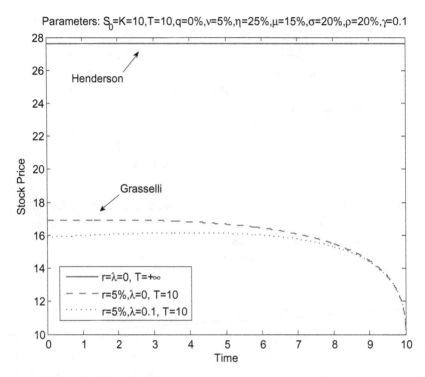

Figure 4.8. **Comparing exercise boundaries**: The model by Grasselli and Henderson (2009) gives a high flat exercise boundary. Grasselli (2005) corresponds to the middle boundary. The bottom boundary from our model accounts for the presence of job termination risk. The parameter values are chosen so that the exercise boundary by Grasselli and Henderson (2009) is finite.

Table 4.1. ESO costs from different valuation models and parameters.

Black–Scholes	Henderson	Grasselli	$+\lambda = 0.1$	+3-year vesting
4.878	4.510	3.412	2.597	2.491

but then job termination risk reduces the cost by a further 17% of the Black–Scholes value, and vesting by yet another 2% in this example.

Remark 4.13. Our formulation can easily be adapted to the case where the job termination time τ^λ is a non-predictable stopping time with a stochastic intensity process. We can define the intensity process $\{\lambda_t\}_{t\geq 0}$ by $\lambda_t = \lambda(Y_t)$ where $\lambda(\cdot)$ is a bounded continuous non-negative function of the firm's stock price Y. In that case, we replace λ with $\lambda(y)$ in our variational inequalities, PDEs, and numerical scheme. However, the estimation of the function $\lambda(\cdot)$ is significantly more difficult than that of a constant parameter. We have implemented the numerical solution with a variety of intensity functions, including that $\lambda(y)$ is decreasing with y. It seems that such generalization does not bring much additional insight to the exercise policy and other features discussed in this section.

4.5. Valuation Model with Multiple Exercises

We extend the model to the case in which the employee is granted multiple ESOs which may be exercised separately. In particular, we are interested in characterizing the employee's optimal timing strategy for multiple exercises. As before, it is sufficient to consider the employee's investment problem with no vesting, and then re-introduce the vesting period when we calculate the cost to the firm.

4.5.1. *The employee's investment problem*

We follow our formulation in Section 4.2. The only difference is that, at time $t \in [0, T]$, the employee is granted n American-styled ESOs with the same strike and maturity. The employee is risk-averse, subject to employment termination risk, and constrained as in Section 4.2. He needs to decide the exercise policies for his options. Let us denote by τ_i the exercise time when i options remain unexercised. Then, τ_n is the first exercise time, and τ_1 is the last one. If we keep track of the number of options exercised, then τ_{n-i} is the exercise time of the $(i+1)$th option. We require that $\tau_i \in \mathscr{T}_{t,T}$, and clearly, we have $\tau_n \leq \cdots \leq \tau_1$. If the employee exercises multiple options at the same time, then some exercise times may coincide.

Throughout the period $[t, T]$, the employee dynamically invests his wealth, using admissible strategies $\theta \in \mathscr{Z}_{t,T}$, in the bank account and the market index. Hence, his trading wealth follows (5.1). At every discretionary exercise time, τ_i, the employee invests the option payoff into his trading portfolio. However, at the job termination time τ^λ, he must exercise *all remaining options*. After exiting from the firm, the employee is assumed to invest the contract proceeds into his trading portfolio and continue trading till time T. Given that the employee has not departed the firm and holds $i \geq 2$ unexercised options at time t, his value function is given by

$$
V^{(i)}(t, x, y)
$$

$$
= \sup_{t \leq \tau_i \leq T} \sup_{\mathscr{L}_{t,\tau_i}} \mathbb{E}_{t,x,y}\{V^{(i-1)}(\tau_i, X_{\tau_i} + (Y_{\tau_i} - K)^+, Y_{\tau_i}) \cdot \mathbf{1}_{\{\tau_i < \tau^\lambda\}}
$$

$$
+ M(\tau^\lambda, X_{\tau^\lambda} + i(Y_{\tau^\lambda} - K)^+) \cdot \mathbf{1}_{\{\tau_i \geq \tau^\lambda\}}\},
$$

with $V^{(1)} = V$ in (4.3) and $V^{(0)} = M$ in (4.2). The second term inside the expectation means that, if the job termination arrives before his next exercise time, the employee must exercise or forgo all i options and invest the proceeds, if any, into the market index and the bank account. Otherwise, as the first term reveals, the employee will exercise his next option at the optimal exercise time, and faces the investment problem again with $i - 1$ unexercised options.

4.5.2. *The free boundary problem*

The value function $V^{(i)}$ solves the variational inequality

$$
\lambda(M(t, x + i(y - K)^+) - V^{(i)}) + V_t^{(i)} + \sup_\theta \mathscr{L} V^{(i)} \leq 0, \quad (4.19)
$$

$$
V^{(i)}(t, x, y) \geq V^{(i-1)}(t, x + (y - K)^+, y),
$$

$$
(\lambda(M(t, x + i(y - K)^+) - V^{(i)}) + V_t^{(i)} + \sup_\theta \mathscr{L} V^{(i)})
$$

$$
\cdot (V^{(i-1)}(t, x + (y - K)^+, y) - V^{(i)}(t, x, y)) = 0,
$$

$(t, x, y) \in [0, T) \times \mathbb{R} \times (0, +\infty)$, with boundary conditions

$$
V^{(i)}(T, x, y) = -e^{-\gamma(x - i(y-K)^+)},
$$

$$
V^{(i)}(t, x, 0) = -e^{-\gamma x e^{r(T-t)}} e^{-\frac{(\mu-r)^2}{2\sigma^2}(T-t)}. \quad (4.20)
$$

Next, we simplify the above variational inequalities by applying the transformation

$$
V^{(i)}(t, x, y) = M(t, x) \cdot H^{(i)}(t, y)^{\frac{1}{(1-\rho^2)}}
$$

so that $H^{(i)}$ satisfies

$$H_t^{(i)} + \tilde{\mathscr{L}} H^{(i)} - (1 - \rho^2)\lambda H^{(i)} + (1 - \rho^2)\lambda b(t,y)^i (H^{(i)})^{-\hat{\rho}} \geq 0, \quad (4.21)$$

$$H^{(i)} \leq \kappa(t,y)H^{(i-1)},$$

$$\left(H_t^{(i)} + \tilde{\mathscr{L}} H^{(i)} - (1 - \rho^2)\lambda H^{(i)} + (1 - \rho^2)\lambda b(t,y)^i (H^{(i)})^{-\hat{\rho}}\right)$$

$$\cdot \left(\kappa(t,y)H^{(i-1)} - H^{(i)}\right) = 0,$$

for $(t,y) \in [0,T] \times [0,+\infty)$. The boundary conditions are

$$H^{(i)}(T,y) = e^{-\gamma(1-\rho^2)i(y-K)^+},$$

$$H^{(i)}(t,0) = 1. \tag{4.22}$$

Associated with each $H^{(i)}$, there is free boundary, denoted by $y_i^\star$: $[0,T] \mapsto \mathbb{R}_+$, such that

$$y_i^\star(t) := \inf\{y \geq 0 : H^{(i)}(t,y) = \kappa(t,y)H^{(i-1)}(t,y)\}, \quad \text{for } t \in [0,T].$$

The boundary $y_i^\star$ represents the employee's optimal exercise boundary for the next option when i options remain unexercised. In Section 4.3, we have solved the problem and obtained $H^{(i)}$ for the case $i = 1$. Given we know $H^{(1)}$, we use our numerical method discussed in Section 4.3.4 to solve the free boundary problem (4.21)–(4.22) for $H^{(2)}$. We continue this procedure to solve for all $H^{(i)}$, and obtain the associated free boundaries, $y_i^\star$, for $i = 1, \ldots, n$.

4.5.3. *The cost of multiple issues*

Given the boundaries $\{y_i^\star, i = 1, 2, \ldots, n\}$, we can calculate the cost of the ESOs to the firm. Following our assumptions in Section 4.2.2, we first consider the value of a vested ESO. For a vesting period of t_v years, the employee's optimal exercise time when there are i options remaining is

$$\tau_i^\star = \inf\{t \leq u \leq T : Y_u = y_i^\star(u)\}, \quad t > t_v, \quad i = 1, 2, \ldots, n.$$

Define $C^{(i)}(t,y)$ as the cost of i vested ESOs at time $t \geq t_v$ when the stock price is y dollars, assuming it is still alive. It satisfies the following recursive relationship:

$$C^{(i)}(t,y) = \mathbb{E}^{\mathbb{Q}}_{t,y}\{e^{-r(\tau^{\lambda}-t)}i(Y_{\tau^{\lambda}} - K)^{+}\mathbf{1}_{\{\tau^{\lambda} \leq \tau_i^{\star}\}}$$
$$+ e^{-r(\tau_i^{\star}-t)}[(Y_{\tau_i^{\star}} - K)^{+} + C^{(i-1)}(\tau_i^{\star}, Y_{\tau_i^{\star}})]\mathbf{1}_{\{\tau^{\lambda} > \tau_i^{\star}\}}\}.$$

The function $C^{(i)}(t,y)$ satisfies the following *inhomogeneous* PDE

$$C_t^{(i)} + \frac{\eta^2}{2}y^2 C_{yy}^{(i)} + (r-q)y C_y^{(i)} - (r+\lambda)C^{(i)} + \lambda i(y-K)^{+} = 0,$$

in the region $\{(t,y) : t_v \leq t \leq T, 0 \leq y \leq y_i^{\star}(t)\}$, and satisfies the boundary conditions

$$\begin{aligned} C^{(i)}(t,0) &= 0, & t_v &\leq t \leq T, \\ C^{(i)}(t,y_i^{\star}(t)) &= (y_i^{\star}(t) - K)^{+} + C^{(i-1)}(t,y_i^{\star}(t)), & t_v &\leq t < T, \\ C^{(i)}(T,y) &= i(y-K)^{+}, & 0 &\leq y \leq y_i^{\star}(T). \end{aligned}$$

To solve this system of PDEs, we apply the implicit finite-difference approximation discussed in Section 4.3.4. Since we have already calculated $C^{(1)}(t,y)$ in Section 4.2, we can use it to solve for $C^{(2)}(t,y), \ldots, C^{(n)}(t,y)$.

Next, we consider the unvested ESOs. Let $\tilde{C}^{(i)}(t,y)$ be the cost of i unvested ESOs at time t when the stock price is y dollars, assuming it is still alive.

$$\tilde{C}^{(i)}(t,y) = \mathbb{E}^{\mathbb{Q}}_{t,y}\{e^{-r(t_v-t)}C^{(i)}(t_v,Y_{t_v})\mathbf{1}_{\{\tau^{\lambda} > t_v\}}\}.$$

We have the following *homogeneous* PDE for $\tilde{C}^{(i)}$:

$$\tilde{C}_t^{(i)} + \frac{\eta^2}{2}y^2 \tilde{C}_{yy}^{(i)} + (r-q)y \tilde{C}_y^{(i)} - (r+\lambda)\tilde{C}^{(i)} = 0$$

in the region $\{(t,y) : 0 \leq t \leq t_v, y \geq 0\}$, with the boundary conditions

$$\begin{aligned} \tilde{C}^{(i)}(t,0) &= 0, & 0 &\leq t \leq t_v, \\ \tilde{C}^{(i)}(t_v,y) &= C^{(i)}(t_v,y), & 0 &\leq y \leq y_i^{\star}(t_v). \end{aligned}$$

Since $C^{(i)}(t_v,y)$ is the terminal condition for the PDE formulation for $\tilde{C}^{(i)}$, we must solve the PDE problem for $C^{(i)}$ before $\tilde{C}^{(i)}$. Again, we use an implicit finite-difference method for both PDE problems.

4.5.4. *Characterization of the employee's exercise boundaries*

Definition 4.14. The employee's indifference price for holding $i \leq n$ ESOs with multiple exercises is defined as the function $p^{(i)} \equiv p^{(i)}(t, x, y)$ such that

$$M(t, x) = V^{(i)}(t, x - p^{(i)}, y).$$

From this, we have $p^{(0)} = 0$ because $V^{(0)}(t, x, y) = M(t, x)$. Also, $p^{(1)}$ is the same as the indifference price in Definition 4.1. Again, due to the exponential utility function, the indifference price is a function of only t and y, and it is related to $H^{(i)}$ and $V^{(i)}$ in the following way.

Proposition 4.15. *The indifference price $p^{(i)}$ satisfies*

$$p^{(i)}(t, y) = -\frac{1}{\gamma(1 - \rho^2)e^{r(T-t)}} \log H^{(i)}(t, y),$$

and

$$V^{(i)}(t, x, y) = M(t, x) \cdot e^{-\gamma p^{(i)}(t,y)e^{r(T-t)}}.$$

Due to this proposition, we obtain a variational inequality that is equivalent to (4.19)–(4.20):

$$p_t^{(i)} + \tilde{\mathscr{L}} p^{(i)} - rp^{(i)} - \frac{1}{2}\gamma(1 - \rho^2)\eta^2 y^2 e^{r(T-t)}(p_y^{(i)})^2$$

$$+ \frac{\lambda}{\gamma}(1 - b(t, y)^i e^{\gamma p^{(i)} e^{r(T-t)}}) \leq 0,$$

$$p^{(i)} \geq p^{(i-1)} + (y - K)^+,$$

$$\left(p_t^{(i)} + \tilde{\mathscr{L}} p^{(i)} - rp^{(i)} - \frac{1}{2}\gamma(1 - \rho^2)\eta^2 y^2 e^{r(T-t)}(p_y^{(i)})^2 \right.$$

$$\left. + \frac{\lambda}{\gamma}(1 - b(t, y)^i e^{\gamma p^{(i)} e^{r(T-t)}}) \right)$$

$$\cdot ((y - K)^+ + p^{(i-1)} - p^{(i)}) = 0,$$

for $(t, y) \in [0, T] \times [0, +\infty)$. The boundary conditions are

$$p^{(i)}(T, y) = i(y - K)^+,$$

$$p^{(i)}(t, 0) = 0.$$

The employee's optimal exercise time for the next option when there are i unexercised ESOs can be expressed in terms of indifference prices.

$$\tau_i^* = \inf\{t \le u \le T : V^{(i)}(u, X_u, Y_u) = V^{(i-1)}(u, X_u + (Y_u - K)^+, Y_u)\}$$
$$= \inf\{t \le u \le T : p^{(i)}(u, Y_u) - p^{(i-1)}(u, Y_u) = (Y_u - K)^+\}.$$

To understand the meaning of this, let us define the following.

Definition 4.16. For a holder with i ESOs, we define $w^{(i+1)} \equiv w^{(i+1)}(t, x, y)$ as the **premium** that this holder is willing to pay in order to receive one extra ESO (i.e. the $(i+1)$th option). In other words, $w^{(i+1)}$ satisfies

$$V^{(i+1)}(t, x - w^{(i+1)}, y) = V^{(i)}(t, x, y). \tag{4.23}$$

From this definition, $w^{(1)}$ equals the employee's indifference price for holding one ESO. The premium can be written as the difference of two indifference prices.

Proposition 4.17. *For $t \le T$ and $y \in \mathbb{R}_+$, we have $w^{(i)}(t, y) = p^{(i)}(t, y) - p^{(i-1)}(t, y)$.*

Proof. We use the defining equation (4.23) to obtain the equality

$$M(t, x) = V^{(i)}(t, x - p^{(i)}, y) = V^{(i-1)}(t, x - p^{(i-1)}, y).$$

From this we have

$$V^{(i)}(t, x, y) = V^{(i-1)}(t, x + p^{(i)} - p^{(i-1)}, y).$$

Therefore, $w^{(i)} := p^{(i)} - p^{(i-1)}$ satisfies (4.23). □

Proposition 4.17 implies that we can rewrite the optimal exercise time as

$$\tau_i^* = \inf\{t \le u \le T : w^{(i)}(u, Y_u) = (Y_u - K)^+\},$$

which means that the employee holding i ESOs should exercise the next option as soon as the payoff from immediate exercise is higher than the amount he is willing to pay for it. Under the assumption of exponential utility, the indifference prices $p^{(i)}$ are wealth-independent, which implies that the premiums $w^{(i)}$ and the optimal exercise time are also wealth-independent. For a general utility function, the indifference prices, premiums, and the optimal exercise time may all depend on wealth.

4.5.5.   *The impact of multiple exercises*

We first study the effect of multiple exercises on the employee's exercise policy. In the traditional no-arbitrage pricing theory for American options, the option holder always exercises all the options at the same time. In our model, the risk-averse employee exercises his ESOs at different critical price levels (see Figure 4.9). This is because the employee's premium for an additional option diminishes with respect to the number of options he already owns. As a result, the employee tends to exercise the first option very early, and the last one much later. Similar exercise behaviors can be found in Grasselli (2005), Rogers and Scheinkman (2007) and Grasselli and Henderson (2009).

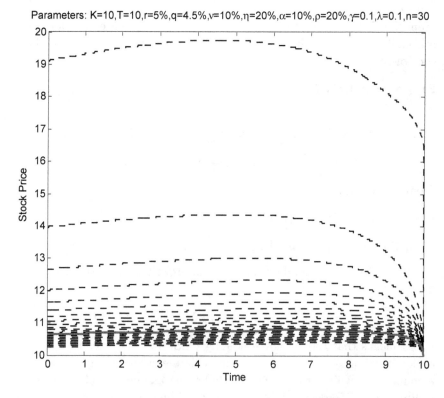

Figure 4.9. **Multiple exercise boundaries**: The dashed curves represent the exercise boundaries for an employee with 30 ESOs with multiple exercise rights. The bottom one corresponds to the first option exercised, and the top one corresponds to the last option exercised. When the employee is granted 30 ESOs with simultaneous exercise constraint, his exercise boundary (solid line) lies somewhere in the middle.

In order to study the impact of multiple exercises, we compare it with the case with simultaneous exercise constraint. This constraint allows the employee to choose only one exercise time for all his ESOs. This is equivalent to the single issue case with the ESO payoff multiplied by the number of options. As Figure 4.9 illustrates, his boundary lies somewhere in the middle.

Finally, we examine the effect of multiple issues on the firm's granting cost. As the number of ESOs increases, the employee tends to adopt a more conservative exercising strategy for every additional option, which in turns results in a diminishing marginal cost. This is depicted in Figure 4.10. When there is no vesting, the cost of ESOs with simultaneous exercise constraint dominates that with multiple exercise rights (see Figure 4.10(a)). This is because the simultaneous exercise constraint prevents the employee from exercising too early, leading to a higher expected discounted payoff.

However, when a two-year vesting period is imposed, the costs are almost the same (see Figure 4.10(b)). In the case of multiple exercises, the majority of the employee's exercise boundaries are very low, so it is very likely that the company stock will be above most of them, leading to exercises at the end of the vesting period. Similarly, in the constrained case, the low boundary implies that the employee will probably exercise all his ESOs at the end of the vesting period. This result is consistent with the well-known early exercise phenomenon in ESO empirical studies. As a result, in the presence of vesting, the right of multiple exercises has negligible influence on the firm's granting cost.

In conclusion, the utility-based approach is effective in accounting for the employee's risk aversion and hedging constraints, and is amenable to incorporating a number of key features of an ESO. This leads to a resulting valuation model that not only accurately calculates the cost of the ESO but also reflects the cost contributions of various factors. Slight variations of this approach can further account for ESO grants with various terms as well as employees' different trading constraints.

4.6. Existence of a Generalized Solution

In this section, we investigate the existence and uniqueness of solution to the nonlinear free boundary problem (4.9)–(4.10). The problem has a singularity as y goes to infinity, that is, when the obstacle term κ approaches zero. To circumvent this difficulty, we alter the obstacle term slightly

$$\hat{\kappa}(t,y) = e^{-\gamma(1-\rho^2)(y \wedge L - K)^+ e^{r(T-t)}},$$

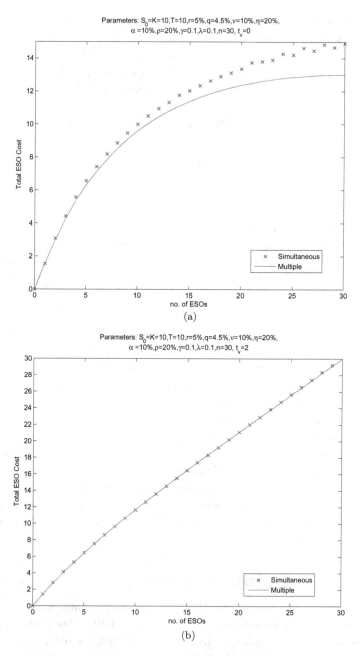

Figure 4.10. **Effect of multiple exercises**: (a) When there is no vesting, the cost of ESOs with simultaneous exercise constraint dominates that with multiple exercise rights. (b) However, when vesting is imposed, the difference in costs almost disappears.

with $L < \infty$. Notice $\hat{\kappa} \geq e^{-\gamma(1-\rho^2)Le^{rT}} =: \epsilon > 0$. This change imposes a positive lower bound on the obstacle, and we can choose L sufficiently large so that the error is negligible. For practical purposes, this free boundary is numerically solved on a bounded domain, which renders the obstacle term bounded away from zero. So far, we have seen that the employee's exercise boundary exists and is bounded above. In such cases, the free boundary problems corresponding to the original obstacle κ and the altered obstacle $\hat{\kappa}$ give the same solution if L is chosen sufficiently large.

For any bounded function $w : [0, T] \times [0, +\infty) \mapsto [\epsilon_L, 1]$ (with constant ϵ_L to be specified later), and stopping time $\tau \in \mathscr{T}_{t,T}$, we define

$$g(t, y; \tau, w) : = \tilde{\mathbb{E}}_{t,y} \left\{ e^{-(1-\rho^2)\lambda(\tau-t)} \hat{\kappa}(\tau, Y_\tau) \right.$$
$$\left. + \int_t^\tau e^{-(1-\rho^2)\lambda(u-t)} \tilde{b}(u, Y_u) w(u, Y_u)^{-\hat{\rho}} \, du \right\},$$

where $\tilde{b}(t, y) := \lambda(1 - \rho^2)b(t, y)$ is bounded:

$$0 \leq \tilde{b}(t, y) \leq \lambda(1 - \rho^2) =: M < \infty.$$

Also, we define an operator Γ by

$$\Gamma w(t, y) = \inf_{\tau \in \mathscr{T}_{t,T}} g(t, y; \tau, w). \tag{4.24}$$

Then, Γw is also bounded in $[\epsilon_L, 1]$. In view of (4.11), the generalized solution to (4.9)–(4.10) is the function that satisfies

$$G(t, y) = \Gamma G(t, y).$$

Note that the solution G appears on both sides of the equation. Moreover, we observe that G is bounded:

$$e^{-(1-\rho^2)\lambda(T-t)} e^{-\gamma(1-\rho^2)(L-K)} \leq G(t, y) \leq \hat{\kappa}(t, y) \leq 1,$$

so we set $\epsilon_L = e^{-(1-\rho^2)(\lambda T + \gamma(L-K))}$. Next, we show that Γ is a contraction mapping and thus has a fixed point.

Proposition 4.18. *The operator Γ is a contraction mapping on the space of functions bounded in $[\epsilon_L, 1]$ with respect to the norm*

$$||v||_\beta := \sup_{(t,y)\in[0,T]\times[0,L]} e^{-\beta(T-t)} |v(t, y)|$$

for $0 < \beta < \infty$ sufficiently large. Also, Γ has a unique fixed point.

Notice the norm $||\cdot||_\beta$ is equivalent to the supremum-norm $||\cdot||_\infty$. We prepare to prove this proposition with two useful inequalities.

Lemma 4.19. *The following inequality holds:*

$$|\Gamma w_1 - \Gamma w_2| \leq \sup_{\tau \in \mathscr{T}_{t,T}} |g(t,y;\tau,w_1) - g(t,y;\tau,w_2)|.$$

Proof.   By its definition in (4.24), the operator satisfies

$$|\Gamma w_1 - \Gamma w_2| = \left| \inf_{\tau \in \mathscr{T}_{t,T}} g(t,y;\tau,w_1) - \inf_{\tau \in \mathscr{T}_{t,T}} g(t,y;\tau,w_2) \right|$$

$$\leq \sup_{\tau \in \mathscr{T}_{t,T}} |g(t,y;\tau,w_1) - g(t,y;\tau,w_2)|.$$

$\square$

Another useful inequality is that, for $a, c > 1$, $\hat{\rho} \in [1, \infty)$, we have

$$|a^{-\hat{\rho}} - c^{-\hat{\rho}}| \leq |a - c|.$$

Now, we can prove the proposition.

Proof of Proposition 4.18. Let w_1 and w_2 be two functions bounded in $[\epsilon_L, 1]$. We obtain

$$e^{-\beta(T-t)} |\Gamma w_1 - \Gamma w_2|$$

$$\leq e^{-\beta(T-t)} \sup_{\tau \in \mathscr{T}_{t,T}} \left| \mathbb{E}_{t,y} \left\{ \int_t^\tau \tilde{b}(s, Y_s) \left(w_1(s, Y_s)^{-\hat{\rho}} - w_2(s, Y_s)^{-\hat{\rho}} \right) ds \right\} \right|$$

$$\leq e^{-\beta(T-t)} \sup_{\tau \in \mathscr{T}_{t,T}} \mathbb{E}_{t,y} \left\{ \int_t^\tau \tilde{b}(s, Y_s) \epsilon_L^{-\hat{\rho}} \left| \left(\frac{w_1(s, Y_s)}{\epsilon_L} \right)^{-\hat{\rho}} \right. \right.$$

$$\left. \left. - \left(\frac{w_2(s, Y_s)}{\epsilon_L} \right)^{-\hat{\rho}} \right| ds \right\}$$

$$\leq e^{-\beta(T-t)} \sup_{\tau \in \mathscr{T}_{t,T}} \mathbb{E}_{t,y} \left\{ \int_t^\tau \tilde{b}(s, Y_s) \epsilon_L^{-\hat{\rho}} \left| \frac{w_1(s, Y_s)}{\epsilon_L} - \frac{w_2(s, Y_s)}{\epsilon_L} \right| ds \right\}$$

$$\leq e^{-\beta(T-t)} M \epsilon_L^{-\hat{\rho}-1} ||w_1 - w_2||_\beta \sup_{\tau \in \mathscr{T}_{t,T}} \mathbb{E}_{t,y} \left\{ \int_t^\tau e^{\beta(T-s)} ds \right\}$$

$$\leq \frac{M \epsilon_L^{-\frac{1}{1-\rho^2}}}{\beta} ||w_1 - w_2||_\beta.$$

If we choose $\beta > M \epsilon_L^{-\frac{1}{1-\rho^2}}$, then Γ is a contraction mapping with respect to the norm $||\cdot||_\beta$. Consequently, Γ has a unique fixed point. $\square$

In conclusion, the problem (4.9)–(4.10) has a unique generalized solution. In particular, the generalized solution can be approximated by the sequence $\{G_n\}_{n\geq 0}$, starting with

$$G_0(t,y) := \inf_{\tau \in \mathscr{T}_{t,T}} \tilde{\mathbb{E}}_{t,y}\{e^{-(1-\rho^2)\lambda(\tau-t)}\hat{\kappa}(\tau, Y_\tau)\},$$

and the rest defined via $G_{n+1}(t,y) = \Gamma G_n(t,y)$, for $n \geq 0$. Then, every member of the sequence is bounded below by ϵ_L, and the contraction mapping property of Γ will ensure convergence to the solution.

Chapter 5

Static–Dynamic Hedging of ESOs

In the standard no-arbitrage pricing theory, option positions are assumed to be hedged perfectly by continuously trading the underlying asset. The option price is computed from the conditional expectation of discounted payoff under a unique risk-neutral pricing measure. However, in many financial applications, the underlying asset is *non-traded*. Some examples include weather derivatives (Davis, 2001), employee stock options (Henderson, 2005; Leung and Sircar, 2009a), options on illiquid assets (Oberman and Zariphopoulou, 2003; Ankirchner *et al.*, 2010).

Instead, derivatives holders manage their risk exposure by trading some liquid assets correlated with the underlying. One candidate hedging instrument is the market index, whose liquidity and relatively low transaction cost permit dynamic trading. Also, standard market-traded options can be used as additional hedging instruments. However, high transaction costs discourage frequent option trades, so several studies, including Carr *et al.* (1998), İlhan and Sircar (2005), and Leung and Sircar (2009b), have focused on static hedging with options, which involves purchasing a portfolio of standard options at initiation and no trades afterwards.

In this chapter, we present a new methodology for hedging long-term employee stock options. Specifically, the hedging strategy proposed herein does not trade the company stock, but combines *dynamic* trading of a correlated liquid asset (e.g. the market index) and *static* positions in market-traded options. Moreover, since most market-traded options are relatively short-term, it is sensible to conduct static hedging sequentially over time till the long-term option expires. For this reason, the proposed strategy is called *sequential static-dynamic* hedging.

The sequential static-dynamic hedging mechanism is applicable to both European and American stock options. Since the market is incomplete, we will adopt a utility maximization approach to determine the optimal static positions at different times, along with the optimal dynamic trading strategy.

5.1. Model Formulation

The financial market consists of a riskless bank account, a market index S, and the firm's stock Y. The prices of S and Y are modeled as lognormal processes

$$\text{(traded)} \qquad dS_t = \mu S_t\, dt + \sigma S_t\, dW_t,$$

$$\text{(non-traded)} \quad dY_t = (\nu - q)Y_t\, dt + \eta Y_t(\rho dW_t + \rho'\, d\hat{W}_t),$$

where the processes W and $\hat{W}$ are two independent standard Brownian motions defined on $(\Omega, \mathscr{F}, (\mathscr{F}_t), \mathbb{P})$, where $\mathscr{F}_t$ is the augmented σ-algebra generated by $(W, \hat{W})$. Also, $\rho \in (-1,1)$ and $\rho' = \sqrt{1-\rho^2}$. We denote the Sharpe ratios of the market index and the firm's stock, respectively, by

$$\lambda = \frac{\mu - r}{\sigma}, \quad \xi = \frac{\nu - q - r}{\eta}.$$

The ESO is a call option written on the firm's stock with finite maturity T. We shall consider European ESOs and American ESOs separately in Sections 5.2 and 5.3, respectively.

The employee cannot trade the firm's stock but dynamically invests in the market index S and the bank account to partially hedge his position. With a dynamic investment strategy θ, the employee's trading wealth evolves according to the process

$$dX_u^\theta = [\theta_u(\mu - r) + rX_u]\, du + \theta_u \sigma\, dB_u, \quad X_t = x, \qquad (5.1)$$

where θ represents the cash amount invested in S. The set of all admissible strategies, Θ, consists of all self-financing $\mathscr{F}_t$-progressively measurable processes $(\theta_t)_{t\geq 0}$ such that the integrability condition $\mathbb{E}\{\int_0^T \theta_t^2\, dt\} < \infty$. For $0 \leq s \leq t \leq T$, we denote by $\Theta_{s,t}$ the set of admissible strategies over the period $[s,t]$.

In addition to dynamic trading, the employee also purchases from the market some put options written on the firm's stock. For the moment, let us consider only European puts all with the same strike K', though in reality there is a wide array of options to choose from, and the choices can be path dependent.[1] To avoid arbitrage opportunities, we assume that the market price of the market-traded puts lie within the no-arbitrage bounds. Since the underlying asset Y follows a geometric Brownian motion, it makes sense to set the market price to be the Black–Scholes put option price, denoted by $\pi(t, y)$.

After every purchase, the employee will hold the put options till expiration. Typically the market-traded options have short maturities, so the employee will repeat this buy-and-hold strategy several times till the ESO expires. To this end, let the maturity of the market-traded puts be $\Delta t = T/N$ where N is some positive integer. Denote $t_n = n\Delta t$, for $n = 0, 1, \ldots, N - 1$. Therefore, the employee make option purchases at times $\{0, t_1, t_2, \ldots, t_{N-1}\}$.

The market is incomplete, so we adopt a utility maximization approach to determine the optimal hedges. In particular, we represent the employee's risk preference by an exponential utility function

$$U(x) = -e^{-\gamma x}, \quad x \in \mathbb{R},$$

with a constant absolute risk-aversion coefficient $\gamma > 0$. We interpret $U(x)$ as the employee's utility of having wealth \$$x$ time T.

5.2. Sequential Static–Dynamic Hedging for European ESOs

In this section, we discuss the static–dynamic hedging of a European ESO with payoff $C(Y_T) = (Y_T - K)^+$.

5.2.1. *Sequential utility maximization*

We shall define the ESO holder's value function recursively backward in time. To start with, suppose at time t_{N-1}, the employee is holding an ESO, along with b_{N-1} units of put options which will expire at time T with payoff $b_{N-1}D(Y_T) = b_{N-1}(K' - Y_T)^+$. Therefore, the employee's value function at time t_{N-1} is given by

$$
\begin{aligned}
&V^{(N-1)}(t_{N-1}, x, y; b_{N-1}) \\
&\quad = \sup_{\theta_{t_{N-1},T}} \mathbb{E}\left\{U\left(X_T + C(Y_T) + b_{N-1}D(Y_T)\right) \mid X_{t_{N-1}} = x, Y_{t_{N-1}} = y\right\}.
\end{aligned}
$$

---

[1] For example, the strike can be an $\mathscr{F}_t$-measurable random variable, such as $g(Y_t)$, instead of a constant K'.

Now, accounting for the market price π of the puts at time t_{N-1}, the employee chooses b_{N-1} so as to maximize the value function:

$$b_{N-1}^*(x,y) = \arg\max_{0 \leq b < \infty} V^{(N-1)}\left(t_{N-1}, x - b\pi(t_{N-1}, y), y; b\right). \qquad (5.2)$$

For convenience, we write the value function and indifference price corresponding to this optimal static hedge as

$$V_*^{(N-1)}(t_{N-1}, x, y)$$
$$= V^{(N-1)}\left(t_{N-1}, x - b_{N-1}^*\pi(t_{N-1}, y), y; b_{N-1}^*\right), \qquad (5.3)$$
$$p_*^{(N-1)}(t_{N-1}, y)$$
$$= p^{(N-1)}(t_{N-1}, x, y; b_{N-1}^*) - b_{N-1}^*\pi(t_{N-1}, y). \qquad (5.4)$$

It is often better for intuitive purposes to work with indifference prices, which we will define next. To do so, we first consider the investment problem in which the risk-averse employee dynamically trades in the market index and bank account without any options till T. This well-studied problem is first introduced by Merton (1969). The employee's maximal expected utility, called the Merton function, is given by

$$M(t,x) = \sup_{\theta_{t,T}} \mathbb{E}\{U(X_T) \mid X_t = x\}$$
$$= -e^{-\gamma x r^{(T-t)}} e^{-\frac{\lambda^2}{2}(T-t)}.$$

At anytime $t \in [t_n, t_{n+1})$, the employee's indifference price $p^{(n)}(t,x,y;b_n)$ for holding the ESO and b_n puts is defined by the equation

$$V^{(n)}(t,x,y;b_n) = M(t, x + p^{(n)}(t,x,y;b_n)),$$

where $V^{(n)}(t,x,y;b_n)$ is the value function for time interval $[t_n, t_{n+1})$ (to be defined in (5.8)). This defining equation allows us to express the optimal static position b_n^* in (5.2) in terms of the indifference price.

$$b_n^*(x,y) = \arg\max_{0 \leq b < \infty} p^{(n)}(t_n, x, y; b) - b\pi(t_n, y). \qquad (5.5)$$

Therefore, the optimal static position is found from the Fenchel–Legendre transform of the employees indifference price as a function of the number of puts, evaluated at the market price. As in (5.3) and (5.4), we denote the value function and indifference price corresponding to this optimal static hedge by

$$V_*^{(n)}(t, x, y) = V^{(n)}\left(t, x - b_n^* \pi(t, y), y; b_n^*\right), \tag{5.6}$$

$$p_*^{(n)}(t, y) = p^{(n)}(t, x, y; b_n^*) - b_n^* \pi(t, y). \tag{5.7}$$

Having defined the value function $V^{(N-1)}$, we can move backward in time to derive the value functions $\{V^{(N-2)}, V^{(N-3)}, \ldots, V^{(0)}\}$. Indeed, the employee's value function at time $t \in [t_n, t_{n+1})$, for $n = N-2, N-3, \ldots, 0$, is given by

$$
\begin{aligned}
&V^{(n)}(t, x, y; b_n) \\
&= \sup_{\theta_{t_n, t_{n+1}}} \mathbb{E}\{V_*^{(n+1)}(t_{n+1}, X_{t_{n+1}} + b_n D(Y_{t_{n+1}}), Y_{t_{n+1}}) \mid X_t = x, Y_t = y\} \\
&= \sup_{\theta_{t_n, t_{n+1}}} \mathbb{E}\{M(t_{n+1}, X_{t_{n+1}} + p_*^{(n+1)}(t_{n+1}, Y_{t_{n+1}}) \\
&\quad + b_n D(Y_{t_{n+1}})) \mid X_t = x, Y_t = y\},
\end{aligned} \tag{5.8}
$$

where $V_*^{(n+1)}$ and $p_*^{(n+1)}$ are defined in (5.6) and (5.7), respectively.

5.2.2. *A recursive system of PDEs*

The value functions $\{V^{(N-1)}, V^{(N-2)}, \ldots, V^{(0)}\}$ lead us to study a system of PDEs. To do so, let us introduce the differential operators:

$$
\begin{aligned}
\mathscr{L} &= \frac{\eta^2 y^2}{2} \frac{\partial^2}{\partial y^2} + \rho \theta \sigma \eta y \frac{\partial^2}{\partial x \partial y} + \frac{\theta^2 \sigma^2}{2} \frac{\partial^2}{\partial x^2} \\
&\quad + (\nu - q) y \frac{\partial}{\partial y} + [\theta(\mu - r) + rx] \frac{\partial}{\partial x},
\end{aligned}
$$

$$
\tilde{\mathscr{L}} u = \frac{\eta^2 y^2}{2} \frac{\partial^2 u}{\partial y^2} + \left(\nu - q - \rho \frac{\mu - r}{\sigma} \eta\right) y \frac{\partial u}{\partial y},
$$

$$
\mathscr{A}^{ql} u = \frac{\partial u}{\partial t} + \tilde{\mathscr{L}} u - ru - \frac{1}{2}\gamma(1 - \rho^2)\eta^2 y^2 e^{r(T-t)} \left(\frac{\partial u}{\partial y}\right)^2.
$$

The operator $\mathscr{L}$ is the infinitesimal generator of (X, Y), $\tilde{\mathscr{L}}$ is the infinitesimal generator of Y under the minimal entropy martingale measure, Q^E, and the last operator $\mathscr{A}^{ql}$ is *quasilinear*.

First, the value function $V^{(N-1)}(t, x, y; b)$ is conjectured to solve the following HJB PDE:

$$V_t^{(N-1)} + \sup_\theta \mathscr{L} V^{(N-1)} = 0,$$

for $(t, x, y) \in [t_{N-1}, T) \times \mathbb{R} \times (0, +\infty)$. The boundary conditions are

$$V^{(N-1)}(T, x, y; b) = -e^{-\gamma(x+C(y)+bD(y))},$$

$$V^{(N-1)}(t, x, 0; b) = -e^{-\gamma(xe^{r(T-t)}+bK)}e^{-\frac{(\mu-r)^2}{2\sigma^2}(T-t)}.$$

Due to the exponential utility function, the value function has a separation of variables (see Oberman and Zariphopoulou, 2003):

$$V^{(N-1)}(t, x, y; b) = M(t, x) \cdot H^{(N-1)}(t, y; b)^{\frac{1}{(1-\rho^2)}}.$$

The function $H^{(N-1)}$ solves a linear PDE

$$H_t^{(N-1)} + \tilde{\mathscr{L}} H^{(N-1)} = 0,$$

for $(t, y) \in [t_{N-1}, T) \times (0, +\infty)$, with boundary conditions

$$H^{(N-1)}(T, y; b) = e^{-\gamma(1-\rho^2)(C(y)+bD(y))},$$

$$H^{(N-1)}(t, 0; b) = e^{-\gamma(1-\rho^2)bK}.$$

5.2.3. *Indifference price*

By the definition of indifference price, this function $H^{(N-1)}$ is connected to the indifference price $p^{(N-1)}$ in the following way:

$$p^{(N-1)}(t, y; b) = -\frac{1}{\gamma(1-\rho^2)e^{r(T-t)}} \log H^{(N-1)}(t, y; b),$$

$$t \in [t_{N-1}, T]. \qquad (5.9)$$

which gives

$$V^{(N-1)}(t, x, y; b) = M(t, x) \cdot e^{-\gamma p^{(N-1)}(t, y; b)e^{r(T-t)}}, \qquad (5.10)$$

and the following PDE

$$\mathscr{A}^{ql} p^{(N-1)} = 0,$$

with boundary conditions

$$p^{(N-1)}(T, y; b) = C(y) + bD(y),$$
$$p^{(N-1)}(t, 0; b) = bKe^{-r(T-t)}.$$

In practice, we numerically solve the PDE for $H^{(N-1)}(t, y; b)$ and use (5.9) to derive the indifference price $p^{(N-1)}(t, y; b)$. Then, we optimize over b (as in (5.5)) to obtain the employee's optimal static hedges b_{N-1}^* at time t_{N-1}, along with the corresponding $V_*^{(N-1)}(t, x, y)$, $H_*^{(N-1)}(t, y)$ and $p_*^{(N-1)}(t, y)$, which will appear in the terminal conditions for $V^{(N-2)}(t, x, y; b)$. All these allow us to iterate backward to derive the PDEs for $V^{(n)}(t, x, y; b)$ and $p^{(n)}(t, y; b)$ for $n = N-2, N-3, \ldots, 0$. To be precise, at time $t \in [t_n, t_{n+1})$, the value function $V^{(n)}(t, x, y; b)$ satisfies the HJB PDE

$$V_t^{(n)} + \sup_\theta \mathscr{L} V^{(n)} = 0,$$

for $(t, x, y) \in [t_n, t_{n+1}) \times \mathbb{R} \times (0, +\infty)$. The boundary conditions are

$$V^{(n)}(t_{n+1}, x, y; b) = V_*^{(n+1)}(t_{n+1}, x + bD(y), y),$$
$$V^{(n)}(t, x, 0; b) = -e^{-\gamma(xe^{r(T-t)}+bK)} e^{-\frac{(\mu-r)^2}{2\sigma^2}(T-t)}.$$

Again, we can simplify the PDE by the transformation

$$V^{(n)}(t, x, y; b) = M(t, x) \cdot H^{(n)}(t, y; b)^{\frac{1}{(1-\rho^2)}}.$$

The function $H^{(n)}(t, y; b)$ satisfies the linear PDE

$$H_t^{(n)} + \tilde{\mathscr{L}} H^{(n)} = 0,$$

for $(t, y) \in [t_n, t_{n+1}) \times (0, +\infty)$, with boundary conditions

$$H^{(n)}(t_{n+1}, y; b) = e^{-\gamma(1-\rho^2)bD(y)} H_*^{(n+1)}(t_{n+1}, y)$$
$$H^{(n)}(t, 0; b) = e^{-\gamma(1-\rho^2)bK}.$$

The indifference price is given by

$$p^{(n)}(t, y; b) = -\frac{1}{\gamma(1-\rho^2)e^{r(T-t)}} \log H^{(n)}(t, y; b), \quad t \in [t_n, t_{n+1}),$$

which yields the PDE

$$\mathscr{A}^{ql} p^{(n)} = 0,$$

for $(t, y) \in [t_n, t_{n+1}) \times (0, +\infty)$, with boundary conditions

$$p^{(n)}(t_{n+1}, y; b) = p_*^{(n+1)}(t_{n+1}, y) + bD(y),$$

$$p^{(n)}(t, 0; b) = bKe^{-r(T-t)}.$$

5.3. Sequential Static–Dynamic Hedging for American ESOs

Now we analyze the sequential hedging problem for an American ESO. Our ultimate objectives are to analyze the optimal static positions over time, and examine the non-trivial effect of static hedges on the optimal ESO exercising strategy. We denote by $\mathscr{T}$ the set of all stopping times with respect to $\mathbb{F}$ taking values in $[0, T]$. This will be the collection of all admissible exercise times for the ESO. For $s, u \in \mathscr{T}$ with $s \leq u$, we denote the set of stopping times in between by $\mathscr{T}_{s,u} := \{\tau \in \mathscr{T} : s \leq \tau \leq u\}$.

5.3.1. *Sequential utility maximization*

We assume that the employee will reinvest the ESO proceeds, if any, into the dynamic trading portfolio. Moreover, after the ESO exercise, there is no need for future static hedges, so the sequential static hedging will terminate by the next expiration date. Precisely, if the ESO has been exercised at time $t \in (t_n, t_{n+1}]$, $n \in \{0, 1, \ldots, N-1\}$, then the employee, who still holds some a units of European puts expiring at t_{n+1}, faces the investment problem

$$u^{(n)}(t, x, y; a) = \sup_{\theta_{t,t_{n+1}}} \mathbb{E}\{M(t_{n+1}, X_{t_{n+1}} + aD(Y_{t_{n+1}})) \mid X_t = x, Y_t = y\}.$$

$$(5.11)$$

This is a standard utility maximization problem with European puts. We can express it in terms of the indifference price for the puts, denoted by $h^{(n)}(t, y; a)$:

$$u^{(n)}(t, x, y; a) = M(t, x + h^{(n)}(t, y; a)).$$

Now suppose the employee is holding the American ESO at t_{N-1}, along with a_{N-1} units of put options. Then, the value function is given by

$$\hat{V}^{(N-1)}(t_{N-1}, x, y; a_{N-1})$$

$$= \sup_{\tau \in \mathcal{T}_{t_{N-1}, T}} \sup_{\theta_{t_{N-1}, T}} \mathbb{E}\{M(\tau, X_\tau + C(Y_\tau)$$

$$+ h^{(N-1)}(\tau, Y_\tau; a_{N-1})) \,|\, X_{t_{N-1}} = x, Y_{t_{N-1}} = y\}.$$

Now, accounting for the market price π of the puts at time t_{N-1}, the employee chooses a_{N-1} so as to maximize the value function:

$$a_{N-1}^*(x, y) = \arg\max_{0 \le a < \infty} \hat{V}^{(N-1)}(t_{N-1}, x - a\pi(t_{N-1}, y), y; a).$$

For any time $t \in [t_n, t_{n+1})$, the employee's indifference price $\hat{p}^{(n)}(t, x, y; a_n)$ for holding the American ESO and a_n puts is defined by the equation

$$\hat{V}^{(n)}(t, x, y; a_n) = M(t, x + \hat{p}^{(n)}(t, x, y; a_n)),$$

where $\hat{V}^{(n)}(t, x, y; a_n)$ is defined in (5.12) below. We can express the optimal static position a_n^* (decided at time t_n) in terms of the indifference price and market price:

$$a_n^*(x, y) = \arg\max_{0 \le a < \infty} \hat{p}^{(n)}(t_n, x, y; a) - a\pi(t_n, y).$$

We write the value function and indifference price with this optimal static hedge as

$$\hat{V}_*^{(n)}(t, x, y) = \hat{V}^{(n)}(t, x - a_n^*\pi(t, y), y; a_n^*),$$

$$\hat{p}_*^{(n)}(t, y) = \hat{p}^{(n)}(t, x, y; a_n^*) - a_n^*\pi(t, y).$$

Then, for $n \in \{N-2, N-3, \ldots, 0\}$, the employee's value function at time $t \in [t_n, t_{n+1})$ with a_n put options is given recursively by

$$\hat{V}^{(n)}(t, x, y; a_n)$$

$$= \sup_{\tau \in \mathcal{T}_{t_n, t_{n+1}}} \sup_{\theta_{t_n, t_{n+1}}} \mathbb{E}\{\hat{V}_*^{(n+1)}$$

$$\times (t_{n+1}, X_{t_{n+1}} + a_n D(Y_{t_{n+1}}), Y_{t_{n+1}}) \cdot \mathbf{1}_{\{\tau = t_{n+1}\}}$$

$$+ u^{(n)}(\tau, X_\tau + C(Y_\tau), Y_\tau; a_n) \cdot \mathbf{1}_{\{\tau < t_{n+1}\}} \,|\, X_t = x, Y_t = y\},$$

$$(5.12)$$

where $u^{(n)}$ is defined in (5.11).

5.3.2.   *A recursive system of free boundary problems*

We proceed to derive the variational inequalities for $\{\hat{V}^{(N-1)}, \hat{V}^{(N-2)}, \ldots, \hat{V}^{(0)}\}$, which will lead to a system of free boundary problems for the corresponding indifference prices.

We first consider the variational inequality for $\hat{V}^{(N-1)}(t, x, y; a)$.

$$\hat{V}_t^{(N-1)} + \sup_\theta \mathscr{L}\, \hat{V}^{(N-1)} \leq 0,$$

$$\hat{V}^{(N-1)} \geq M(t, x + C(y) + h^{(N-1)}(t, y; a)),$$

$$\left(\hat{V}_t^{(N-1)} + \sup_\theta \mathscr{L}\, \hat{V}^{(N-1)} \right) \cdot (M(t, x + C(y) + h^{(N-1)}(t, y; a))$$
$$- \hat{V}^{(N-1)}) = 0,$$

for $(t, x, y) \in [t_{N-1}, T) \times \mathbb{R} \times (0, +\infty)$. The boundary conditions are

$$\hat{V}^{(N-1)}(T, x, y; a) = -e^{-\gamma(x+C(y)+aD(y))},$$

$$\hat{V}^{(N-1)}(t, x, 0; a) = -e^{-\gamma(xe^{r(T-t)}+aK)} e^{-\frac{(\mu-r)^2}{2\sigma^2}(T-t)}.$$

The value function has a separation of variables

$$\hat{V}^{(N-1)}(t, x, y; a) = M(t, x) \cdot \hat{H}^{(N-1)}(t, y; a)^{\frac{1}{(1-\rho^2)}},$$

where $\hat{H}^{(N-1)}$ solves a linear free boundary problem

$$\hat{H}_t^{(N-1)} + \tilde{\mathscr{L}}\, \hat{H}^{(N-1)} \geq 0, \quad \hat{H}^{(N-1)} \leq \kappa_{N-1},$$
$$(\hat{H}_t^{(N-1)} + \tilde{\mathscr{L}}\, \hat{H}^{(N-1)}) \cdot (\kappa_{N-1} - \hat{H}^{(N-1)}) = 0,$$

for $(t, y) \in [t_{N-1}, T) \times (0, +\infty)$, where

$$\kappa_{N-1}(t, y; a) = e^{-\gamma(1-\rho^2)(C(y)+h^{(N-1)}(t,y;a))e^{r(T-t)}}.$$

The boundary conditions are

$$\hat{H}^{(N-1)}(T, y; a) = e^{-\gamma(1-\rho^2)(C(y)+aD(y))},$$
$$\hat{H}^{(N-1)}(t, 0; a) = e^{-\gamma(1-\rho^2)aK}.$$

5.3.3. *Indifference price*

Again, we can express the indifference price in terms of function $H^{(N-1)}$:

$$\hat{p}^{(N-1)}(t,y;a) = -\frac{1}{\gamma(1-\rho^2)e^{r(T-t)}} \log \hat{H}^{(N-1)}(t,y;a), \quad t \in [t_{N-1},T],$$

(5.13)

which gives the following quasilinear variational inequality:

$$\mathscr{A}^{ql}\hat{p}^{(N-1)} \leq 0, \quad \hat{p}^{(N-1)} \geq C(y) + h^{(N-1)}(t,y;a),$$
$$\mathscr{A}^{ql}\hat{p}^{(N-1)} \cdot (C(y) + h^{(N-1)}(t,y;a) - \hat{p}^{(N-1)}) = 0,$$

for $(t,y) \in [t_{N-1},T) \times (0,+\infty)$. The boundary conditions are

$$\hat{p}^{(N-1)}(T,y;a) = C(y) + aD(y),$$
$$\hat{p}^{(N-1)}(t,0;a) = aKe^{-r(T-t)}.$$

Similar to Section 5.2.2, we numerically solve the free boundary problem for $\hat{H}^{(N-1)}(t,y;a)$ and use (5.13) to derive the indifference price $\hat{p}^{(N-1)}(t,y;a)$. Then, we optimize over a to obtain the employee's optimal static hedges a_{N-1}^* at time t_{N-1}, along with the corresponding $\hat{V}_*^{(N-1)}(t,x,y)$ and $\hat{p}_*^{(N-1)}(t,y)$ which will become the terminal conditions for $\hat{V}^{(N-2)}(t,x,y;b)$. All these allow us to iterate backward to derive the variational inequalities for $\hat{V}^{(n)}(t,x,y;a)$ and $\hat{p}^{(n)}(t,y;a)$ for $n = N-2, N-3, \ldots, 0$. At time t_n, the value function $\hat{V}^{(n)}(t,x,y;a)$ satisfies the HJB variational inequality

$$\hat{V}_t^{(n)} + \sup_\theta \mathscr{L}\hat{V}^{(n)} \leq 0, \quad \hat{V}^{(n)} \geq M(t,x + C(y) + h^{(n)}(t,y;a)),$$

$$\left(\hat{V}_t^{(n)} + \sup_\theta \mathscr{L}\hat{V}^{(n)}\right) \cdot (M(t,x + C(y) + h^{(n)}(t,y;a)) - \hat{V}^{(n)}) = 0,$$

for $(t,x,y) \in [t_n,t_{n+1}) \times \mathbb{R} \times (0,+\infty)$. The boundary conditions are

$$\hat{V}^{(n)}(t_{n+1},x,y;a) = \hat{V}_*^{(n+1)}(t_{n+1},x + aD(y),y),$$

$$\hat{V}^{(n)}(t,x,0;a) = -e^{-\gamma(xe^{r(T-t)}+aK)}e^{-\frac{(\mu-r)^2}{2\sigma^2}(T-t)}.$$

Again, the value function admits a separation of variables

$$\hat{V}^{(n)}(t,x,y;a) = M(t,x) \cdot \hat{H}^{(n)}(t,y;a)^{\frac{1}{(1-\rho^2)}},$$

where $\hat{H}^{(n)}$ solves a linear free boundary problem

$$\hat{H}_t^{(n)} + \tilde{\mathscr{L}}\,\hat{H}^{(n)} \geq 0, \quad \hat{H}^{(n)} \leq \kappa_n,$$

$$(\hat{H}_t^{(n)} + \tilde{\mathscr{L}}\,\hat{H}^{(n)}) \cdot (\kappa_n - \hat{H}^{(n)}) = 0,$$

for $(t, y) \in [t_n, t_{n+1}) \times (0, +\infty)$, where

$$\kappa_n(t, y; a) = e^{-\gamma(1-\rho^2)(C(y)+h^{(n)}(t,y;a))e^{r(T-t)}}.$$

The boundary conditions are

$$\hat{H}^{(n)}(t_{n+1}, y; a) = e^{-\gamma(1-\rho^2)(aD(y))}\hat{H}_*^{(n+1)}(t_{n+1}, y),$$

$$\hat{H}^{(n)}(t, 0; a) = e^{-\gamma(1-\rho^2)aK}.$$

The indifference price is given by

$$\hat{p}^{(n)}(t, y; a) = -\frac{1}{\gamma(1-\rho^2)e^{r(T-t)}}\log\hat{H}^{(n)}(t, y; a), \quad t \in [t_n, t_{n-1}),$$

which gives the following quasilinear variational inequality

$$\mathscr{A}^{ql}\hat{p}^{(n)} \leq 0,$$

$$\hat{p}^{(n)} \geq C(y) + h^{(n)}(t, y; a),$$

$$\mathscr{A}^{ql}\hat{p}^{(n)} \cdot (C(y) + h^{(n)}(t, y; a) - \hat{p}^{(n)}) = 0,$$

for $(t, y) \in [t_n, t_{n+1}) \times (0, +\infty)$. The boundary conditions are

$$\hat{p}^{(n)}(t_{n+1}, y; a) = \hat{p}_*^{(n+1)}(t_{n+1}, y) + aD(y),$$

$$\hat{p}^{(n)}(t, 0; a) = aKe^{-r(T-t)}.$$

5.4. Numerical Example

As a special case of the general model, we assume that the employee holds an ESO and purchases $\beta \geq 0$ units of European puts with maturity T and strike K'. For simplicity, we have chosen the same maturity T for both options, so no sequential hedging is needed here.

We take the market price of each European put, denoted by π, as the Black–Scholes price, since we model the company stock price as following a geometric Brownian motion. In practice, the observed market price may well be different, but it does not affect our analysis as long as it is an arbitrage-free price.

In practice, we apply standard finite difference methods to numerically solve the associated variational inequality for the optimal exercise boundary, and compute the indifference price, denoted by $\tilde{p}(t, y; \beta)$ here, for holding an ESO along with $\beta \geq 0$ units of European puts.

The optimal quantity of European puts to purchase, $\beta^\star$, is found from the Fenchel–Legendre transform of the indifference price $\tilde{p}(t, y; \beta)$ as a function of β, evaluated at the market price π, i.e.

$$\beta^\star = \arg\max_{0 \leq \beta < \infty} \tilde{p}(t, y; \beta) - \beta\pi.$$

We illustrate how to determine $\beta^\star$ through an numerical example in Figure 5.1.

The combination of risk aversion and static hedge has a profound impact on the employee's optimal exercising strategy. In the presence of hedging restrictions, it is well-known that a risk-averse employee may find it optimal to exercise an American option early even if the underlying stock pays no dividend (see, for example, Detemple and Sundaresan, 1999). We see a similar effect in our model, but we also identify opposite effects of risk

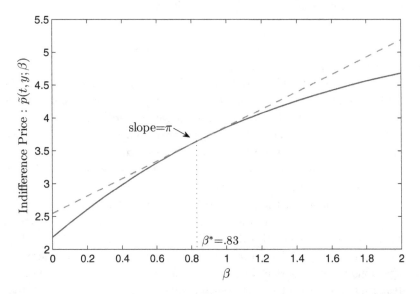

Figure 5.1. The optimal static hedge $\beta^\star$ is the point at which the indifference price (solid curve) has slope equal to the market price π. The parameters are $K = K' = 10$, $T = 10$, $r = 5\%$, $q = 0\%$, $\nu = 8\%$, $\eta = 30\%$, $(\mu - r)/\sigma = 20\%$, $\rho = 30\%$, $\gamma = 0.3$. The Black–Scholes put price is $\pi = 1.322$.

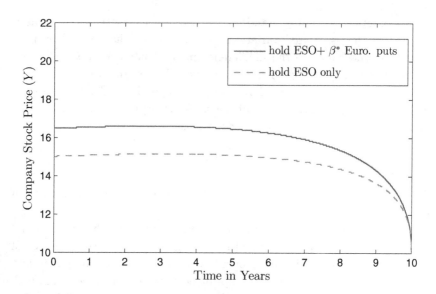

Figure 5.2. The employee who hedges the ESO dynamically will exercise the option as soon as the firm's stock hits the lower dashed boundary. If static–dynamic hedges with European puts are used, the employee will exercise the ESO later at the upper solid boundary. The parameters are the same as those in Figure 5.1.

aversion and static hedges with puts on the employee's optimal exercise policy. Indeed, Leung and Sircar (2009b) show that long positions in European puts will always delay the employee's ESO exercise. In essence, the put options offer protection from the stock's downward movement, which effectively makes the employee less conservative in exercising his ESO. This effect is illustrated in Figure 5.2, where the employee's optimal exercise boundary shifts upward when European puts are used.

This result illustrates a major difference between utility-based optimal exercising policies and risk-neutral exercise times. In the standard no-arbitrage framework, the pricing rule is linear in the quantity of securities, and the optimal exercising strategy for a derivative is unaffected by whether the holder also holds other derivatives, whereas utility-based stopping rules are strongly affected by the holder's hedging strategy. Therefore, in situations where a perfect hedge is unavailable, risk-neutral models are inadequate in predicting the exercise times of early exercisable claims. Since the dynamic–static hedge with European puts induces the employee to delay option exercise and capture more time-value of the option, the ESO cost in general will end up higher than in the case with only dynamic hedge.

5.5. Conclusion

In summary, we have discussed a new utility-based methodology for hedging long-term financial derivatives. The hedging strategy involves *dynamic* trading of a correlated liquid asset (e.g. the market index) combined with *static* positions in market-traded options. In view of the relatively short maturities of most liquid market-traded options, we revise the static hedges *sequentially* over time till the long-term derivative expires. In order to analyze the optimal *sequential static–dynamic* hedging strategy, we study the associated Hamilton–Jacobi–Bellman PDEs and variational inequalities. Working with exponential utility, we apply a series of transformations that reduce the problem for tractability. For future investigation, one meaningful extension is to allow to roll over the short-term positions at random times, rather than a fixed schedule. The rolling decisions will lead to an optimal multiple stopping problem, which involves determining the timing to purchase options (see Leung and Ludkovski, 2011, 2012).

Chapter 6

Hedging and Exercising ESOs in a Regime-Switching Market

6.1. Introduction

In this chapter, we consider the problem of dynamically hedging a long position in early exercisable stock options in a regime-switching market. In the model, the option holder faces the *idiosyncratic risk* from the non-tradability of the underlying stock as well as the *regime-switching risk* in the financial market. These two sources of unhedgeable risks render the market *incomplete*. Since not all risks can be hedged, the holder's risk preferences play a key role in the valuation and investment decisions. We adopt the *utility indifference pricing* methodology, whereby the optimal hedging and exercising strategies are determined through the associated utility maximization problems. In addition, our approach also accounts for the partial hedge with a correlated liquid asset and the multiple early exercises of American stock options.

In our formulation, the holder's utility maximization involves stochastic control (due to dynamic hedging) and optimal stopping (due to early exercises). Our solution approach involves the analytic and numerical studies of the associated variational inequalities (VIs) of Hamilton–Jacobi–Bellman (HJB) type. By a series of transformations, we simplify the fully nonlinear VIs into a semilinear free boundary problems of reaction–diffusion type, and develop an efficient finite-difference method to solve for the optimal exercise boundaries. Our analysis provides both mathematical and financial interpretations for the holder's subjective price, or the *indifference price*, for the American options.

Furthermore, we analyze the dual optimization problem associated with the holder's utility maximization problem. The key idea is the well-known connection between exponential utility and relative entropy minimization; see, among others, Fritelli (2000) and Delbaen *et al.* (2002). Specifically, we first compute explicitly the minimal entropy martingale measure (MEMM) in the regime-switching market. This allows us to construct a duality formula that involves optimizing the expected payoff over a set of stopping times and martingale measures while penalizing by an entropy distance from the MEMM. We apply the duality formula to derive the risk-aversion asymptotics of the holder's indifference price.

In Section 6.2, we study the dynamic hedging of a single American option on a non-traded asset in a regime-switching market. In Section 6.3, we extend our results to the case of American options with multiple exercises. Then, we present the numerical solutions in Section 6.4. In Sections 6.5 and 6.5.3, we establish the duality results and study the asymptotics of the holder's indifference price.

6.2. Dynamic Hedging of a Single American Option

We fix a probability space $(\Omega, \mathscr{F}, P)$, where P is the historical measure. Let ξ be a continuous-time irreducible finite-state Markov chain with state space $E = \{1, 2, \ldots, m\}$. The generator matrix of ξ is denoted by A, which has constant entries $A(i, j) = a_{ij}$ for $i, j \in E$, such that $a_{ij} \geq 0$ for $i \neq j$ and $\sum_{j \in E} a_{ij} = 0$ for each $i \in E$. This Markov chain represents the changing regime of the financial market, and it influences the dynamics of assets.

The financial market consists of a *liquid* asset S and a *non-traded* asset Y, along with the riskless money market account with a constant interest rate $r \geq 0$. Throughout, we shall work with *discounted* cash flows. The discounted prices of (S, Y) are modeled as correlated regime-switching geometric Brownian motions:

$$\mathrm{d}S_t = \mu(\xi_t)S_t \, \mathrm{d}t + \sigma(\xi_t)S_t \, \mathrm{d}W_t,$$

$$\mathrm{d}Y_t = \nu(\xi_t)Y_t \, \mathrm{d}t + \eta(\xi_t)Y_t \left(\rho(\xi_t) \, \mathrm{d}W_t + \tilde{\rho}(\xi_t) \, \mathrm{d}\tilde{W}_t \right),$$

with correlation coefficient $\rho(i) \in (-1, 1)$ for $i \in E$, and $\tilde{\rho}(i) = \sqrt{1 - \rho^2(i)}$. The processes W and $\tilde{W}$ are two independent Brownian motions under P, and are independent of ξ. We define the filtration $\mathbb{F} = (\mathscr{F}_t)_{0 \leq t \leq T}$ with $\mathscr{F}_t$ being the augmented σ-algebra generated by $\{W_u, \tilde{W}_u, \xi_u; 0 \leq u \leq t\}$. For each $i \in E$, the coefficients $\mu(i), \nu(i), \sigma(i), \eta(i)$ are known constants, with

$\sigma(i), \eta(i) > 0$. The Sharpe ratios of S and Y are, respectively,

$$\lambda(i) = \frac{\mu(i)}{\sigma(i)} \quad \text{and} \quad \kappa(i) = \frac{\nu(i)}{\eta(i)}.$$

For convenience, we may use the subscript notation for these constants, e.g. $\mu_i \equiv \mu(i)$, and $\rho_i \equiv \rho(i)$.

We consider the problem of hedging a long position in an American options, which is written on the non-traded asset Y, with a payoff $g_\tau := g(\tau, Y_\tau, \xi_\tau)$ at any exercise time $\tau \leq T$. The set of admissible exercise times, denoted by $\mathscr{T}$, consists of all stopping times with respect to $\mathbb{F}$ taking values in $[0, T]$. For any two stopping times $s, u \in \mathscr{T}$ with $s \leq u$, we define $\mathscr{T}_{s,u} := \{\tau \in \mathscr{T} : s \leq \tau \leq u\}$.

We assume that the holder measures utility from wealth at the terminal time T by an exponential utility function

$$U(x) = -e^{-\gamma x}, \quad x \in \mathbb{R},$$

with a constant absolute risk aversion $\gamma \in (0, \infty)$. The option holder can partially hedge by dynamically trading in S and the money market account throughout $[0, T]$. A trading strategy $(\theta_t)_{0 \leq t \leq T}$ is the discounted cash amount invested in S. As is standard (see Karatzas and Shreve, 1998), a strategy θ is deemed admissible if it is self-financing, $\mathscr{F}_t$-progressively measurable, and satisfies the integrability condition $\mathbb{E}\{\int_0^T \theta_t^2 \, dt\} < \infty$. Denote by $\mathscr{Z}_{s,u}$ the set of admissible strategies over the period $[s, u]$ with $s \leq u$. For any strategy θ, the holder's trading wealth follows

$$dX_t^\theta = \theta_t \frac{dS_t}{S_t} = \theta_t \mu(\xi_t) \, dt + \theta_t \sigma(\xi_t) \, dW_t. \tag{6.1}$$

Note that dynamic trading in S hedges against the risk from W, but there exist the *idiosyncratic risk* due to $\tilde{W}$ and the *regime-switching risk* from ξ. These two unhedgeable sources of risk render the market incomplete.

Remark 6.1. Our model also address the cases with $|\rho(i)| = 1$ for some or all states i. During a regime with perfect correlation, the idiosyncratic risk disappears until ξ switches into another state j with $|\rho(j)| < 1$. Furthermore, if $|\rho(i)| = 1$ *for every* $i \in E$, then the idiosyncratic risk completely vanishes, and Y is effectively "traded" via the proxy asset S. However, the market is still *incomplete* due to the unhedgeable regime-switching risk.

The *utility indifference pricing* methodology is based on the comparison of maximal expected utilities corresponding to dynamic investments with and without the options. The first is the Merton (Merton, 1969) portfolio optimization problem without any options, modified here to incorporate regime-switching price dynamics. With initial wealth x at $t \in [0, T]$, the investor's *Merton value function* is

$$M(t, x, i) = \sup_{\theta \in \mathscr{Z}_{t,T}} \mathbb{E}\{U(X_T^\theta) \,|\, X_t = x, \xi_t = i\}. \tag{6.2}$$

Numerous variations of this classical problem have been developed; for example, see Fleming and Sheu (1999) for a risk-sensitive control approach.

Next, we consider the dynamic investment problem including the American option g. The holder selects the optimal trading strategy and exercise time in order to maximize his expected utility from trading wealth plus the option payoff. Upon exercise of the option, the holder will re-invest the option payoff, if any, into his portfolio, and continue to trade up to time T. Therefore, the holder faces the Merton problem during $[\tau, T]$, and his value function is given by

$$V(t, x, y, i) = \sup_{\substack{\tau \in \mathscr{T}_{t,T} \\ \theta \in \mathscr{Z}_{t,\tau}}} \mathbb{E}_{t,x,y,i}\{M(\tau, X_\tau^\theta + g_\tau, \xi_\tau)\}, \tag{6.3}$$

where the notation $\mathbb{E}_{t,x,y,i}\{\cdot\} \equiv \mathbb{E}\{\cdot \,|\, X_t = x, Y_t = y, \xi_t = i\}$.

The holder's *indifference price* of the American option g is defined as the cash amount p such that he is indifferent between optimally investing without the claim, and optimally investing with the claim at an initial cost p.

Definition 6.2. The American option holder's indifference price $p \equiv p(t, x, y, i)$ is defined by the indifference relation:

$$M(t, x, i) = V(t, x - p, y, i). \tag{6.4}$$

As we shall see in Proposition 6.4, exponential utility yields wealth-independent indifference prices, and hence the x-argument of p will be dropped. We shall analyze p through M and V by studying their associated HJB PDEs and VIs.

6.2.1. *Merton portfolio optimization with regime-switching*

First, we provide a closed-form formula for M.

Theorem 6.3. *The Merton function admits a separation of variables*

$$M(t, x, i) = -e^{-\gamma x} F_i(t), \tag{6.5}$$

for $(t, x, i) \in [0, T] \times \mathbb{R}_+ \times E$, where $F(t) := (F_1(t), \ldots, F_m(t))'$ is given by

$$F(t) = \exp\{(A - D)(T - t)\}\mathbf{1}, \tag{6.6}$$

where $D = \mathrm{diag}(\frac{\lambda_1^2}{2}, \ldots, \frac{\lambda_m^2}{2})$, A is the generator matrix, $\mathbf{1}$ is a vector of ones, and $\exp$ is the matrix exponential. In addition, each $F_i(t)$ admits the probabilistic representation

$$F_i(t) = \mathbb{E}\left\{ \exp\left(-\int_t^T \frac{\lambda^2(\xi_s)}{2} ds \right) \mid \xi_t = i \right\}. \tag{6.7}$$

Proof. The Hamilton–Jacobi–Bellman (HJB) equation associated with $M(t, x, i)$ is

$$M_t^i + \max_\theta \left(\frac{\theta^2 \sigma_i^2}{2} M_{xx}^i + \theta \mu_i M_x^i \right) + \sum_{j \in E} a_{ij} M^j = 0, \tag{6.8}$$

$$M(T, x, i) = U(x).$$

on $[0, T] \times \mathbb{R} \times E$, where the notation $M^i \equiv M(t, x, i)$. Then, substituting (6.5) into (6.8) yields the system of linear ODEs:

$$F'(t) = (D - A)F,$$
$$F(T) = \mathbf{1}. \tag{6.9}$$

Direct computation shows that (6.6) solves (6.9), and (6.7) is the corresponding Feynman–Kac representation. $\qquad\square$

By performing the maximization over θ in (6.8), we obtain the optimal trading strategy for the Merton problem:

$$\hat{\theta}(t, i) = \frac{\lambda_i}{\gamma \sigma_i}. \tag{6.10}$$

Note that $\hat{\theta}$ is inversely proportional to risk aversion γ, but is independent of wealth x. It stays constant in each regime but jumps when ξ switches states. When there is only one regime, $\hat{\theta}$ coincides with the standard Merton solution (Merton, 1969).

In view of (6.5) and (6.7), $F_i(t)$ acts as a regime-dependent discounting factor to the utility function $U(x)$. In fact, one can view the Merton function $M(t, x, i)$ as a *dynamic regime-dependent utility* function. Precisely, it measures utility of wealth at intermediate time t in regime i by accounting for the investment opportunity available to the investor over the period $[0, T]$. This perspective gives another intuitive explanation for its role in the definition of V in (7.36).

Furthermore, the Merton function satisfies the following *dynamic programming principle*:

$$M(t, x, i) = \sup_{\theta \in \mathscr{Z}_{t, \tau}} \mathbb{E}\{M(\tau, X_\tau, \xi_\tau) \mid X_t = x, \xi_t = i\},$$

for every $\tau \in \mathscr{T}_{t, T}$. This is a specific example of Proposition 2.6 of Leung and Sircar (2009b) which establishes this property of the Merton function in a general semimartingale market.

6.2.2.   *The indifference price*

Next, we establish a direct connection between the holder's value function V and the indifference price p. To facilitate presentation, we introduce the differential operators

$$\mathscr{L}_i u = \frac{\eta_i^2 y^2}{2} \frac{\partial^2 u}{\partial y^2} + \nu_i y \frac{\partial u}{\partial y},$$

$$\mathscr{L}_i^0 u = \mathscr{L}_i u - \rho_i \eta_i \lambda_i y \frac{\partial u}{\partial y},$$

$$\mathscr{A}_i u = \frac{\partial u}{\partial t} + \mathscr{L}_i^0 u - \frac{1}{2} \gamma (1 - \rho_i^2) \eta_i^2 y^2 \left(\frac{\partial u}{\partial y} \right)^2,$$

and the Hamiltonian

$$\tilde{H}_i(u_{xx}, u_{xy}, u_x) = \max_\theta \left(\frac{\theta^2 \sigma_i^2}{2} u_{xx} + \theta (\rho_i \sigma_i \eta_i y u_{xy} + \mu_i u_x) \right).$$

Note that $\mathscr{L}_i$ is the infinitesimal generator of Y under measure P, while $\mathscr{L}_i^0$ is the infinitesimal generator of Y under the *minimal martingale measure* Q^0 (see Definition 6.7 below). Also, $\mathscr{A}_i$ is semilinear and depends on γ.

Theorem 6.4. *The holder's value function is given by*

$$V(t,x,y,i) = M(t,x,i)\,e^{-\gamma p(t,y,i)}, \tag{6.11}$$

for $(t,x,y,i) \in [0,T] \times \mathbb{R} \times \mathbb{R}_+ \times E$, *where* $p(t,y,i)$ *is the holder's indifference price (defined in (7.37)). In addition,* $p(t,y,i)$ *satisfies the system of VIs*

$$\mathscr{A}_i p(t,y,i) + \frac{1}{\gamma} \sum_{j \in E\backslash\{i\}} a_{ij} \frac{F_j(t)}{F_i(t)}(1 - e^{-\gamma(p(t,y,j)-p(t,y,i))}) \leq 0,$$

$$p(t,y,i) \geq g(t,y,i),$$

$$\left(\mathscr{A}_i p(t,y,i) + \frac{1}{\gamma} \sum_{j \in E\backslash\{i\}} a_{ij} \frac{F_j(t)}{F_i(t)}(1 - e^{-\gamma(p(t,y,j)-p(t,y,i))})\right) \tag{6.12}$$

$$\cdot\, (g(t,y,i) - p(t,y,i)) = 0,$$

for $(t,y,i) \in [0,T) \times \mathbb{R}_+ \times E$, *and*

$$p(T,y,i) = g(T,y,i), \quad \text{for } (y,i) \in \mathbb{R}_+ \times E.$$

Proof. We present the main steps of the proof. First, we derive the HJB VI for the value function, namely

$$V_t^i + \mathscr{L}_i V^i + \tilde{H}_i(V_{xx}^i, V_{xy}^i, V_x^i) + \sum_{j \in E} a_{ij} V^j \leq 0,$$

$$V(t,x,y,i) \geq M\,(t, x + g(t,y,i), i)\,,$$

$$\left(V_t^i + \mathscr{L}_i V^i + \tilde{H}_i(V_{xx}^i, V_{xy}^i, V_x^i) + \sum_{j \in E} a_{ij} V^j\right) \tag{6.13}$$

$$\cdot\, (M\,(t, x + g(t,y,i), i) - V(t,x,y,i)) = 0,$$

for $(t,x,y,i) \in [0,T) \times \mathbb{R} \times \mathbb{R}_+ \times E$, *and*

$$V(T,x,y,i) = U(x + g(T,y,i)), \quad \text{for } (x,y,i) \in \mathbb{R} \times \mathbb{R}_+ \times E,$$

where the shorthand notation $V^i \equiv V(t, x, y, i)$. Maximizing over θ in (6.13) gives the optimal strategy in feedback form:

$$\theta^*(t, x, y, i) = -\frac{\lambda_i}{\sigma_i} \frac{V_x(t, x, y, i)}{V_{xx}(t, x, y, i)} - \frac{\rho_i \eta_i}{\sigma_i} y \frac{V_{xy}(t, x, y, i)}{V_{xx}(t, x, y, i)}. \tag{6.14}$$

Then, substituting (6.5) and (6.11) into (6.13) gives the VI for $p(t, y, i)$ in (6.12) as claimed. By (6.5) and (6.11), $p(t, y, i)$ satisfies $V(t, x, y, i) = M(t, x + p(t, y, i), i)$, implying that $p(t, y, i)$ is indeed the holder's indifference price by Definition 6.2. $\qquad\square$

Formula (6.11) in Theorem 6.4 allows us to express the holder's optimal hedging strategy in terms of p. By substituting (6.11) to (6.14), we obtain

$$\theta^*(t, y, i) = \frac{\lambda_i}{\gamma \sigma_i} - \rho_i \frac{\eta_i}{\sigma_i} y p_y(t, y, i),$$

which is again wealth independent. The first part of the strategy resembles the Merton strategy $\hat{\theta}$ given in (6.10), while the second part represents the residual investment in S arising from hedging the option g. In particular, if the correlation $\rho(k) = 0$ for some $k \in E$, then the second term vanishes and we have $\theta^*(t, y, k) = \hat{\theta}(t, y, k)$. This is intuitive because zero correlation between W and $\tilde{W}$ implies that trading S does not reduce the risk from Y, leading the holder to adopt the Merton strategy in this case.

By Definition 6.2, we deduce that the holder's optimal exercise time

$$\tau^* = \inf\{0 \leq t \leq T : V(t, X_t^{\theta^*}, Y_t, \xi_t) = M(t, X_t^{\theta^*} + g_t)\}$$

$$= \inf\{0 \leq t \leq T : p(t, Y_t, \xi_t) = g(t, Y_t, \xi_t)\}. \tag{6.15}$$

See also Leung and Sircar (2009b) for details. This provides an intuitive interpretation for the holder's optimal exercising strategy: the holder will exercise as soon as his indifference price equals the option payoff. The optimal exercising strategy depends on the underlying price Y_t and the Markov chain ξ_t, but, like the indifference price p, it is wealth-independent. For other utility functions, the optimal exercise time has the same interpretation but it may depend on wealth.

6.3. Dynamic Hedging of American Options with Multiple Exercises

We proceed to study indifference pricing for American options with multiple exercises. We consider the holder of $N \geq 2$ integer units of American option

g that can be exercised separately. We denote by $\tau_n \in \mathscr{T}_{t,T}$ the exercise time of the next unit of American option when $n \leq N$ units remain unexercised at time $t \in [0, T]$. After exercising one American option at τ_n, the holder has $(n - 1)$ options left. If the holder decides to exercise multiple options at the same time, then some exercise times may coincide.

As in Section 6.2, the holder dynamically trades S and the money market account throughout $[0, T]$, and his trading wealth follows the SDE (6.1). Upon exercising each American option, the holder reinvests the option payoff, if any, into the portfolio till T. Therefore, the holder's value function for holding $n \geq 2$ units of American options g is defined recursively by

$$V^{(n)}(t, x, y, i) = \sup_{\substack{\tau_n \in \mathscr{T}_{t,T} \\ \theta \in \mathscr{L}_{t,\tau_n}}} \mathbb{E}_{t,x,y,i}\{V^{(n-1)}(\tau_n, X_{\tau_n} + g_{\tau_n}, Y_{\tau_n}, \xi_{\tau_n})\}, \quad (6.16)$$

with $V^{(1)}(t, x, y, i) = V(t, x, y, i)$ in (7.36) and $V^{(0)}(t, x, y, i) = M(t, x, i)$ with no option. We remark that (6.16) is a stochastic control problem with *optimal multiple stopping*.

Definition 6.5. The holder's indifference price $p_i^{(n)} \equiv p^{(n)}(t, y, i)$ for $n \in \mathbb{N}$ units of American option g satisfies

$$M(t, x, i) = V^{(n)}(t, x - p_i^{(n)}, y, i). \quad (6.17)$$

Note that $p^{(1)}(t, y, i) = p(t, y, i)$ in (7.37), and $p^{(0)} = 0$.

Applying (6.17) into (6.16) yields that

$$V^{(n)}(t, x, y, i) = \sup_{\substack{\tau_n \in \mathscr{T}_{t,T} \\ \theta \in \mathscr{L}_{t,\tau_n}}} \mathbb{E}_{t,x,y,i}\{M(\tau_n, X_{\tau_n} + g_{\tau_n}$$

$$+ p^{(n-1)}(\tau_n, Y_{\tau_n}, \xi_{\tau_n}), \xi_{\tau_n})\}$$

$$= V(t, x, y, i; g + p^{(n-1)}), \quad (6.18)$$

where $V(t, x, y, i; g + p^{(i-1)})$ is the value function (7.36) for an American option with payoff $g(\tau, Y_\tau, \xi_\tau) + p^{(n-1)}(\tau, Y_\tau, \xi_\tau)$ at any $\tau \in \mathscr{T}$. The last equality (6.18) represents a crucial connection between the cases with single exercise and multiple exercises. It allows us to tackle the optimal multiple stopping problem by solving the single optimal stopping problem *sequentially*. With this simplification, we can apply the results from Section 6.2

to study the indifference price $p_i^{(n)}$ and the corresponding hedging and exercising strategies.

Proposition 6.6. *The value function $V^{(n)}$ is given by*

$$V^{(n)}(t, x, y, i) = M(t, x, i)\, e^{-\gamma p^{(n)}(t,y,i)}, \qquad (6.19)$$

where $p^{(n)}(t, y, i)$ satisfies the VI:

$$\mathscr{A}_i p_i^{(n)} + \frac{1}{\gamma} \sum_{j \in E \backslash \{i\}} a_{ij} \frac{F_j(t)}{F_i(t)} \left(1 - e^{-\gamma(p_j^{(n)} - p_i^{(n)})}\right) \leq 0,$$

$$p^{(n)}(t, y, i) \geq g(t, y, i) + p^{(n-1)}(t, y, i),$$

$$\left(\mathscr{A}_i p_i^{(n)} + \frac{1}{\gamma} \sum_{j \in E \backslash \{i\}} a_{ij} \frac{F_j(t)}{F_i(t)} \left(1 - e^{-\gamma(p_j^{(n)} - p_i^{(n)})}\right)\right) \qquad (6.20)$$

$$\cdot \left(g(t, y, i) + p^{(n-1)}(t, y, i) - p^{(n)}(t, y, i)\right) = 0,$$

for $(t, y, i) \in [0, T) \times \mathbb{R}_+ \times E$,

$$p^{(n)}(T, y, i) = ng(T, y, i), \text{ for } (y, i) \in \mathbb{R}_+ \times E.$$

This result follows directly from Theorem 6.4 by replacing the payoff g with $g + p^{(n-1)}$ and by induction. With multiple exercises, we obtain chain of VIs for the indifference prices. In order to solve for $\{p_i^{(n)}\}_{i \in E}$, we first solve for $\{p_i^{(1)}\}_{i \in E}$ via the variational inequality (6.12), and sequentially solve for $\{p_i^{(2)}\}_{i \in E}$, $\{p_i^{(3)}\}_{i \in E}$, and so on, via (6.20) above.

In view of (6.15), the holder's optimal exercise time for the next option when n options remain unexercised is

$$\tau^{(n)*} = \inf\{t \leq T : p^{(n)}(t, Y_t, \xi_t) - p^{(n-1)}(t, Y_t, \xi_t) = g(t, Y_t, \xi_t)\}.$$

This implies that the holder, while holding n options, will exercise the next option as soon as the indifference price increment $p^{(n)} - p^{(n-1)}$ reaches the value of the option payoff g.

6.4. Numerical Solution of the Indifference Price

Theorem 6.4 yields a system of semilinear free boundary problems of reaction–diffusion type. The regime-switching dynamics of asset prices gives rise to the reaction–diffusion terms (the summation terms in (6.12)). In this section, we discuss an analytic simplification and a numerical scheme applicable for both VIs (6.12) and (6.20).

First, for $n \in \mathbb{N}$, we apply the transformation

$$p^{(n)}(t, y, i) = -\frac{\delta_i}{\gamma} \log w^{(n)}(t, y, i), \qquad (6.21)$$

with $\delta_i = (1 - \rho_i^2)^{-1}$ for $i \in E$. By direct substitution of (6.21) into (6.12) yields the system of VIs:

$$\frac{\partial w_i^{(n)}}{\partial t} + \mathcal{L}_i^0 w_i^{(n)} - \frac{1}{\gamma \delta_i} w_i^{(n)} \sum_{j \in E \setminus \{i\}} \hat{A}_{ij}(t) \left(1 - \frac{(w_j^{(n)})^{\delta_j}}{(w_i^{(n)})^{\delta_i}} \right) \geq 0,$$

$$w^{(n)}(t, y, i) \leq w^{(n-1)}(t, y, i) e^{-\gamma(1 - \rho_i^2) g(t, y, i)},$$

$$\left(\frac{\partial w_i^{(n)}}{\partial t} + \mathcal{L}_i^0 w_i^{(n)} - \frac{1}{\gamma \delta_i} w_i^{(n)} \sum_{j \in E \setminus \{i\}} \hat{A}_{ij}(t) \left(1 - \frac{(w_j^{(n)})^{\delta_j}}{(w_i^{(n)})^{\delta_i}} \right) \right) \qquad (6.22)$$

$$\cdot \left(w^{(n-1)}(t, y, i) e^{-\gamma(1 - \rho_i^2) g(t, y, i)} - w^{(n)}(t, y, i) \right) = 0,$$

for $(t, y, i) \in [0, T) \times \mathbb{R}_+ \times E$,

$$w^{(n)}(T, y, i) = e^{-\gamma(1 - \rho_i^2) n g(T, y, i)}, \text{ for } (y, i) \in \mathbb{R}_+ \times E.$$

Here, we have used the notations

$$w_i^{(n)} \equiv w^{(n)}(t, y, i), \quad \text{and} \quad \hat{A}_{ij}(t) \equiv a_{ij} \frac{F_j(t)}{F_i(t)} \quad \text{for } i, j \in E.$$

Note that the differential operator in (6.22) is *linear*, and nonlinearity comes only through the summation term. Working with a linear operator significantly simplifies the numerical solution to this problem.

Applying (6.21) and the Feynman–Kac representation of $w(t, y, i)$, we obtain an alternative expression for the indifference price:

$$p(t, y, i) = -\frac{\delta_i}{\gamma} \log \inf_{\tau \in \mathcal{T}_{t,T}} \mathbb{E}^0 \{ e^{-\gamma(1 - \rho^2(\xi_\tau)) g_\tau} \,|\, Y_t = y, \xi_t = i \}, \qquad (6.23)$$

where the expectation $\mathbb{E}^0$ is taken under the minimal martingale measure Q^0 (see Definition 6.24). As a result, the holder's utility maximization with optimal stopping reduces to a pure optimal stopping problem.

We apply an implicit–explicit finite-difference method to solve for the indifference prices and optimal exercise boundaries in all regimes. Specifically, we discretize the differential inequalities in (6.22) using central differences for the y-derivatives, backward difference for the t-derivative, and explicit approximation for the summation term.

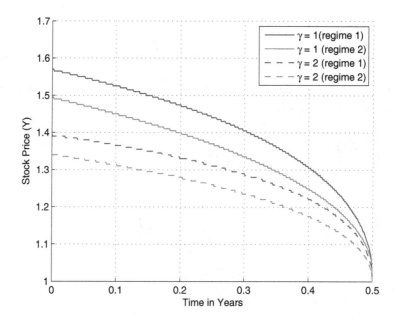

Figure 6.1. The holder's exercise boundary in regime 1 (good state) is higher than that in regime 2 (bad state) (see top two curves for $\gamma = 1$, or bottom two curves for $\gamma = 2$). Increasing the risk aversion from 1 to 2 results in a lower exercise boundary in each regime, leading to earlier exercise. Here, the parameters are $K = 1$, $T = .5$, $r = 3\%$, $\mu = (9\%, 8\%)$, $\sigma = (30\%, 20\%)$, $\nu = (11\%, 7\%)$, $q = (2\%, 1\%)$, $\eta = (40\%, 28\%)$, $\rho = 30\%$, $\gamma = 1$, $a_{12} = a_{21} = 1$.

Our numerical method iterates backward in time starting at maturity T. At each time step, the constraints is enforced by the projected successive-over-relaxation (PSOR) algorithm, which iteratively solves the implicit time-stepping equations, while preserving the constraint between iterations. Similar numerical schemes can be found in Li (2016), Leung and Sircar (2009a) and Wilmott *et al.* (1995).

In Figure 6.1, we illustrate the case of exercising a single American call option on a non-tradable stock in a two-regime market. Regime 1 is a state of more bullish market condition than regime 2. The holder will exercise the call as soon as the underlying price Y exceeds the exercise boundary in the current regime. The holder's optimal exercise boundary in regime 1 is higher than in regime 2, meaning that he intends to exercise the call earlier in regime 2 than in regime 1. Moreover, a more risk-averse holder tends to exercise the option earlier, which we will prove in Proposition 6.15.

In Figure 6.2, we show that optimal exercise boundaries for five American calls in the two-regime market. In either regime, the holder will

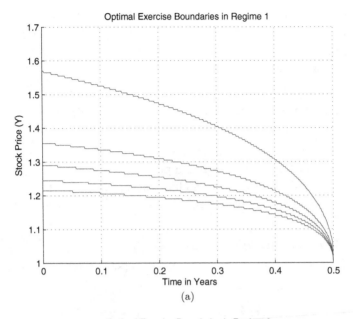

(a)

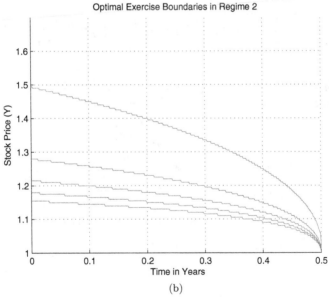

(b)

Figure 6.2. In each regime, the holder exercises the first call at the lowest exercise boundary, and subsequent ones at higher boundaries. The exercise boundaries in regime 1 dominate the corresponding ones in regime 2. Here, $\gamma = 1$, and other parameters are taken from Figure 6.1. The highest boundaries from these two graphs correspond to the top two boundaries in Figure 6.1.

exercise the first option as soon as the underlying price Y exceeds the lowest boundary, and then the subsequent options at higher boundaries. Observe that holding more options makes the holder more willing to exercise the additional options at lower underlying prices.

6.5. Indifference Pricing via Entropic Penalization with Optimal Stopping

An alternative interpretation of indifference pricing is through its dual representation, which involves selecting a pricing measure via relative entropy penalization. This is related to finding the optimal risk premia for the idiosyncratic and regime-switching risks due to $\tilde{W}$ and ξ, respectively.

6.5.1. *Minimal entropy risk premia*

We begin by defining the set of equivalent local martingale measures in the regime-switching market.

Definition 6.7. We define the probability measure Q^ϕ by

$$\frac{\mathrm{d}Q^\phi}{\mathrm{d}P} = \exp\left(-\frac{1}{2}\int_0^T (\lambda^2(\xi_s) + \phi_s^2)\,\mathrm{d}s - \int_0^T \lambda(\xi_s)\mathrm{d}W_s - \int_0^T \phi_s \mathrm{d}\tilde{W}_s\right),$$

(6.24)

where $(\phi_t)_{t\geq 0}$ is a $\mathscr{F}_t$-adapted process and $\mathbb{E}^{Q^\phi}\{\int_0^T \phi_t^2 \mathrm{d}t\} < \infty$. Its density process is denoted by

$$Z_t^\phi = \mathbb{E}\left\{\frac{\mathrm{d}Q^\phi}{\mathrm{d}P}\,\bigg|\,\mathscr{F}_t\right\}.$$

By Girsanov's theorem, (S, Y) under Q^ϕ satisfies

$$\mathrm{d}S_t = \sigma(\xi_t)S_t\,\mathrm{d}W_t^\phi,$$

$$\mathrm{d}Y_t = (\nu(\xi_t) - \rho(\xi_t)\eta(\xi_t)\lambda(\xi_t) - \tilde{\rho}(\xi_t)\eta(\xi_t)\phi_t)\,Y_t\,\mathrm{d}t$$
$$+ \eta(\xi_t)Y_t(\rho(\xi_t)\,\mathrm{d}W_t^\phi + \tilde{\rho}(\xi_t)\,\mathrm{d}\tilde{W}_t^\phi),$$

where

$$W_t^\phi = W_t + \int_0^t \lambda(\xi_s)\mathrm{d}s,$$

$$\tilde{W}_t^\phi = \tilde{W}_t + \int_0^t \phi_s\mathrm{d}s$$

are independent Brownian motions under Q^ϕ. The discounted price S is a Q^ϕ-local martingale, so Q^ϕ is an equivalent local martingale measure. When $\phi = 0$, we obtain the well-known minimal martingale measure Q^0 (see Föllmer and Sondermann, 1986).

The process ϕ is the *risk premium* accounting for $\tilde{W}$ only, and we need to specify the premium for the regime-switching risk. To this end, we summarize Girsanov's theorem for Markov Chain (see Chapter IV.22 of Rogers and Williams, 2000).

Theorem 6.8. *Define the probability measure $Q^{\phi,\alpha}$ by*

$$\frac{dQ^{\phi,\alpha}}{dP} = \frac{dQ^\phi}{dP} \frac{dQ^{\phi,\alpha}}{dQ^\phi},$$

with $\frac{dQ^\phi}{dP}$ defined in (6.24) and

$$\frac{dQ^{\phi,\alpha}}{dQ^\phi} = \exp\left(-\int_0^T (\tilde{A}_s(\xi_s,\xi_s) - A(\xi_s,\xi_s))\, ds\right)$$

$$\cdot \prod_{\substack{0\le s\le T \\ \xi_{s-}\ne\xi_s}} \alpha_s(\xi_{s-},\xi_s), \tag{6.25}$$

where $\{\alpha_t(i,j)\}_{i\ne j}$ is a family of positive bounded adapted processes, and

$$\tilde{A}_t(i,j) = \begin{cases} \alpha_t(i,j)A(i,j) & \text{if } i \ne j, \\ -\sum_{k\ne i} \tilde{A}_t(i,k) & \text{if } i = j. \end{cases} \tag{6.26}$$

Then, the measure $Q^{\phi,\alpha}$ is equivalent to Q^ϕ, and thus to P.

In addition, to preserve the Markovian property of ξ under the new measure $Q^{\phi,\alpha}$, we require that all $\alpha_t(i,j)$ be Markovian. Then, under $Q^{\phi,\alpha}$, the generator matrix of ξ is $\tilde{A} = [\tilde{A}_s(i,j)]_{i,j\in E}$. In view of (6.26), the collection $\{\alpha_t(i,j)\}_{i\ne j}$ can be considered as the *risk premium factors* for the regime-switching risk. As a result, the set of the equivalent local martingale measures with respect to P, denoted by $\mathcal{M}(P) := \{Q^{\phi,\alpha}\}_{\phi,\alpha}$, is parameterized by the risk premia pair (ϕ, α).

For any measure Q, the relative entropy of Q with respect to P is defined as

$$H(Q|P) := \begin{cases} \mathbb{E}^Q \left\{ \log \dfrac{dQ}{dP} \right\}, & Q \ll P, \\ +\infty, & \text{otherwise.} \end{cases}$$

The minimal entropy martingale measure (MEMM), $\hat{Q}$, minimizes the relative entropy with respect to P over the set of equivalent local martingale measures $\mathcal{M}(P)$:

$$\hat{Q} = \arg\min_{Q \in \mathcal{M}(P)} H(Q|P).$$

A common condition for the existence of a unique MEMM is the existence of an equivalent local martingale measure with finite relative entropy with respect to P (see Theorem 2.1 and 2.2 of Fritelli, 2000); this clearly holds in our model due to the condition we impose on $Q^{\phi,\alpha}$ (see also Remark 6.12).

Definition 6.9. For any $Q^{\phi,\alpha} \in \mathcal{M}(P)$, the conditional relative entropy of Q with respect to P at time $t \in [0, T]$ is

$$H_t^T(Q^{\phi,\alpha}|P) := \mathbb{E}^{Q^{\phi,\alpha}} \left\{ \log \frac{Z_T^{\phi,\alpha}}{Z_t^{\phi,\alpha}} \middle| \mathscr{F}_t \right\}, \qquad (6.27)$$

where $Z_t^{\phi,\alpha} := \mathbb{E}\{ \frac{dQ^{\phi,\alpha}}{dP} | \mathscr{F}_t \}$ is the related density process.

As is well known, it follows from Jensen's inequality that $H_t^T(Q^{\phi,\alpha}|P) \geq 0$ for any $Q^{\phi,\alpha} \in \mathcal{M}(P)$. It turns out that the MEMM $\hat{Q}$ also minimizes the conditional relative entropy (see Proposition 4.1 of Kabanov and Stricker, 2002). Namely, for any $t \in [0, T]$,

$$\operatorname*{ess\,inf}_{Q \in \mathcal{M}(P)} H_t^T(Q|P) = H_t^T(\hat{Q}|P), \quad t \in \mathscr{T}.$$

Next, we consider the relative entropy minimization

$$h(t, i) = \inf_{Q^{\phi,\alpha} \in \mathcal{M}(P)} \mathbb{E}^{Q^{\phi,\alpha}} \left\{ \log \frac{Z_T^{\phi,\alpha}}{Z_t^{\phi,\alpha}} \middle| \xi_t = i \right\},$$

and provide explicit formulae for $h(t, i)$ and $\hat{Q}$.

Theorem 6.10. *The MEMM is given by* $\hat{Q} = Q^{\hat{\phi},\hat{\alpha}}$, *where the* minimal entropy risk premia *are*

$$\hat{\phi}_t = 0, \quad and \quad \hat{\alpha}_t(i,j) = F_j(t)/F_i(t), \quad i \neq j. \tag{6.28}$$

The minimal relative entropy $H_t^T(\hat{Q}|P) = h(t, \xi_t)$, *where*

$$h(t,i) = -\log F_i(t) \tag{6.29}$$

$$= -\log\left(\mathbb{E}\left\{\exp\left(-\int_t^T \frac{\lambda^2(\xi_s)}{2}\,ds\right) \mid \xi_t = i\right\}\right), \tag{6.30}$$

with $F_i(t)$ *given in* (6.6).

Proof. Applying (6.25) to (6.27), the conditional relative entropy of Q with respect to P is given by

$$\mathbb{E}^{Q^{\phi,\alpha}}\left\{\log\frac{Z_T^{\phi,\alpha}}{Z_t^{\phi,\alpha}} \mid \xi_t = i\right\}$$

$$= \mathbb{E}^{Q^{\phi,\alpha}}\left\{\frac{1}{2}\int_t^T (\lambda^2(\xi_s) + \phi_s^2)\,\mathrm{d}s\right.$$

$$+ \int_{(t,T]}\sum_{j \in E} \mathbf{1}_{\{\xi_{s-}\neq j\}}(1 - \alpha_s(\xi_{s-},j))\,A(\xi_{s-},j)$$

$$\left. + \alpha_s(\xi_{s-},j)A_s(\xi_{s-},j)\log\alpha_s(\xi_{s-},j)\mathrm{d}s \mid \xi_t = i\right\}.$$

The HJB equations associated with $h_i(t) \equiv h(t,i)$ are

$$h_i'(t) + \frac{\lambda_i^2}{2} + \inf_\phi \frac{\phi^2}{2}$$

$$+ \inf_{\alpha^{ij}}\left(\sum_{j \in E\setminus\{i\}}(1 - \alpha^{ij})a_{ij} + \alpha^{ij}a_{ij}\log\alpha^{ij} + a_{ij}\alpha^{ij}(h_j(t) - h_i(t))\right) = 0,$$

for $(t,i) \in [0,T) \times E$, with $h_i(T) = 0$ for $i \in E$.

Minimizing over ϕ and α^{ij} in the equation above yields the optimal controls $\hat{\phi} = 0$ and

$$\hat{\alpha}_t(i,j) = e^{-(h_j(t)-h_i(t))}, \tag{6.31}$$

and leads to the system of first-order nonlinear ODEs:

$$h_i'(t) + \frac{\lambda_i^2}{2} - \sum_{j \in E} a_{ij}\, e^{-(h_j(t) - h_i(t))} = 0, \tag{6.32}$$

for $(t, i) \in [0, T) \times E$, with $h_i(T) = 0$, $i \in E$.

Direct substitution of $h_i(t) = -\log F_i(t)$ into (6.32) leads to (6.9), and (6.29) follows. Finally, applying (6.30) to (6.31) gives $\hat{\alpha}_t(i, j)$ in (6.28). $\square$

Remark 6.11. By formula (6.30), the minimal entropy is bounded:

$$\frac{\lambda_*^2}{2}(T - t) \le h_i(t) \le \frac{\lambda^{*2}}{2}(T - t), \quad \text{for } (t, i) \in [0, T] \times E.$$

Also, we can deduce from (6.28) that the minimal entropy risk premia $\hat{\alpha}_t(i, j)$ are also bounded.

This theorem has a number of important implications. First, applying (6.29) to (6.2) yields a duality formula for the Merton function, namely

$$M(t, x, i) = -e^{-\gamma x} e^{-h(t, i)}. \tag{6.33}$$

In turn, this implies that

$$U^{-1}(M(t, 0, i)) = \frac{1}{\gamma} h(t, i).$$

Therefore, the minimal relative entropy, when scaled by risk aversion, can be viewed as the *certainty equivalent* of the Merton investment with zero initial wealth.

From (6.28) and (6.33), we observe that ξ becomes a *time-inhomogeneous* Markov chain under the MEMM $\hat{Q}$ with the generator matrix $\hat{A}$, whose off-diagonal elements are

$$\hat{A}_t(i, j) = A(i, j)\frac{F_j(t)}{F_i(t)} = A(i, j)\frac{M(t, x, j)}{M(t, x, i)}, \quad \text{for } i \ne j.$$

This indicates that $\hat{Q}$ scales the transition rates $A(i, j)$ by the ratio of the discounting factors $F_j(t)$ and $F_i(t)$, or equivalently, by the relative Merton investment performances. As a result of changing from P to $\hat{Q}$, the Markov chain ξ is more likely to switch to the states with higher M values.

Remark 6.12. When $\phi = 0$ and $\alpha(i, j) = 1$ for $i \ne j$, the resulting measure $Q^{0,1} \equiv Q^0$ is the minimal martingale measure, and it does *not* minimize the relative entropy with respect to P, despite the contrary claim by Elliot et al. (2005). Indeed,

$$H_t^T(Q^0|P) = \mathbb{E}^{Q^0}\left\{\frac{1}{2}\int_t^T \lambda^2(\xi_s)\,ds\Big|\mathscr{F}_t\right\}$$

$$= \mathbb{E}\left\{\frac{1}{2}\int_t^T \lambda^2(\xi_s)\,ds\Big|\mathscr{F}_t\right\}$$

$$\geq -\log\left(\mathbb{E}\{e^{-\int_t^T \frac{\lambda^2(\xi_s)}{2}ds}|\mathscr{F}_t\}\right) = H_t^T(\hat{Q}|P),$$

by (6.30) and Jensen's inequality. The inequality is strict unless there is no regime switching. This shows that $Q^0 \neq \hat{Q}$.

6.5.2. *Duality formula for the indifference price*

The MEMM $\hat{Q}$ also plays a crucial role in the indifference price characterization. To illustrate, we first consider the relative entropy with respect to $\hat{Q}$ instead of P. Following Theorem 6.8, we define the Radon–Nikodym derivative

$$\frac{dQ^{\phi,\alpha}}{d\hat{Q}} = \frac{dQ^{\phi,\alpha}}{dP}\frac{dP}{d\hat{Q}}$$

$$= \exp\left(-\frac{1}{2}\int_0^T \phi_s^2\,ds - \int_0^T \phi_s d\tilde{W}_s^{\hat{Q}}\right)$$

$$\cdot \exp\left(-\int_0^T \tilde{A}_s(\xi_s,\xi_s) - \hat{A}(\xi_s,\xi_s)\,ds\right)\prod_{\substack{0 \leq s \leq T \\ \xi_{s-} \neq \xi_s}} \frac{\alpha_s(\xi_{s-},\xi_s)}{\hat{\alpha}_s(\xi_{s-},\xi_s)}.$$

$$(6.34)$$

Here, $\tilde{W}^{\hat{Q}}$ is a $\hat{Q}$-standard Brownian motion, and we have $\tilde{W}^{\hat{Q}} = \tilde{W}$ since $\hat{\phi} = 0$. Denote the associated density process by $\hat{Z}_t^{\phi,\alpha} := \mathbb{E}^{\hat{Q}}\{\frac{dQ^{\phi,\alpha}}{d\hat{Q}}|\mathscr{F}_t\}$, and the conditional relative entropy of $Q^{\phi,\alpha}$ with respect to $\hat{Q}$ over the period $[t,\tau]$ by

$$\hat{H}_{\phi,\alpha}^\tau(t,y,i) := \mathbb{E}_{t,y,i}^{Q^{\phi,\alpha}}\left\{\log\frac{\hat{Z}_\tau^{\phi,\alpha}}{\hat{Z}_t^{\phi,\alpha}}\right\},\qquad(6.35)$$

with $\mathbb{E}_{t,y,i}^{Q^{\phi,\alpha}}\{\cdot\} \equiv \mathbb{E}^{Q^{\phi,\alpha}}\{\cdot|Y_t = y, \xi_t = i\}$.

Note that $\hat{H}^\tau_{\phi,\alpha}(t,y,i) \geq 0$ by Jensen's inequality, and it vanishes when $Q^{\phi,\alpha} = \hat{Q}$. This entropy term represents the penalty in our indifference price formula.

Theorem 6.13. *The indifference price is given by*

$$p(t,y,i) = \sup_{\tau \in \mathscr{T}_{t,T}} \inf_{\phi,\alpha} \left(\mathbb{E}^{Q^{\phi,\alpha}}_{t,y,i}\{g_\tau\} + \frac{1}{\gamma}\hat{H}^\tau_{\phi,\alpha}(t,y,i) \right). \tag{6.36}$$

Proof.   By (6.34) and (6.35), the entropy term is

$$\hat{H}^\tau_{\phi,\alpha}(t,y,i) = \mathbb{E}^{Q^{\phi,\alpha}}_{t,y,i}\left\{ \frac{1}{2}\int_t^\tau \phi_s^2\,\mathrm{d}s + \int_{(t,\tau]}\sum_{j\in E}1_{\{\xi_{s-}\neq j\}}(\tilde{A}(\xi_{s-},j)\right.$$

$$-\hat{\alpha}_s(\xi_{s-},j)A(\xi_{s-},j))\,\mathrm{d}s$$

$$\left. + \int_{(t,\tau]}\sum_{j\in E}1_{\{\xi_{s-}\neq j\}}\tilde{A}_s(\xi_{s-},j)\left(\log\frac{\alpha_s(\xi_{s-},j)}{\hat{\alpha}_s(\xi_{s-},j)}\right)\,\mathrm{d}s \right\}.$$

Let us denote $f^i \equiv f(t,y,i)$ as the right-hand side of (6.36), and write down the variational inequality for f^i:

$$f^i_t + \mathscr{L}^0_i f^i + \inf_\phi \left(-\tilde{\rho}_i\eta_i y f^i_y \phi + \frac{\phi^2}{2\gamma} \right)$$

$$+ \inf_{\alpha^{ij}}\left(\sum_{j\in E\backslash\{i\}}\frac{1}{\gamma}a_{ij}[(\alpha^{ij}-\hat{\alpha}_t(i,j))\right.$$

$$\left. + \alpha^{ij}(\log\alpha^{ij} - \log\hat{\alpha}_t(i,j))] + \alpha^{ij}a_{ij}(f^j - f^i) \right) \leq 0,$$

$$f(t,y,i) \geq g(t,y,i),$$

$$\left(f^i_t + \mathscr{L}^0_i f^i + \inf_\phi\left(-\tilde{\rho}_i\eta_i y f^i_y \phi + \frac{\phi^2}{2\gamma} \right) \right.$$

$$+ \inf_{\alpha^{ij}}\left(\sum_{j\in E\backslash\{i\}}\frac{1}{\gamma}a_{ij}[(\alpha^{ij}-\hat{\alpha}_t(i,j)) + \alpha^{ij}(\log\alpha^{ij}-\log\hat{\alpha}_t(i,j))] \right.$$

$$\left.\left. + \alpha^{ij}a_{ij}(f^j - f^i) \right) \right) \cdot (g(t,y,i) - f(t,y,i)) = 0,$$

for $(t,y,i) \in [0,T) \times \mathbb{R}_+ \times E$,

$$f(T,y,i) = g(T,y,i), \quad \text{for } (y,i) \in \mathbb{R}_+ \times E.$$

The optimal controls are given by

$$\phi^*(t, y, i) = -\gamma \tilde{\rho}_i \eta_i y f_y(t, y, i),$$

$$\alpha^*(t, y, i, j) = \hat{\alpha}_t(i, j) e^{-\gamma(f(t,y,j)-f(t,y,i))}, \quad i \neq j,$$

(6.37)

and the first inequality for f becomes

$$f_t^i + \mathscr{L}_i^0 f^i - \frac{1}{2}\gamma(1 - \rho_i^2)\eta_i^2 y^2 (f_y^i)^2$$

$$+ \frac{1}{\gamma} \sum_{j \in E \setminus \{i\}} a_{ij} \hat{\alpha}_t(i, j)(1 - e^{-\gamma(f^j - f^i)}) \leq 0.$$

By comparing this with VI (6.12) and using that $\hat{\alpha}_t(i, j) = F_j(t)/F_i(t)$, we conclude that $f(t, y, i) = p(t, y, i)$. □

The duality formula (6.36) shows that the option holder selects a pricing measure that minimizes the expected discounted payoff plus a relative entropic penalty up to the exercise time τ. Note that the holder's risk aversion γ plays the role of scaling the penalty term.

By (6.11) and (6.37), we can express the risk premium α^* as

$$\alpha^*(t, y, i, j) = A(i, j)\frac{V(t, x, y, j)}{V(t, x, y, i)}, \quad \text{for } i \neq j.$$

This provides a financial interpretation that the holder assigns the optimal risk premium factor α^* to ξ by scaling the transition rates according to the relative values of the value function in different states.

Finally, we directly apply Theorem 6.13 to American options with multiple exercises.

Proposition 6.14. *The indifference price $p^{(n)}(t, y, i)$ satisfies*

$$p^{(n)}(t, y, i) = \sup_{\tau_n \in \mathscr{T}_{t,T}} \inf_{\phi, \alpha} \left(\mathbb{E}_{t,y,i}^{Q^{\phi,\alpha}} \{g_{\tau_n} + p^{(n-1)}(\tau_n, Y_{\tau_n}, \xi_{\tau_n})\} + \frac{1}{\gamma}\hat{H}_{\phi,\alpha}^{\tau_n}(t, y, i) \right).$$

6.5.3. *Risk-aversion asymptotics*

Next, we apply the dual formula (6.36) to analyze some properties of the indifference price, with an emphasis on the impact of the risk aversion γ and correlation coefficient $\rho(i)$.

Let us denote the indifference price and optimal exercise time respectively by $p^{(\gamma)}(t, y, i)$ and $\tau^{(\gamma)*}$ to highlight its dependence on γ. Next, we show that higher risk aversion reduces the option holder's indifference price and directly leads to an earlier exercise time.

Proposition 6.15. *If* $\gamma_2 \geq \gamma_1 > 0$, *then we have* $p^{(\gamma_2)}(t, y, i) \leq p^{(\gamma_1)}(t, y, i)$, *and* $\tau^{(\gamma_2)*} \leq \tau^{(\gamma_1)*}$ *almost surely.*

Proof. For any τ, ϕ, and α, the entropic penalty in (6.36), $\gamma^{-1} \hat{H}_{\phi,\alpha}^{\tau}(t, y, i)$, is non-negative and non-increasing in γ. This yields $p^{(\gamma_2)}(t, y, i) \leq p^{(\gamma_1)}(t, y, i)$. By (6.15), this implies that $p^{(\gamma_2)}$ reaches the payoff g earlier than $p^{(\gamma_1)}$ almost surely, and therefore, $\tau^{(\gamma_2)*} \leq \tau^{(\gamma_1)*}$ almost surely. □

This is reflected in Figure 6.1, where the holder's optimal exercise boundary shifts downward as risk aversion increases.

We observe that, as $\gamma \uparrow \infty$, the entropic penalty in (6.36) vanishes. Consequently, we obtain the limit price:

$$\lim_{\gamma \to \infty} p^{(\gamma)}(t, y, i) = \sup_{\tau \in \mathcal{T}_{t,T}} \inf_{\phi,\alpha} \mathbb{E}^{Q^{\phi,\alpha}} \{g(\tau, Y_\tau, \xi_\tau) \mid Y_t = y, \xi_t = i\}.$$

This price is commonly referred to as the sub-hedging price (see Karatzas and Kou, 1998). On the other hand, as $\gamma \downarrow 0$, we deduce from (6.36) that it is optimal not to deviate from $\hat{Q}$, resulting in zero penalty. The limit price is

$$\lim_{\gamma \to 0} p^{(\gamma)}(t, y, i) = \sup_{\tau \in \mathcal{T}_{t,T}} \mathbb{E}^{\hat{Q}} \{g(\tau, Y_\tau, \xi_\tau) \mid Y_t = y, \xi_t = i\}.$$

Here, the MEMM is the pricing measure — it assigns zero risk premium ($\hat{\phi} = 0$) to $\tilde{W}$, but places a time-varying premium $\hat{\alpha}_t(i, j)$ to the regime-switching risk (see (6.28)).

Next, we turn to the case with perfect correlation across all states, namely, $|\rho(i)| = 1$ for every $i \in E$. In this case, $\tilde{W}$ vanishes from the dynamics of Y, and both S and Y are driven by the same Brownian motion W (in addition to ξ). Consequently, Y is effectively "traded" via the proxy asset S. To avoid arbitrage, we require that $\lambda(i) = \kappa(i)$ for every $i \in E$. However, the market is still incomplete due to the unhedgeable regime-switching risk. Using these facts, Theorem 6.4 can be directly applied to obtain the VI for the indifference price — the only change here is that the differential operator $\mathscr{A}_i$ in (6.12) reduces to a linear one:

$$\mathscr{A}_i u = \frac{\partial u}{\partial t} + \frac{1}{2} \eta_i^2 y^2 u_{yy}.$$

Also, the duality formula (6.36) also holds, with $\phi = 0$ due to the absence of a second Brownian motion. Hence, the entropy minimization is conducted over the collections of measures $\{Q^{0,\alpha}\}$.

$$p(t,y,i) = \sup_{\tau \in \mathscr{T}_{t,T}} \inf_{\alpha} \left(\mathbb{E}^{Q^{0,\alpha}}_{t,y,i} \{g_\tau\} + \frac{1}{\gamma}\hat{H}^\tau_{0,\alpha}(t,y,i) \right).$$

Applying this to (6.12), the variational inequality for the indifference price simplifies to

$$\frac{\partial p_j}{\partial t} + \frac{1}{2}\eta_j^2 y^2 \frac{\partial^2 p_j}{\partial y^2} + \frac{1}{\gamma} \sum_{k \in E_1 \setminus \{j\}} \hat{A}_{jk}(t)(1 - e^{-\gamma(p(t,y,k)-p(t,y,j))}) \le 0,$$

$$p(t,y,j) \ge g(t,y,j),$$

$$\left(\frac{\partial p_j}{\partial t} + \frac{1}{2}\eta_j^2 y^2 \frac{\partial^2 p_j}{\partial y^2} + \frac{1}{\gamma} \sum_{k \in E_1 \setminus \{j\}} \hat{A}_{jk}(t)(1 - e^{-\gamma(p(t,y,k)-p(t,y,j))}) \right) \qquad (6.38)$$

$$\cdot (g(t,y,j) - p(t,y,j)) = 0, \quad \text{for } (t,y,j) \in [0,T) \times \mathbb{R}_+ \times E,$$

$$p(T,y,j) = g(T,y,j), \quad \text{for } (y,j) \in \mathbb{R}_+ \times E,$$

where we have used the notation $p_i = p(y,t,i)$ for $i \in E$. Again, notice that the system (6.22)–(6.38) involves only *linear* differential operators. This provides a significant advantage in obtaining the numerical solutions (see Section 6.4).

The market is incomplete even if the underlying is tradable, and there are many candidate pricing measures. It is still meaningful to determine the suitable pricing measure under a given risk preference. This question of assigning a financially reasonable risk premium for the regime-switching risk. This essentially amounts to relating the dynamics of the Markov chain under the pricing measure and historical measure, which is often ignored in the literature on option pricing under regime-switching dynamics.

6.6. Conclusion

We have discussed the indifference pricing of American options in an incomplete regime-switching market. We analyze the primal and dual problems of combined stochastic control and optimal stopping type. Our model yields the optimal hedging and exercising strategies that are *adaptive* to the market conditions. In particular, we have studied both analytically and numerically the behavior of the holder's regime-dependent optimal exercise boundaries. Our results are useful for estimating the ESO holder's exercise times under different market conditions and calculate the associated option costs to the firm.

Chapter 7

Forward Indifference Valuation
of ESOs

7.1. Introduction

In this chapter, we develop an ESO valuation methodology based on the forward performance criterion. As discussed in Chapter 1, this approach specifies the investor's utility at an initial time, and allows the risk preferences at subsequent times to evolve forward without reference to any specific ultimate time horizon. This results in a stochastic utility process, which evolves forward in time rather than deduced backward in traditional utility maximization approaches. This is called the *forward performance process*, which satisfies certain properties so that it evolves consistently with the random market conditions (see, for example, Musiela and Zariphopoulou, 2008). Hence, this approach necessarily connects risk preferences with market models.

To introduce the theory, we first study the valuation of a long position in an American option in an incomplete diffusion market model. This leads us to study a combined stochastic control and optimal stopping problem. In Section 7.2, our main objective is to analyze the optimal trading and exercising strategies that maximize the option holder's forward performance from the dynamic portfolio together with the option payoff upon exercise. We also study the holder's *forward indifference price* for the American option, which is defined by comparing the optimal expected forward performance with and without the derivative.

In Section 7.3, we discuss the exponential forward indifference valuation of an American option in a stochastic volatility model. Using the analytical properties of the exponential forward performance, we show that the forward indifference price is wealth-independent and admits other properties.

In Section 7.4, we assume a forward performance criterion for the employee. By numerically solving the nonlinear variational inequality associated with the employee's maximal expected forward performance, we obtain an optimal exercise boundary representing the critical stock prices at different times and wealth levels. We investigate the effects of various factors, such as wealth and risk tolerance function, on the employee's exercise timing. Among our findings, the forward indifference valuation model suggests that the employee tends to exercise the ESO earlier when the wealth approaches zero.

In Section 7.5, we introduce an alternative valuation mechanism for early exercisable stock options based on the marginal forward performance. As is well known in the classical utility framework, the *marginal utility price* represents the per-unit price that a risk-averse investor is willing to pay for an infinitesimal position in a contingent claim. In general, the marginal utility price is closely linked to the investor's utility function and the market setup, and it only becomes wealth-independent under very special circumstances. We adapt the classical definition to our forward performance framework and give a definition of the *marginal forward indifference price*. In contrast to the classical marginal utility price, the marginal forward indifference price turns out to be independent of the holder's wealth and forward performance criterion, and is equivalent to pricing under the *minimal martingale measure*.

We also provide a comparative analysis between the forward and classical exponential indifference prices. For instance, we show that the forward indifference price representation involves a relative entropy minimization (up to a stopping time) with respect to the *minimal martingale measure* (MMM), as opposed to the *minimal entropy martingale measure* (MEMM) that arises in the classical exponential utility indifference price for European claims (Rouge and El Karoui, 2000; Delbaen *et al.*, 2002) and American claims (Leung and Sircar, 2009b). This contrasting difference is also reflected in the asymptotics results of indifference prices discussed here.

7.2. Forward Investment Performance Measurement and Indifference Valuation

In the background, we fix a filtered probability space $(\Omega, \mathscr{F}, \mathbb{P})$, with a filtration $(\mathscr{F}_t)_{t\geq 0}$ that satisfies the usual conditions of right continuity and completeness. In addition, all stochastic processes considered herein are processes with continuous paths. The financial market consists of two liquidly traded assets, namely, a riskless money market account and a stock. The money market account has the price process B that satisfies

$$dB_t = r_t B_t \, dt,$$

with $B_0 = 1$, where $(r_t)_{t \geq 0}$ is a non-negative $\mathscr{F}_t$-adapted interest rate process. We shall work with discounted cash flows throughout.

The discounted stock price S is modeled as a continuous Itô process satisfying

$$dS_t = S_t \sigma_t \left(\lambda_t \, dt + dW_t \right), \tag{7.1}$$

with $S_0 > 0$, where $(W_t)_{t \geq 0}$ is an $\mathscr{F}_t$-adapted standard Brownian motion. The Sharpe ratio $(\lambda_t)_{t \geq 0}$ is a bounded $\mathscr{F}_t$-adapted process, and the volatility coefficient $(\sigma_t)_{t \geq 0}$ is strictly positive bounded $\mathscr{F}_t$-adapted process. Moreover, we assume that a strong solution exists for the SDE (7.1).

Starting with initial endowment $x \in \mathbb{R}$, the investor dynamically rebalances his portfolio allocations between the stock S and the money market account B. Under the self-financing trading condition, the discounted wealth satisfies

$$dX_t^\pi = \pi_t \sigma_t (\lambda_t \, dt + dW_t), \tag{7.2}$$

where $(\pi_t)_{t \geq 0}$ represents the discounted cash amount invested in S. As is a common choice for Itô markets (see Section 6C of Duffie (2001)), the set of admissible strategies $\mathscr{L}$ consists of all self-financing $\mathscr{F}_t$-adapted processes $(\pi_t)_{t \geq 0}$ such that $\mathbb{E}\{ \int_0^s \sigma_t^2 \pi_t^2 \, dt \} < \infty$ for each $s > 0$. For $0 \leq t \leq s$, we denote by $\mathscr{L}_{t,s}$ the set of admissible strategies over the period $[t, s]$.

In the standard Merton portfolio optimization problem, risk aversion is modeled by a deterministic utility function $\hat{U}(x)$ defined at some fixed terminal time T and the investor's risk preferences (or indirect utility) at intermediate times are inferred backwards. Starting at time $t \leq T$ with $\mathscr{F}_t$-measurable wealth X_t, the Merton value function is given by

$$M_t(X_t) = \operatorname*{ess\,sup}_{\pi \in \mathscr{L}_{t,T}} \mathbb{E} \left\{ \hat{U}(X_T^\pi) \middle| \mathscr{F}_t \right\}. \tag{7.3}$$

When the *dynamic programming principle* holds, the Merton problem can be written as

$$M_t(X_t) = \operatorname*{ess\,sup}_{\pi \in \mathscr{L}_{t,s}} \mathbb{E} \left\{ M_s(X_s^\pi) \middle| \mathscr{F}_t \right\}, \quad 0 \leq t \leq s \leq T. \tag{7.4}$$

The dynamic programming principle (7.4) is taken as the defining characteristic of the forward performance criterion.

Nevertheless, in the forward performance framework, the investor's utility function $u_0(x)$ is defined at time 0, and his performance criterion evolves forward in time. We adapt the definition of the forward performance process given by Musiela and Zariphopoulou (2008).

Definition 7.1. An $\mathscr{F}_t$-adapted process $(U_t(x))_{t\geq 0}$ is a forward performance process if:

(1) it satisfies the initial datum $U_0(x) = u_0(x)$, $x \in \mathbb{R}$, where $u_0 : \mathbb{R} \mapsto \mathbb{R}$ is an increasing and strictly concave function of x,
(2) for each $t \geq 0$, the mapping $x \mapsto U_t(x)$ is increasing and strictly concave in $x \in \mathbb{R}$, and
(3) for $0 \leq t \leq s < \infty$, we have

$$U_t(X_t) = \operatorname*{ess\,sup}_{\pi \in \mathscr{Z}_{t,s}} \mathbb{E}\{U_s(X_s^\pi)| \mathscr{F}_t\}, \qquad (7.5)$$

with any $\mathscr{F}_t$-measurable starting wealth X_t.

As condition (3) indicates, the forward performance process $(U_t(X_t^\pi))_{t\geq 0}$ is a $(\mathbb{P}, \mathscr{F}_t)$ supermartingale for any strategy π, and a martingale if there exists an optimal admissible strategy π^* for (7.5). In related studies, this is also referred to as the horizon-unbiased condition in Henderson and Hobson (2007) and the self-generating condition in Zitkovic (2009).

The above definition does not explicitly require the existence of π^*. As is common in the classical utility maximization, the existence and characterization of the optimal strategy are challenging questions and depend on the market structure and utility function used. In this chapter, however, our analysis will focus on a class of explicit forward performance processes (see Theorem 7.3), whose optimal strategies are completely characterized (see Berrier *et al.*, 2009; Musiela and Zariphopoulou, 2010). Our first objective is to apply forward performance to the indifference pricing of American options.

7.2.1.   *Forward indifference price*

We introduce the forward indifference valuation from the perspective of the holder of an American option. The option payoff is characterized by an $\mathscr{F}_t$-adapted bounded process $(g_t)_{0\leq t\leq T}$ with a finite expiration date T. The collection of admissible exercise times is the set of stopping times with respect to $\mathscr{F}_{0,T} = (\mathscr{F}_t)_{0 \le t \le T}$ taking values in $[0, T]$. For $0 \le t \le s \le T$, we denote by $\mathscr{T}_{t,s}$ the set of stopping times bounded by $[t, s]$.

The option holder chooses his dynamic trading strategy π and exercise time τ so as to maximize his expected forward performance from investing in S and the money market account and from receiving the option payoff. This leads to a combined stochastic control and optimal stopping problem. The holder's maximal expected forward performance process, with current wealth X_t, is defined as

$$V_t(X_t) = \operatorname*{ess\,sup}_{\tau \in \mathscr{T}_{t,T}} \operatorname*{ess\,sup}_{\pi \in \mathscr{X}_{t,\tau}} \mathbb{E}\left\{ U_\tau(X_\tau^\pi + g_\tau) \mid \mathscr{F}_t \right\}, \quad t \in [0, T], \tag{7.6}$$

which is the holder's value process starting at time t with wealth X_t.

In the classical case with a terminal utility function $\hat{U}$, the holder's optimal investment problem is to solve

$$\operatorname*{ess\,sup}_{\tau \in \mathscr{T}_{t,T}} \operatorname*{ess\,sup}_{\pi \in \mathscr{X}_{t,\tau}} \mathbb{E}\left\{ M_\tau(X_\tau^\pi + g_\tau) \mid \mathscr{F}_t \right\},$$

where M is the solution to the Merton problem defined in (7.3). In this formulation, M plays the role of intermediate utility at times $\tau \le T$, and corresponds to specifying that option proceeds received at exercise time τ are re-invested in the Merton optimal strategy, up till time T. In contrast, the forward performance process U specifies utilities at all times, without reference to any specific horizon.

The forward indifference valuation methodology is based on the comparison of investment opportunities with and without the American option. The holder's forward indifference price p_t for the American option g is defined as the cash amount such that the option holder is indifferent between two positions: optimal investment with the American option, and optimal investment without the American option but with extra wealth p_t.

Definition 7.2. The holder's forward indifference price process $(p_t)_{0 \le t \le T}$ for the American option is defined by the equation

$$V_t(X_t) = U_t(X_t + p_t), \quad t \in [0, T], \tag{7.7}$$

where V_t and U_t are given in Eq. (7.6) and Definition 7.1 respectively.

The forward indifference price is useful for characterizing the option holder's optimal exercise time τ^*. Under quite general conditions, the optimal stopping time is recovered as usual as the first time the value process reaches the reward process.

From (7.6) and (7.7), we have

$$\tau_t^* = \inf\left\{t \le s \le T \ : \ V_s(X_s) = U_s(X_s + g_s)\right\}$$
$$= \inf\left\{t \le s \le T \ : \ U_s(X_s + p_s) = U_s(X_s + g_s)\right\}$$
$$= \inf\left\{t \le s \le T \ : \ p_s = g_s\right\}. \tag{7.8}$$

The representation (7.8) implies that the option holder will exercise the American option as soon as the forward indifference price reaches (from above) the option payoff. It allows us to analyze the holder's optimal exercise policy through his forward indifference price.

Next, we investigate the forward indifference valuation of an early exercisable stock option under two market configurations and risk preferences. In Section 7.3, the underlying stock S exhibits stochastic volatility and the option holder has a forward performance criterion of *exponential* type (to be defined in (7.19)). In Section 7.4, the option holder partially hedges the ESO with a correlated asset under a general forward performance criterion.

7.2.2. *Forward performance of generalized CARA/CRRA type*

Henceforth, we will use a special class of forward performance processes introduced by Musiela and Zariphopoulou (2008), namely, the time-monotone ones. They are represented by the compilation of a deterministic function $u(x, t)$ which models the investor's dynamic risk preference, and an increasing process $(A_t)_{t \ge 0}$ that solely depends on the market. Recently, Berrier *et al.* (2009) and Musiela and Zariphopoulou (2010) studied various properties of this family of forward performance and gave a dual representation.

Theorem 7.3 (Proposition 3 of Musiela and Zariphopoulou (2008)). *Define the stochastic process*

$$A_t = \int_0^t \lambda_s^2 \, ds, \quad t \ge 0.$$

Suppose $u : \mathbb{R} \times \mathbb{R}_+ \mapsto \mathbb{R}$ is $\mathscr{C}^{3,1}$, strictly concave, increasing in the first argument, and satisfies the partial differential equation

$$u_t = \frac{1}{2}\frac{u_x^2}{u_{xx}}, \tag{7.9}$$

with initial condition $u(x,0) = u_0(x)$, where $u_0 \in \mathcal{C}^3(\mathbb{R})$. Then, the process $U_t(x)$ defined by

$$U_t(x) = u(x, A_t), \quad t \geq 0,$$

is a forward performance process. Moreover, the strategy π^* defined by

$$\pi_t^* = -\frac{\lambda_t}{\sigma_t} \frac{u_x(X_t^*, A_t)}{u_{xx}(X_t^*, A_t)}, \quad t \geq 0, \tag{7.10}$$

where $X^* = X^{\pi^*}$ is the associated wealth process following (7.2), is the candidate optimal strategy in (7.5).

A quantity that plays a crucial role in the description of the wealth and portfolio processes (X^*, π^*) is the so-called *local risk tolerance* function $R : \mathbb{R} \times \mathbb{R}_+ \mapsto \mathbb{R}_+$ defined by

$$R(x,t) = -\frac{u_x(x,t)}{u_{xx}(x,t)}. \tag{7.11}$$

With this notation, the dynamics of X^* is

$$dX_t^* = R(X_t^*, A_t)\lambda_t \left(\lambda_t \, dt + dW_t\right). \tag{7.12}$$

Indeed, if we define the *risk tolerance process* by $R_t^* = R(X_t^*, A_t)$, then it follows from (7.10) that the portfolio process π^* in (7.5) is given by $\pi_t^* = \frac{\lambda_t}{\sigma_t} R_t^*$. Furthermore, it was shown in Musiela and Zariphopoulou (2008) that the processes X_t^* and R_t^* solve the system of stochastic differential equations:

$$\begin{aligned} dX_t^* &= R_t^* \lambda_t \left(\lambda_t \, dt + dW_t\right), \\ dR_t^* &= r_x(X_t^*, A_t) \, dX_t^*, \end{aligned} \tag{7.13}$$

with $X_0^* = x$, and $R_0^* = R(x,0)$.

Furthermore, if $u \in \mathcal{C}^4$, then, by differentiation, R is solution of the fast diffusion equation, namely

$$R_t + \frac{1}{2}R^2 R_{xx} = 0.$$

One way to construct forward performance criteria is to look for solutions of this partial differential equation (PDE). In Zariphopoulou and Zhou (2008), the following two-parameter family of risk tolerance functions was

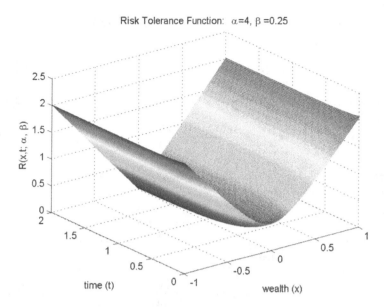

Figure 7.1. The risk tolerance function $R(x, t; \alpha, \beta)$ with $\alpha = 4$, and $\beta = 0.25$. For any fixed wealth x, the risk tolerance decreases over time. At any fixed time, the risk tolerance increases as wealth decreases or increases away from zero.

introduced:

$$R(x, t; \alpha, \beta) = \sqrt{\alpha x^2 + \beta e^{-\alpha t}}, \quad \alpha, \beta > 0. \qquad (7.14)$$

We illustrate an example of this risk tolerance in Figure 7.1.

There are several reasons to work with this family. First, it yields, in the limit, risk tolerance functions that resemble those related to the three most popular cases, specifically, the *exponential*, *power* and *logarithmic*. Indeed,

$$\lim_{\alpha \to 0} R(x, t; \alpha, \beta) = \sqrt{\beta} \qquad \text{(exponential)},$$

$$\lim_{\beta \to 0} R(x, t; \alpha, \beta) = \alpha x, \quad x \geq 0 \quad \text{(power)}, \qquad (7.15)$$

$$\lim_{\beta \to 0} R(x, t; 1, \beta) = x, \quad x > 0 \quad \text{(logarithmic)}.$$

We remark that $R(x, t; \alpha, \beta)$ is well-defined for wealth $x \in (-\infty, \infty)$, except in the limit case $\beta \downarrow 0$. In Figure 7.2, we illustrate the limit in (7.15) where the risk tolerance function converges to the constant $\sqrt{\beta}$ as $\alpha \downarrow 0$. As we will see in Section 7.3, the constant risk tolerance corresponds to the forward performance measure of exponential type.

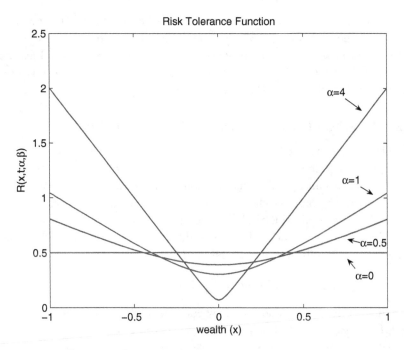

Figure 7.2. As α decreases from 4 to 0, with $\beta = 0.25$ and $t = 1$, the risk tolerance function $R(x, t; \alpha, \beta)$ converges to the constant level $\sqrt{\beta} = 0.5$, as predicted by the limit in (7.15).

Zariphopoulou and Zhou (2008) compute the corresponding dynamic risk preference function $u(x, t)$.

Proposition 7.4 (Proposition 3.2 of Zariphopoulou and Zhou (2008)). *The dynamic risk preference function* $u(x, t; \alpha, \beta)$ *associated with* $R(x, t; \alpha, \beta)$ *in* (7.14) *is given by*

$$u(x, t; \alpha, \beta) = m \frac{\kappa^{1 + \frac{1}{\kappa}}}{\alpha - 1} e^{\frac{1-\kappa}{2} t} \frac{\frac{\beta}{\kappa} e^{-\alpha t} + (1 + \kappa) x (\kappa x + \sqrt{\alpha x^2 + \beta e^{-\alpha t}})}{(\kappa x + \sqrt{\alpha x^2 + \beta e^{-\alpha t}})^{1 + \frac{1}{\kappa}}} + n,$$

$$\alpha \neq 1,$$

$$u(x, t; 1, \beta) = \frac{m}{2} \left(\log(x + \sqrt{x^2 + \beta e^{-t}}) \right.$$

$$\left. - \frac{e^{-t}}{\beta} x \left(x - \sqrt{x^2 + \beta e^{-t}} \right) - \frac{t}{2} \right) + n, \quad \alpha = 1,$$

where $\kappa = \sqrt{\alpha}$, *and* $m > 0, n \in \mathbb{R}$ *are constants of integration.*

As mentioned earlier, in the context of the domain of the local risk tolerance, the function $u(x, t; \alpha, \beta)$ is also well-defined for all $x \in \mathbb{R}$, except in the limit case $\beta \downarrow 0$. This property is particularly useful in indifference valuation for it eliminates the non-negativity constraints on the investor's wealth (with and without the claim in hand).

7.3. American Options under Stochastic Volatility

In this section, we study the forward indifference valuation of an American option in a stochastic volatility model. We work with the exponential forward performance, which, as mentioned in the previous section, corresponds to the parameter choice $\alpha = 0$. A comparative analysis with the classical exponential utility indifference pricing is provided in Section 7.3.4.

The underlying stock price S, discounted by the money market account, is modeled as a diffusion process satisfying

$$dS_t = S_t \sigma(Y_t)(\lambda(Y_t)\, dt + dW_t). \tag{7.16}$$

The Sharpe ratio $\lambda(Y_t)$ and volatility coefficient $\sigma(Y_t)$ are driven by a *non-traded* stochastic factor Y which evolves according to

$$dY_t = b(Y_t)\, dt + c(Y_t)\left(\rho dW_t + \sqrt{1 - \rho^2} d\hat{W}_t\right), \tag{7.17}$$

with correlation coefficient $\rho \in (-1, 1)$. The processes W and $\hat{W}$ are two independent standard Brownian motions defined on $(\Omega, \mathscr{F}, (\mathscr{F}_t)_{t \geq 0}, \mathbb{P})$, where $\mathscr{F}_t$ is taken to be the augmented σ-algebra generated by $((W_u, \hat{W}_u); 0 \leq u \leq t)$. The volatility function $\sigma(\cdot)$ and the diffusion coefficient $c(\cdot)$ are smooth, positive and bounded. The Sharpe ratio $\lambda(\cdot)$ is bounded continuous, and $b(\cdot)$ is Lipschitz continuous on $\mathbb{R}$. The American option yields payoff $g(S_\tau, Y_\tau, \tau)$ at exercise time $\tau \in [0, T]$, where $g(\cdot, \cdot, \cdot)$ is a smooth and bounded function.

The holder of the American option g dynamically trades in S and the money market. His discounted trading wealth follows

$$dX_t^\pi = \pi_t \sigma(Y_t)(\lambda(Y_t)\, dt + dW_t), \tag{7.18}$$

where $(\pi_t)_{t \geq 0}$ is the discounted cash amount invested in S.

7.3.1. *Exponential forward indifference price*

We model the American option holder's risk preferences by the exponential forward performance process. By setting the parameter $\alpha = 0$ in (7.14), the risk tolerance becomes a constant $\sqrt{\beta}$ (see (7.15) and Figure 7.2). In turn, (7.9) and (7.11) yield the corresponding exponential risk preference function $u(x,t)$:

$$u(x,t) = -e^{-\gamma x + \frac{t}{2}},$$

with $\gamma = 1/\sqrt{\beta}$. The parameter γ can be considered as the investor's *local risk version*. Applying Theorem 7.3, we obtain the exponential forward performance process

$$U_t^e(x) = -e^{-\gamma x + \frac{1}{2}\int_0^t \lambda(Y_s)^2 ds}, \quad t \geq 0. \tag{7.19}$$

As defined in (7.6), the holder's forward performance value process is given by

$$V_t^e(X_t) = \operatorname*{ess\,sup}_{\tau \in \mathscr{T}_{t,T}} \operatorname*{ess\,sup}_{\pi \in \mathscr{Z}_{t,\tau}} \mathbb{E}\{-e^{-\gamma(X_\tau^\pi + g(S_\tau, Y_\tau, \tau))} e^{\frac{1}{2}\int_0^\tau \lambda(Y_s)^2 ds} \mid \mathscr{F}_t\}$$

$$= e^{\frac{1}{2}\int_0^t \lambda(Y_s)^2 ds} \operatorname*{ess\,sup}_{\tau \in \mathscr{T}_{t,T}} \operatorname*{ess\,sup}_{\pi \in \mathscr{Z}_{t,\tau}}$$

$$\mathbb{E}\{-e^{-\gamma(X_\tau^\pi + g(S_\tau, Y_\tau, \tau))} e^{\frac{1}{2}\int_t^\tau \lambda(Y_s)^2 ds} \mid \mathscr{F}_t\}. \tag{7.20}$$

We observe that the second term in (7.20) is the value of a combined stochastic control and optimal stopping problem. Working under the Markovian stochastic volatility market (7.16)–(7.17), we look for a candidate optimal $\mathscr{F}_t$-adapted Markovian strategy by studying the associated Hamilton–Jacobi–Bellman (HJB) variational inequality.

To facilitate notation, we introduce the following differential operators and Hamiltonian:

$$\mathscr{L}_{SY}v = \frac{1}{2}\sigma(y)^2 s^2 v_{ss} + \rho c(y)\sigma(y) s v_{sy} + \frac{1}{2}c(y)^2 v_{yy} + \lambda(y)\sigma(y) s v_s + b(y)v_y,$$

$$\mathscr{L}_{SY}^0 v = \frac{1}{2}\sigma(y)^2 s^2 v_{ss} + \rho c(y)\sigma(y) s v_{sy} + \frac{1}{2}c(y)^2 v_{yy} + (b(y) - \rho c(y)\lambda(y))v_y,$$

and

$$\tilde{H}(v_{xx}, v_{xy}, v_{xs}, v_x)$$

$$= \max_\pi \left(\frac{\pi^2 \sigma(y)^2}{2} v_{xx} + \pi \left(\rho\sigma(y)c(y)v_{xy} + \sigma(y)^2 s v_{xs} + \lambda(y)\sigma(y)v_x \right) \right).$$

Note that $\mathscr{L}^{SY}$ and $\mathscr{L}_{SY}^0$ are, respectively, the infinitesimal generators of the Markov process $(S_t, Y_t)_{t \geq 0}$ under the historical measure $\mathbb{P}$ and the minimal martingale measure Q^0 (to be defined in (7.26)).

Next, we consider the HJB variational inequality

$$V_t + \mathscr{L}_{SY} V + \tilde{H}(V_{xx}, V_{xy}, V_{xs}, V_x) + \frac{\lambda(y)^2}{2} V \leq 0,$$

$$V(x, s, y, t) \geq -e^{-\gamma(x+g(s,y,t))},$$

$$\left(V_t + \mathscr{L}_{SY} V + \tilde{H}(V_{xx}, V_{xy}, V_{xs}, V_x) + \frac{\lambda(y)^2}{2} V \right) \tag{7.21}$$

$$\cdot \left(-e^{-\gamma(x+g(s,y,t))} - V(x, s, y, t) \right) = 0,$$

$$V(x, s, y, T) = -e^{-\gamma(x+g(s,y,T))},$$

for $(x, s, y, t) \in \mathbb{R} \times \mathbb{R}_+ \times \mathbb{R} \times [0, T]$.

Given a solution $V(x, s, y, t)$ to (7.21) that is $\mathscr{C}^{2,2,2,1}$ except across a lower dimensional optimal exercise boundary, one can show by standard verification arguments (see Theorem 4.2 of Oksendal and Sulem (2005)) that V is the value function for the combined optimal control/stopping problem in (7.20). Therefore, we can write

$$V_t^e(X_t) = e^{\frac{1}{2} \int_0^t \lambda(Y_s)^2 ds} V(X_t, S_t, Y_t, t). \tag{7.22}$$

Remark 7.5. As is usual in classical indifference pricing problems, the existence of a solution (in the appropriate regularity class) to the HJB equation or variational inequality is a non-trivial issue, and is typically verified in specific cases. For instance, in the classical exponential utility indifference pricing for American options, Musiela and Zariphopoulou (2004b) show the viscosity (weak) solution of the HJB equation for the value function. For our analysis in this section, we assume the existence of a unique solution to the variational inequality (7.21) with the regularity needed for the verification arguments.

Applying (7.19) and (7.22) to Definition 7.2, the option holder's exponential forward indifference price function $p(x, s, y, t)$ is given by

$$p(x, s, y, t) = -\frac{1}{\gamma} \log(-V(x, s, y, t)) - x. \tag{7.23}$$

Then, we substitute (7.23) into the variational inequality (7.21) to derive the variational equality for $p(x, s, y, t)$. As it turns out, the indifference price is independent of the wealth argument x and it solves the free boundary problem

$$p_t + \mathscr{L}^0_{SY}p - \frac{1}{2}\gamma(1 - \rho^2)c(y)^2 p_y^2 \leq 0,$$

$$p(s, y, t) \geq g(s, y, t),$$

$$\left(p_t + \mathscr{L}^0_{SY}p - \frac{1}{2}\gamma(1 - \rho^2)c(y)^2 p_y^2\right) \cdot (g(s, y, t) - p(s, y, t)) = 0, \tag{7.24}$$

$$p(s, y, T) = g(s, y, T),$$

for $(s, y, t) \in \mathbb{R}_+ \times \mathbb{R} \times [0, T]$.

By the first-order condition in (7.21) and the formula (7.23), the optimal hedging strategy $(\tilde{\pi}^*_t)_{0 \leq t \leq T}$ can be expressed in terms of the indifference price, namely,

$$\tilde{\pi}^*_t = \frac{\lambda(Y_t)}{\gamma\sigma(Y_t)} + \frac{S_t}{\gamma}p_s(S_t, Y_t, t) + \frac{\rho c(Y_t)}{\gamma\sigma(Y_t)}p_y(S_t, Y_t, t).$$

The first term in this expression is the optimal strategy in (7.10) when there is no claim, while the second and third terms correspond to the extra demand in stock S due to changes in S and the stochastic factor Y, respectively.

The optimal exercise time is the first time that the indifference price reaches the option payoff:

$$\tau^*_t = \inf\{t \leq u \leq T : p(S_u, Y_u, u) = g(S_u, Y_u, u)\}.$$

In practice, one can numerically solve the variational inequality (7.24) to obtain the optimal exercise boundary which represents the critical levels of S and Y at which the option should be exercised. We remark that the indifference price, the optimal hedging and exercising strategies are all wealth-independent. The same phenomenon occurs in the classical indifference valuation with exponential utility.

7.3.2. *Dual representation*

The option holder's forward performance maximization in (7.22) can be considered as the primal optimization problem, and it yields the first expression for the forward indifference price in (7.23). Our objective is to derive a dual representation for the forward indifference price, which turns out to be related to pricing the American option with entropic penalty. This result will allow us to express the price in a way analogous to the classical exponential indifference price. We carry out this comparison in Section 7.3.4.

First, we denote by $\mathscr{M}(\mathbb{P})$ the set of equivalent local martingale measures with respect to $\mathbb{P}$ on $\mathscr{F}_T$. By Proposition 6.1 of Frey (1997), these measures are characterized as follows.

Proposition 7.6. *A probability measure Q^ϕ belongs to $\mathscr{M}(\mathbb{P})$ if and only if there exists a progressively measurable process $(\phi_t)_{0 \leq t \leq T}$ with $\int_0^T \phi_s^2 \, ds < \infty$ $\mathbb{P}$-a.s., and $dQ^\phi/d\mathbb{P} = Z_T^\phi$ where $(Z_t^\phi)_{0 \leq t \leq T}$ is a local martingale defined by*

$$
Z_t^\phi = \exp\left(-\frac{1}{2} \int_0^t \left(\lambda(Y_s)^2 + \phi_s^2 \right) ds - \int_0^t \lambda(Y_s) \, dW_s - \int_0^t \phi_s \, d\hat{W}_s \right)
\tag{7.25}
$$

with $\mathbb{E}\{Z_T^\phi\} = 1$.

By Girsanov's theorem, it follows that

$$
W_t^\phi = W_t + \int_0^t \lambda(Y_s) ds \quad \text{and} \quad \hat{W}_t^\phi = \hat{W}_t + \int_0^t \phi_s \, ds
$$

are independent Q^ϕ-Brownian motions. The process ϕ is commonly referred to as the *volatility risk premium* for the second Brownian motion $\hat{W}$.

When $\phi = 0$, we obtain the minimal martingale measure (MMM) Q^0, given by

$$
\frac{dQ^0}{d\mathbb{P}} = \exp\left(-\frac{1}{2} \int_0^T \lambda(Y_s)^2 \, ds - \int_0^T \lambda(Y_s) \, dW_s \right).
\tag{7.26}
$$

In fact, we can express Q^ϕ in terms of Q^0, namely,

$$
\frac{dQ^\phi}{dQ^0} = \frac{dQ^\phi}{d\mathbb{P}} \bigg/ \frac{dQ^0}{d\mathbb{P}}
$$

$$
= \exp\left(-\frac{1}{2} \int_0^T \phi_s^2 \, ds - \int_0^T \phi_s \, d\hat{W}_s^0 \right).
\tag{7.27}
$$

We also denote the density process of Q^ϕ with respect to Q^0 by

$$
Z_t^{\phi,0} = \mathbb{E}^{Q^0}\left\{ \frac{dQ^\phi}{dQ^0} \,\bigg|\, \mathscr{F}_t \right\}.
$$

Treating Q^0 as the prior risk-neutral measure, we define the conditional relative entropy $H_t^\tau(Q^\phi|Q^0)$ of Q^ϕ with respect to Q^0 over the interval $[t, \tau]$ as

$$H_t^\tau(Q^\phi|Q^0) = \mathbb{E}^{Q^\phi}\left\{\log \frac{Z_\tau^{\phi,0}}{Z_t^{\phi,0}}\middle| \mathscr{F}_t\right\}.$$

Direct computation from (7.27) shows that this relative entropy is, in fact, a quadratic penalization on the risk premium ϕ. In other words,

$$H_t^\tau(Q^\phi|Q^0) = \frac{1}{2}\mathbb{E}^{Q^\phi}\left\{\int_t^\tau \phi_s^2\,ds\middle| \mathscr{F}_t\right\}.$$

Let us denote the set of equivalent local martingale measures with finite relative entropy (with respect to Q^0) as

$$\mathscr{M}_f := \left\{Q^\phi \in \mathscr{M}(\mathbb{P}) : \mathbb{E}^{Q^\phi}\left\{\int_0^T \phi_t^2\,dt\right\} < \infty\right\}.$$

Next, we give a duality result for the exponential forward indifference price.

Proposition 7.7. *Let $p(s, y, t)$ be the solution to (7.24). Define Q^{ϕ^*} by $dQ^{\phi^*}/d\mathbb{P} = Z_T^{\phi^*}$ (as in (7.25)) with*

$$\phi_t^* = -\gamma c(Y_t)\sqrt{1 - \rho^2}\,p_y(S_t, Y_t, t), \quad 0 \le t \le T, \tag{7.28}$$

and assume that $Q^{\phi^*} \in \mathscr{M}_f$. Then, $p(s, y, t)$ is the solution of the following combined stochastic control and optimal stopping problem:

$$p(S_t, Y_t, t) = \operatorname*{ess\,sup}_{\tau \in \mathscr{T}_{t,T}}\operatorname*{ess\,inf}_{Q^\phi \in \mathscr{M}_f}\left(\mathbb{E}^{Q^\phi}\{g(S_\tau, Y_\tau, \tau)|\mathscr{F}_t\} + \frac{1}{\gamma}H_t^\tau(Q^\phi|Q^0)\right),$$
$$\tag{7.29}$$

and Q^{ϕ^*} is the associated optimal measure.

Proof. It is straightforward to check that the HJB variational inequality for the stochastic control/stopping problem in (7.29) is identical to (7.24). The associated optimal control ϕ^* is given in (7.28), and Q^{ϕ^*} is the corresponding optimal probability measure. $\qquad\square$

The dual representation (7.29) provides an alternative interpretation of the forward indifference price. In essence, the holder tries to value the American option over a set of equivalent local martingale measures, and his selection criterion for the optimal pricing measure is based on relative entropic penalization. Indeed, the second term in (7.29) is the relative entropy of a candidate measure Q^ϕ with respect to the MMM Q^0 up to the exercise time. This leads the holder to assign the corresponding optimal risk premium ϕ^* in (7.28). We will compare this result to its classical analog in Section 7.3.4.

7.3.3. *Risk aversion and volume asymptotics*

Proposition 7.7 provides a convenient representation for analyzing the exponential forward indifference price's sensitivity with respect to risk aversion and the number of options held. First, let us consider a risk-averse investor with local risk aversion γ who holds $a > 0$ units of American options, and suppose that all a units are constrained to be exercised simultaneously. In this case, the holder's indifference price $p(s, y, t; \gamma, a)$ is again given by (7.29) but with the payoff $g(S_\tau, Y_\tau, \tau)$ replaced by $ag(S_\tau, Y_\tau, \tau)$. The optimal exercise time $\tau^*(a, \gamma)$ is the first time that the forward indifference price reaches the payoff from exercising all a units:

$$\tau^*(a, \gamma) = \inf\{t \le u \le T \,:\, p(S_u, Y_u, u; \gamma, a) = ag(S_u, Y_u, u)\}. \quad (7.30)$$

Proposition 7.8. *Fix $a > 0$ and $t \in [0, T]$. If $\gamma_2 \ge \gamma_1 > 0$, then we have*

$$p(s, y, t; \gamma_2, a) \le p(s, y, t; \gamma_1, a),$$

and

$$\tau^*(a, \gamma_2) \le \tau^*(a, \gamma_1),$$

almost surely.

Proof.   For $\gamma_2 \ge \gamma_1 > 0$, it follows from (7.29) that $p(s, y, t; \gamma_2, a) \le p(s, y, t; \gamma_1, a)$. Therefore, as γ increases, $p(s, y, t; \gamma, a)$ decreases, while the payoff $ag(s, y, t)$ does not depend on γ. By (7.30), this implies a shorter exercise time (almost surely). □

Furthermore, we observe that, as γ increases to infinity, the penalty term in the indifference price representation (7.29) vanishes. Consequently, we deduce the following limit:

$$\lim_{\gamma \to \infty} p(s, y, t; \gamma, a) = a \cdot \sup_{\tau \in \mathcal{T}_{t,T}} \inf_{Q^\phi \in \mathcal{M}_f} \mathbb{E}^{Q^\phi} \left\{ g(S_\tau, Y_\tau, \tau) | S_t = s, Y_t = y \right\}.$$

$$(7.31)$$

This limiting price is commonly referred to as the sub-hedging price of the American options (Karatzas and Kou, 1998). On the other hand, as the holder's risk aversion γ decreases to zero, one can deduce from (7.29) that it is optimal not to deviate from the prior measure Q^0 (i.e. $\phi = 0$), yielding zero entropic penalty. This leads to valuing the American options under the MMM Q^0, namely,

$$\lim_{\gamma \to 0} p(s, y, t; \gamma, a) = a \cdot \sup_{\tau \in \mathcal{T}_{t,T}} \mathbb{E}^{Q^0} \left\{ g(S_\tau, Y_\tau, \tau) | S_t = s, Y_t = y \right\}. \quad (7.32)$$

We have provided the formal arguments for these risk-aversion limits. For more technical details, we refer the reader to Leung and Sircar (2009b) who have shown these asymptotic results for the traditional exponential indifference price of American options in a general semimartingale framework, and their proofs can be easily adapted here.

Finally, we observe from (7.29) the volume-scaling property:

$$\frac{p(s, y, t; \gamma, a)}{a} = p(s, y, t; a\gamma, 1).$$

Hence, as the number of options held increases, the holder's average indifference price $p(s, y, t; \gamma, a)/a$ decreases, and by (7.30) the options will be exercised earlier. Moreover, the indifference price limits in (7.31)–(7.32) lead to the following limits:

$$\lim_{a \to \infty} \frac{p(s, y, t; \gamma, a)}{a} = \sup_{\tau \in \mathcal{T}_{t,T}} \inf_{Q^\phi \in \mathcal{M}_f} \mathbb{E}^{Q^\phi} \left\{ g(S_\tau, Y_\tau, \tau) | S_t = s, Y_t = y \right\},$$

$$\lim_{a \to 0} \frac{p(s, y, t; \gamma, a)}{a} = \sup_{\tau \in \mathcal{T}_{t,T}} \mathbb{E}^{Q^0} \left\{ g(S_\tau, Y_\tau, \tau) | S_t = s, Y_t = y \right\}.$$

7.3.4. *Comparison with the classical exponential utility indifference price*

In this section, we provide a comparative analysis between the classical and forward indifference valuation. We start with a brief review of the classical indifference pricing with exponential utility under stochastic volatility models. We refer the reader to, for example, Sircar and Zariphopoulou (2005) and Benth and Karlsen (2005) for European options, and Oberman and Zariphopoulou (2003) for American options.

In the traditional setting, the investor's risk preferences at time T are modeled by the exponential utility function $-e^{-\gamma x}$, $\gamma > 0$. In the stochastic volatility model described in (7.16)–(7.17), the value function of the Merton problem is

$$M(x,y,t) = \sup_{\pi \in \mathscr{Z}_{t,T}} \mathbb{E}\{-e^{-\gamma X_T^\pi} \,|\, X_t = x, Y_t = y\}, \qquad (7.33)$$

with $(X_t^\pi)_{t\geq 0}$ given by (7.18). As is well known, the function M admits a separation of variables due to the exponential utility.

Proposition 7.9. *The value function $M(x,y,t)$ is given by*

$$M(x,y,t) = -e^{-\gamma x} f(y,t)^{\frac{1}{1-\rho^2}}, \qquad (7.34)$$

where ρ is the correlation coefficient in (7.17), and f solves

$$f_t + \mathscr{L}_Y^0 f = \frac{1}{2}(1-\rho^2)\lambda(y)^2 f, \qquad (7.35)$$

for $(x,t) \in \mathbb{R} \times [0,T)$, with $f(y,T) = 1$, for $y \in \mathbb{R}$. The operator $\mathscr{L}_Y^0$ is the infinitesimal generator of Y under the MMM Q^0, and is given by

$$\mathscr{L}_Y^0 f = (b(y) - \rho c(y)\lambda(y)) f_y + \frac{1}{2}c(y)^2 f_{yy}.$$

Details can be found, for example, in Theorem 2.2 of Sircar and Zariphopoulou (2005).

If the American option g is held, then the investor seeks the optimal trading strategy and exercise time to maximize the expected utility from trading wealth plus the option's payoff. Upon exercise of the option, the investor will reinvest the contract proceeds, if any, to his trading portfolio, and continue to trade up to time T. As a consequence, the holder faces the optimization problem

$$\hat{V}(x,s,y,t) = \sup_{\tau \in \mathscr{T}_{t,T}} \sup_{\pi \in \mathscr{Z}_{t,\tau}} \mathbb{E}\{M(X_\tau^\pi + g(S_\tau, Y_\tau, \tau), Y_\tau, \tau) \,|\, X_t = x,$$

$$S_t = s, Y_t = y\}, \qquad (7.36)$$

where M is defined in (7.33).

The indifference price of the American option $\hat{p}$ is found from the equation

$$M(x, y, t) = \hat{V}(x - \hat{p}(x, s, y, t), s, y, t). \tag{7.37}$$

Using (7.34) and (7.37), we obtain the formula

$$\hat{V}(x, s, y, t) = -e^{-\gamma(x + \hat{p}(x,s,y,t))} f(y, t)^{\frac{1}{1-\rho^2}}. \tag{7.38}$$

To derive the variational inequality for the indifference price, one can use the variational inequality for V and then apply the transformation (7.38). Again, the choice of exponential utility yields wealth-independent indifference prices, i.e. $\hat{p}(x, s, y, t) = \hat{p}(s, y, t)$. We obtain

$$\hat{p}_t + \mathscr{L}_{SY}^E \hat{p} - \frac{1}{2}\gamma(1 - \rho^2)c(y)^2 \hat{p}_y^2 \leq 0,$$

$$\hat{p}(s, y, t) \geq g(s, y, t),$$

$$\left(\hat{p}_t + \mathscr{L}_{SY}^E \hat{p} - \frac{1}{2}\gamma(1 - \rho^2)c(y)^2 \hat{p}_y^2 \right) \cdot (g(s, y, t) - \hat{p}(s, y, t)) = 0, \tag{7.39}$$

$$\hat{p}(s, y, T) = g(s, y, T),$$

for $(s, y, t) \in \mathbb{R}_+ \times \mathbb{R}_+ \times [0, T]$. Here,

$$\mathscr{L}_{SY}^E w = \mathscr{L}_{SY}^0 w + l(y, t)c(y)\sqrt{1 - \rho^2} w_y,$$

where

$$l(y, t) = \frac{1}{\sqrt{1 - \rho^2}} c(y) \frac{f_y(y, t)}{f(y, t)}.$$

As shown in Section 2 of Sircar and Zariphopoulou (2005), $l(y, t)$ is smooth and bounded, and is the risk premium corresponding to the MEMM Q^E, namely,

$$\frac{dQ^E}{d\mathbb{P}} = \exp\left(-\frac{1}{2} \int_0^T (\lambda(Y_s)^2 + l(Y_s, s)^2) \, ds \right.$$

$$\left. - \int_0^T \lambda(Y_s) \, dW_s + \int_0^T l(Y_s, s) \, d\hat{W}_s \right). \tag{7.40}$$

Therefore, the operator $\mathscr{L}_{SY}^E$ is the infinitesimal generator of (S, Y) under Q^E.

It is important to notice that the fundamental difference between variational inequalities (7.24) and (7.39) lies in the operators $\mathscr{L}_{SY}^0$ and $\mathscr{L}_{SY}^E$. Indeed, these variational inequalities reflect the special roles of the MMM in the forward indifference setting and the MEMM in the classical model. The MEMM also arises in the dual representation of $\hat{p}$. Namely, one can show that (see Proposition 2.8 of Leung and Sircar (2009b))

$$\hat{p}(S_t, Y_t, t) = \operatorname*{ess\,sup}_{\tau \in \mathscr{T}_{t,T}} \operatorname*{ess\,inf}_{Q^\phi \in \mathscr{M}_f} \left(\mathbb{E}^{Q^\phi} \{ g(S_\tau, Y_\tau, \tau) | \mathscr{F}_t \} + \frac{1}{\gamma} H_t^\tau(Q^\phi | Q^E) \right).$$

This duality result bears a striking resemblance to (7.29), except here the relative entropy term is computed with respect to Q^E rather than with respect to Q^0.

In the classical setting, the computation of the indifference price involves two steps, namely, first solving PDE (7.35) followed by variational inequality (7.39). However, in the forward indifference valuation, the indifference price can be obtained by solving only one variational inequality (7.24). Hence, with exponential performance, the forward indifference formulation allows for more efficient computation than in the classical framework.

Remark 7.10. If the claim is written on Y only, say with payoff function $g(y, t)$, then the indifference price does not depend on S. Applying a logarithmic transformation to the variational inequality (7.24), the nonlinear variational inequality can be linearized. As a result, in addition to (7.29), the forward indifference price admits the representation:

$$p(y, t) = -\frac{1}{\gamma(1-\rho^2)} \log \inf_{\tau \in \mathscr{T}_{t,T}} \mathbb{E}^{Q^0} \{ e^{-\gamma(1-\rho^2)g(Y_\tau, \tau)} | Y_t = y \}.$$

In contrast, the classical exponential utility indifference price of an American option with the same payoff function $g(y, t)$ can be found in Oberman and Zariphopoulou (2003), and it is given by

$$\hat{p}(y, t) = -\frac{1}{\gamma(1-\rho^2)} \log \inf_{\tau \in \mathscr{T}_{t,T}} \mathbb{E}^{Q^E} \{ e^{-\gamma(1-\rho^2)g(Y_\tau, \tau)} | Y_t = y \},$$

with Q^E given in (7.40). Again, we see that Q^0 in the forward performance framework plays a similar role as Q^E in the classical setting.

In summary, we have studied the exponential forward indifference price through its associated variational inequality and dual representation, which have very desirable structures and interpretations due to the nice analytic properties of the exponential forward performance. We have also seen that higher risk aversion leads to earlier exercise times.

7.4. Modeling Early Exercises of Employee Stock Options

Now, we consider the problem of partially hedging and exercising employee stock options (ESOs) under a forward performance criterion. Recall that a typical ESO contract prohibits the employee from selling the option and from hedging by short selling the firm's stock. The sale and hedging restrictions may induce the employee to exercise the ESO early and invest the option proceeds elsewhere. In fact, empirical studies (for example, Bettis *et al.*, 2005) show that employees tend to exercise their ESOs very early.

Recent studies, for example, Henderson (2005) and Leung and Sircar (2009a), apply classical indifference pricing to ESO valuation. In those papers, the employee was assumed to have a classical exponential utility specified at the expiration date T of the options. Here, we assume a forward performance criterion for the employee, which is not anchored to a specific future time, and then compute the optimal exercise strategy. Modeling the employee's exercise timing is crucial to the accurate valuation of ESOs.

We assume that the employee dynamically trades in a liquid correlated market index and a riskless money market account in order to partially hedge against his ESO position. Alternative hedging strategies for ESOs have also been proposed. For instance, Leung and Sircar (2009b) considered combining static hedges with market-traded European or American puts with the dynamic investment in the market index.

We focus our study on the case of a single vested ESO. Typically, ESOs have a vesting period during which they cannot be exercised early. The incorporation of a vesting period amounts to lifting the employee's pre-vesting exercise boundary to infinity to prevent exercise, but leaving the post-vesting policy unchanged. The case with multiple ESOs can be studied as a straightforward extension to our model though the numerical computations will be more complex and time-consuming. Our main objective is to examine the non-trivial effects of forward investment performance criterion on the employee's optimal exercise timing.

7.4.1. *The employee's optimal forward performance with an ESO*

We assume that the money market account yields a constant interest rate $r \geq 0$. The *discounted* prices of the market index and the firm's stock are modeled as correlated lognormal processes, namely,

$$dS_t = S_t \sigma(\lambda\, dt + dW_t) \qquad\qquad \text{(traded)},$$
$$dY_t = bY_t dt + cY_t(\rho dW_t + \sqrt{1 - \rho^2}\, d\hat{W}_t) \quad \text{(non-traded)},$$

where λ, σ, b, c are constant parameters. The discounted ESO payoff, with expiration date T, is given by

$$g(Y_\tau, \tau) = (Y_\tau - Ke^{-r\tau})^+, \quad \text{for } \tau \in \mathcal{T}_{0,T}.$$

Note that this market setup is nested in the Itô diffusion market described in Section 7.2. Here, the Sharpe ratio λ of S is now a constant, and the option payoff is independent of S. The employee dynamically trades in the index Y and the money market account, so his discounted wealth process satisfies

$$dX_t^\pi = \pi_t \sigma(\lambda\, dt + dW_t).$$

We proceed with the employee's forward performance criterion $U_t(x)$. First, we adopt the risk tolerance function in (7.14), namely, $R(x,t) = \sqrt{\alpha x^2 + \beta e^{-\alpha t}}$, and the corresponding dynamic risk preference function $u(x, t)$ given in Proposition 7.4. Then, we apply Theorem 7.3 to obtain the employee's forward performance $U_t(x) = u(x, \lambda^2 t)$. In turn, the employee's maximal forward performance in the presence of the ESO is given by

$$V(x, y, t) = \sup_{\tau \in \mathcal{T}_{t,T}} \sup_{\pi \in \mathcal{Z}_{t,\tau}} \mathbb{E}\left\{ u(X_\tau^\pi + g(Y_\tau, \tau), \lambda^2 \tau) \,|\, X_t = x, Y_t = y \right\}.$$

In contrast to the stochastic volatility problem in Section 7.3, the state variable S is no longer needed, but we work with a more general forward performance criterion than the exponential one.

To solve for the employee's value function, we look for a solution to the following HJB variational inequality:

$$V_t + \mathcal{L}_Y V - \frac{(\rho cy V_{xy} + \lambda V_x)^2}{2V_{xx}} \le 0,$$

$$V(x, y, t) \ge u(x + g(y, t), \lambda^2 t),$$

$$\left(V_t + \mathcal{L}_Y V - \frac{(\rho cy V_{xy} + \lambda V_x)^2}{2V_{xx}} \right) \cdot (u(x + g(y, t), \lambda^2 t) - V(x, y, t)) = 0,$$

$$V(x, y, T) = u(x + g(y, T), \lambda^2 T), \qquad\qquad\qquad (7.41)$$

for $(x, y, t) \in \mathbb{R} \times \mathbb{R}_+ \times [0, T]$.

Then, by Definition 7.2, the ESO holder's forward indifference price $p(x, y, t)$ can be found from the indifference equation

$$V(x, y, t) = u(x + p(x, y, t), \lambda^2 t). \tag{7.42}$$

We remark that the variational inequality (7.41) is highly nonlinear, and it can be simplified only for very special local utility functions (e.g. the exponential utility). Here, we do not attempt to address the related existence, uniqueness, and regularity questions.

7.4.2. *Numerical solutions*

We apply a *fully explicit* finite-difference scheme to numerically solve the variational inequality in (7.41) for the employee's optimal exercising strategy. First, we restrict the domain $\mathbb{R} \times \mathbb{R}_+ \times [0, T]$ to a finite domain $\mathscr{D} = \{(x, y, t) : -L_1 \leq x \leq L_2, 0 \leq y \leq L_3, 0 \leq t \leq T\}$, where L_k, $k = 1, 2, 3$, are chosen to be sufficiently large to preserve the accuracy of the numerical solutions. The numerical scheme also requires a number of boundary conditions. For $y = 0$, we have $Y_t = 0$, $t \geq 0$, and thus the ESO becomes worthless. Therefore, we set

$$V(x, 0, t) = u(x, \lambda^2 t).$$

When Y hits the high level L_3, we assume that the employee will exercise the ESO there, implying the condition

$$V(x, L_3, t) = u(x + g(L_3, t), \lambda^2 t).$$

We also need to set appropriate boundary conditions along $x = -L_1$ and $x = L_2$. To this end, we adopt the Dirichlet boundary conditions

$$V(-L_1, y, t) = u(-L_1 + g(y, t), \lambda^2 t),$$
$$V(L_2, y, t) = u(L_2 + g(y, t), \lambda^2 t),$$

which imply that the employee will exercise the ESO at these boundaries.

Then, a uniform grid is applied on $\mathscr{D}$ with nodes $\{(x_i, y_j, t_n) : i = 0, ..., I; j = 0, ..., J; n = 0, ..., N\}$, with $\Delta x = (L_1 + L_2)/I$, $\Delta y = L_3/J$, and $\Delta t = T/N$ being the grid spacings. Next, we use the discrete approximations $V_{i,j}^n \approx V(x_i, y_j, t_n)$ where $x_i = i\Delta x$, $y_j = j\Delta y$, and

$t_n = n\Delta t$. Also, we discretize the partial differential inequality in (7.41) by approximating the x and y derivatives with central differences:

$$\frac{\partial V}{\partial x}(x_i, y_j, t_n) \approx \frac{V_{i+1,j}^n - V_{i-1,j}^n}{2\Delta x},$$

$$\frac{\partial^2 V}{\partial x^2}(x_i, y_j, t_n) \approx \frac{V_{i+1,j}^n - 2V_{i,j}^n + V_{i-1,j}^n}{\Delta x^2},$$

$$\frac{\partial V}{\partial y}(x_i, y_j, t_n) \approx \frac{V_{i,j+1}^n - V_{i,j-1}^n}{2\Delta y},$$

$$\frac{\partial^2 V}{\partial y^2}(x_i, y_j, t_n) \approx \frac{V_{i,j+1}^n - 2V_{i,j}^n + V_{i,j-1}^n}{\Delta y^2},$$

and

$$\frac{\partial^2 V}{\partial x \partial y}(x_i, y_j, t_n) \approx \frac{V_{i+1,j+1}^n - V_{i+1,j-1}^n + V_{i-1,j-1}^n - V_{i-1,j+1}^n}{4\Delta x \Delta y}.$$

The t-derivative is approximated by the backward difference

$$\frac{\partial V}{\partial t}(x_i, y_j, t_n) \approx \frac{V_{i,j}^{n+1} - V_{i,j}^n}{\Delta t}.$$

This results in an explicit finite-difference scheme which solves for all $V_{i,j}^n$ iteratively backward in time starting at $t_N = T$.

During each time step, the inequality constraint $V(x, y, t) \geq u(x + g(y, t), \lambda^2 t)$ is enforced. By comparing the value function and the obstacle term, we identify the *continuation region* $\mathscr{C}$ where the ESO is not exercised, and the *exercise region* $\mathscr{E}$ where the ESO is exercised, namely

$$\mathscr{C} = \{(x, y, t) \in \mathbb{R} \times \mathbb{R}_+ \times [0, T] : V(x, y, t) > u(x + g(y, t), \lambda^2 t)\},$$

$$\mathscr{E} = \{(x, y, t) \in \mathbb{R} \times \mathbb{R}_+ \times [0, T] : V(x, y, t) = u(x + g(y, t), \lambda^2 t)\}.$$

From the numerical example in Figure 7.3, we observe that the value function dominates the obstacle term. At any time t and wealth x, we locate the optimal stock price level $y^*(x, t)$ that separates the two regions $\mathscr{C}$ and $\mathscr{E}$. As a result, the employee will exercise the ESO as soon as Y_t hits the threshold $y^*(X_t, t)$:

$$\tau^* = \inf\{0 \leq t \leq T : Y_t = y^*(X_t, t)\}.$$

In the case of call options, the boundary lies above the strike K. Figure 7.4 shows an example of the optimal exercise boundary for the ESO. It follows

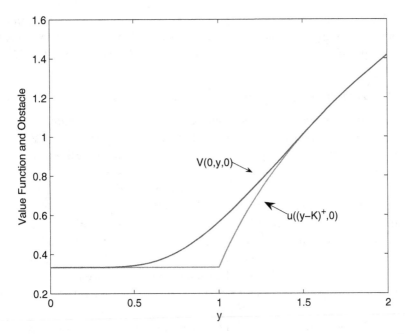

Figure 7.3. The value function $V(x, y, t)$ dominates the obstacle term $u(x+g(y, t), \lambda^2 t)$. The parameters are $\lambda = 33\%$, $\sigma = 35\%$, $b = 6\%$, $c = 40\%$, $\rho = 50\%$, $r = 1\%$, $K = 1$, $T = 1$, $\alpha = 4$, $\beta = 0.25$. At $t = 0$ and $x = 0$, the critical stock price $y^*(0, 0) = 1.58$ is the point at which the value function touches the obstacle term (above the strike).

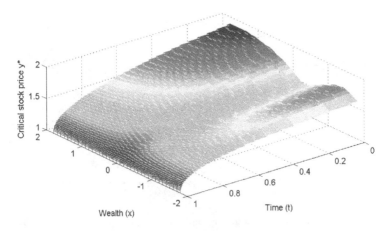

Figure 7.4. The optimal exercise policy is characterized by the critical stock price $y^*(x, t)$ as a function of wealth x and time t. It decreases as time approaches maturity. In addition, it tends to shift lower as wealth is near zero.

from (7.42) that $p(x, y, t) > g(y, t)$ in $\mathscr{C}$, and $p(x, y, t) = g(y, t)$ in $\mathscr{E}$. Therefore, the optimal exercise time τ^* is also the first time that the holder's forward indifference price reaches the option payoff, as pointed out in (7.8).

7.4.3. *Behavior of the optimal exercise policy*

We illustrate the employee's optimal exercise boundary in Figure 7.4. Not surprisingly, the exercise boundary $y^*(x, t)$ decreases with respect to time, which implies that the employee is willing to exercise the ESO at a lower stock price as it gets closer to expiry.

From Figure 7.5, we observe that the exercise boundary is wealth-dependent. The employee tends to delay exercising the ESO when his wealth deviates away from zero. We can gain some intuition from our choice of risk tolerance function $R(x, t; \alpha, \beta)$. As wealth approaches zero, the employee's risk tolerance decreases (recall Figure 7.1), or equivalently, risk aversion increases. Higher risk aversion influences the employee to exercise earlier to secure small gains rather than waiting for future uncertain payoffs.

Finally, we show in Figure 7.6 that the exercise boundary tends to shift upward for higher values of α and β, given the initial wealth $x = 0$. The effect of β is intuitive because the risk tolerance function is increasing with respect to β. Therefore, the option holder with a higher β is effectively less risk-averse and may be willing to hold on to the ESO longer.

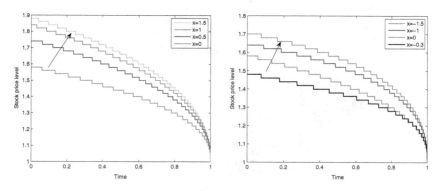

Figure 7.5.   Left: The exercise boundary shifts upward as wealth increases from zero. Right: The exercise boundary is the lowest when wealth $x = -0.3$. As wealth further decreases from -0.3 to -1.5, the exercise boundary rises again. The parameters here are the same as in Figure 7.3.

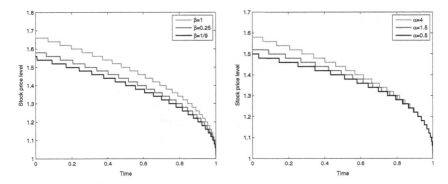

Figure 7.6. Left: A higher value of β leads to a higher exercise boundary (at initial wealth $x = 0$). Right: A higher value of α shifts the exercise boundary upward (initial wealth $x = 0$). The parameters here are taken to be same as those in Figure 7.3, except for α and β specified in the figures above.

7.5. Marginal Forward Indifference Price of American Options

In this section, we introduce the marginal forward indifference price of American options. A related concept in the classical utility framework is the *marginal utility price*, which is useful as an approximation for pricing a small number of claims. For completeness and the upcoming comparison with the forward analog, we provide a brief review of the marginal utility price in the diffusion market.

7.5.1. *Review of the classical marginal utility price*

In traditional utility maximization, risk aversion is modeled by a deterministic utility function $\hat{U}(x)$ defined at time T. In the Itô diffusion market introduced in Section 7.2, the investor dynamically trades between the money market and stock S, and his wealth process follows SDE (7.2). The corresponding Merton portfolio optimization problem is given in (7.3).

Next, suppose that the investor decides to buy δ units of a European claim, each offering payoff $C_T \in \mathscr{F}_T$. The marginal utility price is the per-unit price that the investor is willing to pay for an infinitesimal position ($\delta \approx 0$) in the claim. This problem has been studied in detail by Davis (1997, 2001), who shows by a formal small δ expansion that the investor's marginal utility price at time t is given by

$$\hat{h}_t = \frac{\mathbb{E}\left\{\hat{U}'(\hat{X}_T^*)C_T \mid \mathscr{F}_t\right\}}{M_t'(X_t)}, \quad t \in [0, T], \tag{7.43}$$

where $\hat{X}_T^*$ is the optimal terminal wealth in the Merton value process $M_t(X_t)$ given in (7.3). Kramkov and Sirbu (2006) adopt (7.43) as the definition of the marginal utility price, which we also adapt to the case of American options.

Definition 7.11. The marginal utility price process $(h_t)_{0 \leq t \leq T}$ for an American option with payoff process $(g_t)_{0 \leq t \leq T}$ is defined as

$$h_t = \frac{\operatorname{ess\,sup}_{\tau \in \mathscr{T}_{t,T}} \mathbb{E}\left\{M_\tau'(\hat{X}_\tau^*)\, g_\tau \mid \mathscr{F}_t\right\}}{M_t'(X_t)}, \tag{7.44}$$

where $M_t(X_t)$ is given in (7.3).

Among others, one important question is under what conditions does the marginal utility price become independent of the investor's wealth. In the classical setting for options without early exercise, wealth-independence of marginal utility prices is very rare. In fact, Kramkov and Sirbu (2006) show that only exponential and power utilities yield wealth-independent marginal utility prices for any payoff and in any financial market.

In the following proposition, we show that, if the Merton satisfies a separation of variables in the stochastic volatility model in Section 7.3, then the corresponding marginal utility price is wealth-independent.

Proposition 7.12. *In the stochastic volatility model, where S and Y follow* (7.16)–(7.17), *we consider the value function of the Merton problem*

$$M(x, y, t) = \sup_{\pi \in \mathscr{Z}_{t,T}} \mathbb{E}\left\{\hat{U}(X_T^\pi) \mid X_t = x, Y_t = y\right\},$$

for $(x, y, t) \in \mathbb{R} \times \mathbb{R}_+ \times [0, T]$. Assume that M satisfies the separation of variables:

$$M(x, y, t) = k(x, t)w(y, t), \tag{7.45}$$

where $w : \mathbb{R}_+ \times [0, T] \mapsto \mathbb{R}$ *is continuously differentiable in the first argument. Define* Q^φ *by*

$$\frac{dQ^\varphi}{d\mathbb{P}} = \exp\left(-\frac{1}{2}\int_0^T \left(\lambda(Y_s)^2 + \varphi(Y_s, s)^2\right)ds\right.$$

$$\left. -\int_0^T \lambda(Y_s)\,dW_s + \int_0^T \varphi(Y_s, s)\,d\hat{W}_s\right),$$

with $\varphi(y, t) = \sqrt{1 - \rho^2}c(y)w_y(y, t)$, *and assume* $Q^\varphi \in \mathcal{M}_f$. *Then, the marginal utility price for an American option with payoff function* $g(s, y, t)$ *is given by*

$$h(s, y, t) = \sup_{\tau \in \mathscr{T}_{t,T}} \mathbb{E}^{Q^\varphi}\left\{g(S_\tau, Y_\tau, \tau) \,|\, S_t = s, Y_t = y\right\}. \qquad (7.46)$$

Proof. First, we recall the associated HJB equation of the Merton value function, namely,

$$M_t = \frac{(\rho\sigma(y)c(y)M_{xy} + \lambda(y)\sigma(y)M_x)^2}{2\sigma(y)^2 M_{xx}} - b(y)M_y - \frac{c(y)^2}{2}M_{yy}, \qquad (7.47)$$

with $M(x, y, T) = \hat{U}(x)$. The optimal strategy is given in the feedback form

$$\hat{\pi}_t^* = -\frac{\rho c(Y_t)M_{xy}(\hat{X}_t^*, Y_t, t) + \lambda(Y_t)M_x(\hat{X}_t^*, Y_t, t)}{\sigma(Y_t)M_{xx}(\hat{X}_t^*, Y_t, t)}. \qquad (7.48)$$

By Ito's formula, the process $M_x\left(\hat{X}_t^*, Y_t, t\right)$ satisfies the SDE

$$dM_x(\hat{X}_t^*, Y_t, t) = \left(M_{xt} + \frac{\hat{\pi}_t^{*2}\sigma^2(Y_t)}{2}M_{xxx} + \hat{\pi}_t^*\sigma(Y_t)\lambda(Y_t)M_{xx}\right.$$

$$\left. + b(Y_t)M_{xy} + \frac{c^2(Y_t)}{2}M_{xyy} + \hat{\pi}_t^*\rho\sigma(Y_t)c(Y_t)M_{xxy}\right)dt$$

$$+ \hat{\pi}_t^*\sigma(Y_t)M_{xx}\,dW_t + c(Y_t)M_{xy}(\rho dW_t + \sqrt{1 - \rho^2}d\hat{W}_t).$$

$$(7.49)$$

Next, we show that the drift in (7.49) vanishes. Indeed, by differentiating (7.47) with respect to x, we get

$$M_{xt} = \rho^2 c(y)^2 \frac{M_{xy} M_{xxy}}{M_{xx}} - \frac{\rho^2 c(y)^2}{2} \frac{M_{xy}^2 M_{xxx}}{M_{xx}^2}$$

$$+ \lambda(y)^2 M_x - \frac{\lambda(y)^2}{2} \frac{M_x^2 M_{xxx}}{M_{xx}^2}$$

$$+ \rho\lambda(y)c(y) \left(M_{xy} + \frac{M_{xxy} M_x}{M_{xx}} - \frac{M_{xy} M_x M_{xxx}}{M_{xx}^2} \right)$$

$$- b(y) M_{xy} - \frac{c(y)^2}{2} M_{xyy},$$

which, combined with (7.48), eliminates the drift. Consequently, the SDE for $M_x\left(\hat{X}_t^*, Y_t, t\right)$ simplifies to

$$dM_x(\hat{X}_t^*, Y_t, t) = (\hat{\pi}_t^* \sigma(Y_t) M_{xx} + \rho c(Y_t) M_{xy})\, dW_t + \sqrt{1-\rho^2} c(Y_t) M_{xy}\, d\hat{W}_t$$

$$= -M_x \left(\lambda(Y_t) dW_t - \sqrt{1-\rho^2} c(Y_t) w_y(Y_t, t)\, d\hat{W}_t \right),$$

where the second equality follows from (7.48) and (7.45).

This implies that the process $(M_x(\hat{X}_t^*, Y_t, t))_{t \geq 0}$ is given by the stochastic exponential

$$M_x(\hat{X}_t^*, Y_t, t) = \exp\left(-\frac{1}{2} \int_0^t (\lambda(Y_s)^2 + \varphi(Y_s, s)^2)\, ds \right.$$

$$\left. - \int_0^t \lambda(Y_s)\, dW_s + \int_0^t \varphi(Y_s, s)\, d\hat{W}_s \right),$$

with $\varphi(y, t) = \sqrt{1-\rho^2} c(y) w_y(y, t)$. This provides the necessary change of measure from $\mathbb{P}$ to Q^φ that leads (7.44) to (7.46).   □

Examples where M admits the separation of variables include the exponential or power utilities (also see Corollary 7.13 for the exponential case).

We observe from Proposition 7.12 that the marginal utility price is *wealth-independent*. Nevertheless, the associated pricing measure Q^φ depends on the function w, and therefore on the utility function.

As we discuss next, in the special example with exponential utility, the measure Q^φ turns out to be the MEMM and is independent of both wealth and utility function. However, this measure is *not* independent of the horizon choice. The following proposition is a straightforward generalization of this well-known result to the case of American options; see, for example, Becherer (2001) for the case of claims without early exercise opportunities.

Proposition 7.13. *Assume $\hat{U}(x) = -e^{-\gamma x}$. Then, the marginal utility price is given by*

$$h(s, y, t) = \sup_{\tau \in \mathscr{T}_{t,T}} \mathbb{E}^{Q^E} \left\{ g(S_\tau, Y_\tau, \tau) \,|\, S_t = s, Y_t = y \right\},$$

where Q^E is the MEMM given in (7.40).

Proof. This is a direct application of Proposition 7.12. According to the Merton solution for exponential utility in (7.34), it is immediate that (7.45) is satisfied, and

$$w_y(y, t) = \frac{1}{(1 - \rho^2)} \frac{f_y(y, t)}{f(y, t)}.$$

Then, we have

$$\varphi(y, t) = \sqrt{1 - \rho^2} c(y) w_y(y, t) = l(y, t),$$

where $l(y, t)$ is the risk premium associated with the MEMM Q^E defined in (7.40). As a result, the pricing formula (7.13) follows from (7.46). $\quad\square$

Next, we consider a special situation where the coefficients $\lambda(\cdot)$ and $\sigma(\cdot)$ of S are constant. In this case, the process Y does not affect the dynamics of S, but plays the role of a non-traded asset on which the claim g is written. Therefore, the market is still incomplete. We show that in this case *every* utility function will yield the *same* wealth-independent marginal utility price, given as an expectation under the MMM (defined in (7.26)).

Proposition 7.14. *If the Sharpe ratio $\lambda(\cdot)$ and volatility coefficient $\sigma(\cdot)$ of S (see (7.16)) are constant, then the marginal utility price is independent of the holder's wealth and risk preferences, and it is given by*

$$h(s, y, t) = \sup_{\tau \in \mathscr{T}_{t,T}} \mathbb{E}^{Q^0} \left\{ g(S_\tau, Y_\tau, \tau) \,|\, S_t = s, Y_t = y \right\}, \tag{7.50}$$

where Q^0 is the MMM defined by

$$dQ^0/d\mathbb{P} = e^{-\frac{\lambda^2}{2}T - \lambda W_T}.$$

Proof. With $\sigma(\cdot)$ being constant, the investor's wealth X^π does not depend on Y. The HJB equation (7.47) then reduces to

$$M_t = \frac{\lambda^2}{2} \frac{M_x^2}{M_{xx}}, \tag{7.51}$$

with $M(x,T) = \hat{U}(x)$. In turn, the optimal feedback strategy simplifies to

$$\hat{\pi}_t^* = -\frac{\lambda}{\sigma} \frac{M_x(\hat{X}_t^*, t)}{M_{xx}(\hat{X}_t^*, t)}. \tag{7.52}$$

By Ito's formula, we then get

$$dM_x(\hat{X}_t^*, t) = \left(M_{xt} + \hat{\pi}_t^* \lambda \sigma M_{xx} + \frac{\hat{\pi}_t^{*2} \sigma^2}{2} M_{xxx} \right) dt + \hat{\pi}_t^* \sigma M_{xx} \, dW_t$$

$$= -\lambda M_x(\hat{X}_t^*, t) \, dW_t,$$

where the second equality follows from (7.52) and differentiating (7.51). As a result, $(M_x(\hat{X}_t^*, t))_{t \geq 0}$ is given by the stochastic exponential

$$M_x\left(\hat{X}_t^*, t\right) = e^{-\frac{\lambda^2}{2}t - \lambda W_t}.$$

This yields the change of measure from $\mathbb{P}$ to Q^0, which leads (7.44) to (7.50). □

7.5.2. *The marginal forward indifference price formula*

Following the classical formulation, we introduce the marginal forward indifference price for our model. Henceforth, we will give the definitions and results based on the Itô diffusion market settings described in Section 7.2, where the discounted stock price S follows (7.1) and the option holder's trading wealth X_t follows (7.2).

Definition 7.15. Let $U_t(x) = u(x, A_t)$ (see Theorem 7.3) be the investor's forward performance process. The marginal forward indifference price process $(\tilde{p}_t)_{0 \leq t \leq T}$ for an American option with an $\mathscr{F}_t$-adapted bounded payoff process $(g_t)_{0 \leq t \leq T}$ is defined as

$$\tilde{p}_t = \frac{\text{ess sup}_{\tau \in \mathscr{T}_{t,T}} \mathbb{E}\left\{ u_x\left(X_\tau^*, A_\tau\right) g_\tau | \mathscr{F}_t \right\}}{u_x(X_t, A_t)}, \tag{7.53}$$

where $A_t = \int_0^t \lambda_s^2 ds$ and the optimal wealth process X^* follows (7.13).

At first glance, the marginal forward indifference price in (7.53) might depend on the holder's risk preferences and wealth. Nevertheless, as the following proposition shows, the marginal forward indifference price is *independent* of both of these elements, and is simply given as the expected discounted payoff under the MMM, regardless of the investor's forward performance criterion.

Proposition 7.16. *The marginal forward indifference price of an American option with payoff process* $(g_t)_{0 \leq t \leq T}$ *is given by*

$$\tilde{p}_t = \operatorname*{ess\,sup}_{\tau \in \mathscr{T}_{t,T}} \mathbb{E}^{Q^0}\{g_\tau \mid \mathscr{F}_t\}, \qquad (7.54)$$

where Q^0 *is the MMM. Consequently,* $\tilde{p}_t$ *is independent of both the holder's wealth and his forward performance.*

Proof. Comparing (7.53) and (7.54), we observe that it is sufficient to show that

$$\frac{u_x\left(X_\tau^*, A_\tau\right)}{u_x\left(X_t^*, A_t\right)} = \exp\left(-\frac{1}{2}\int_t^\tau \lambda_s^2 \, ds - \int_t^\tau \lambda_s \, dW_s\right), \qquad \tau \in \mathscr{T}_{t,T}. \quad (7.55)$$

Since λ is bounded, this leads to the desired measure change from the historical measure $\mathbb{P}$ to the MMM Q^0.

Applying Itô's formula to $u_x(X_t^*, A_t)$ and using the SDE (7.13) for X^* gives

$$du_x\left(X_t^*, A_t\right) = \lambda_t^2 \left(u_{xt}(X_t^*, A_t) + R(X_t^*, A_t)u_{xx}(X_t^*, A_t)\right.$$

$$\left. + \frac{R(X_t^*, A_t)^2}{2} u_{xxx}(X_t^*, A_t)\right) dt$$

$$+ \lambda_t R(X_t^*, A_t)u_{xx}(X_t^*, A_t)\, dW_t. \qquad (7.56)$$

Next, we show that the drift vanishes. First, it follows from differentiating $u(x,t)$ in (7.9) that

$$u_{xt} = u_x - \frac{u_x^2 u_{xxx}}{2u_{xx}^2}.$$

Applying this and the fact that $R(x,t) = -u_x(x,t)/u_{xx}(x,t)$ to (7.56), we eliminate the drift term. As a result, the SDE (7.56) simplifies to

$$du_x(X_t^*, A_t) = \lambda_t R(X_t^*, A_t) u_{xx}(X_t^*, A_t)\, dW_t$$
$$= \lambda_t u_x(X_t^*, A_t)\, dW_t.$$

This implies that the process $(u_x(X_t^*, A_t))_{t \geq 0}$ is given by the stochastic exponential representation in (7.55). Hence, by a change of measure, we obtain Eq. (7.54). $\qquad\qquad\square$

Corollary 7.17. *In the stochastic volatility model where S and Y follow* (7.16)–(7.17), *the marginal forward indifference price for an American option with payoff function $g(s, y, t)$ is given by*

$$\tilde{p}(s, y, t) = \sup_{\tau \in \mathcal{T}_{t,T}} \mathbb{E}^{Q^0} \{ g(S_\tau, Y_\tau, \tau) \mid S_t = s, Y_t = y \}, \qquad (7.57)$$

where Q^0 is the MMM defined in (7.26).

Proposition 7.16 illustrates a crucial feature of the forward indifference pricing mechanism. If we consider that, in a general Itô diffusion market, different investors adopt different forward performances according to Theorem 7.3, then their marginal forward indifference prices for an American claim will necessarily be the same, regardless of their wealth and choices of forward performance. However, in the traditional setting, the marginal utility price for a general utility function is both wealth and utility independent only in a correlated geometric Brownian motions model (see Kramkov and Sirbu (2006) and Proposition 7.14 above). Due to the simple structure of this special market model, the marginal forward indifference price and the marginal utility price have the same form (see Proposition 7.14 and Corollary 7.17) even though they are derived from very different mechanisms.

The probabilistic representation (7.57) in Corollary 7.17 shows that the marginal indifference price of an American option under the stochastic volatility model amounts to pricing under the minimal martingale measure. Consequently, the marginal forward indifference price is independent of the holder's wealth and forward performance criterion.

While the forward indifference valuation yields a nonlinear pricing rule, the marginal pricing rule is linear with respect to the quantity of options. In contrast to the nonlinear variational inequalities in (7.21) and (7.41) in Markovian models such as those in Sections 7.3 and 7.4, the marginal forward utility price yields a linear free boundary problem with reduced dimension due to its wealth-independence. Therefore, the marginal formulation is more amenable for computations, and can potentially be used as an efficient approximation for valuing and hedging a small position.

7.6. Conclusion

In summary, we have discussed the forward indifference valuation for American-style stock options. The methodology is used to model the exercise timing of ESOs under a general risk criterion. The risk-averse option holder's optimal hedging and exercising strategies are found from solving the associated variational inequalities.

The forward indifference valuation mechanism is profoundly different from the one in the classical approach. This is best illustrated in Section 7.3, in which the exponential forward indifference price for the stock option is expressed in terms of relative entropy minimization with respect to the MMM, rather than the MEMM that arises in the traditional setting. The MMM also plays a crucial role as the pricing measure for the marginal forward indifference price. In contrast to the classical marginal utility price, the marginal forward indifference price is independent of both the investor's wealth and risk preferences. This drastically simplifies the marginal pricing problem and is applicable to a variety of European or American contingent claims.

Several challenges and interesting problems are to be further investigated. The nonlinearity of the variational inequalities requires the development of efficient numerical schemes to capture the optimal exercise timing and ESO value. Moreover, even though we have focused on the valuation of ESOs as American options, it is important to examine the impact of forward performance on ESOs with other features, such as reloading, repricing, knockout, and performance hurdles. In many utility maximization problems, exponential utility is chosen for its convenient analytic properties. Forward performance provides a convenient tool to move away from exponential utility and remove the horizon dependence.

Bibliography

Aboody, D. and Kasznik, R. (2000). CEO stock option awards and the timing of corporate voluntary disclosures, *Journal of Accounting and Economics* **29**, 1, pp. 73–100.

Acharya, V. V., John, K. and Sundaram, R. K. (2000). On the optimality of resetting executive stock options, *Journal of Financial Economics* **57**, 1, pp. 65–101.

Alix, S. (2016). CFO journal: More firms move to reprice options — stock-option exchanges help keep employees happy when share drop hurts award's valuation, *Wall Street Journal*, p. B7.

Ankirchner, S., Imkeller, P. and dos Reis, G. (2010). Pricing and hedging of derivatives based on non-tradable underlying, *Mathematical Finance* **20**, 2, pp. 289–312.

Armstrong, C. S., Jagolinzer, A. D. and Larcker, D. F. (2007). Timing of employee stock option exercises and the cost of stock option grants, Working paper.

Bayraktar, E. and Xing, H. (2009). Analysis of the optimal exercise boundary of American options for jump diffusions, *SIAM Journal on Mathematical Analysis* **41**, 8, pp. 825–860.

Bebchuk, L. A. and Fried, J. M. (2003). Executive compensation as an agency problem, *Journal of Economic Perspectives* **17**, 3, pp. 71–92.

Becherer, D. (2001). Rational hedging and valuation with utility-based preferences, Doctoral dissertation, Technical University of Berlin.

Becherer, D. (2004). Utility indifference hedging and valuation via reaction diffusion systems, *Stochastic Analysis with Applications to Mathematical Finance* **460**, pp. 27–51.

Becherer, D. and Schweizer, M. (2005). Classical solutions to reaction diffusion systems for hedging problems with interacting Itô and point processes, *Annals of Applied Probability* **15**, pp. 1111–1144.

Benth, F. and Karlsen, K. (2005). A PDE representation of the density of the minimal entropy martingale measure in stochastic volatility markets, *Stochastics and Stochastics Reports* **77**, 2, pp. 109–137.

Berrier, F., Rogers, L. and Tehranchi, M. (2009). A characterization of forward utility functions, Preprint, University of Cambridge.

Bettis, J. C., Bizjak, J. M. and Lemmon, M. L. (2001). Managerial ownership, incentive contracting, and the use of zero-cost collars and equity swaps by corporate insiders, *Journal of Financial and Quantitative Analysis* **36**, pp. 345–370.

Bettis, J. C., Bizjak, J. M. and Lemmon, M. L. (2005). Exercise behaviors, valuation, and the incentive effects of employee stock options, *Journal of Financial Economics* **76**, pp. 445–470.

Black, F. and Scholes, M. (1973). The pricing of options and corporate liabilities, *Journal of Political Economy* **3**, pp. 637–654.

Bova, F. and Vance, M. (2019). Uncertainty avoidance and the timing of employee stock option exercise, *Journal of International Business Studies* **50**, 5, pp. 740–757.

Brisley, N. (2006). Executive stock options: Early exercise provisions and risk-taking incentives, *Journal of Finance* **61**, pp. 2487–2509.

Callaghan, S., Subramaniam, C. and Youngblood, S. (2003). Does option repricing retain executives and improve future performance? Working paper.

Carmona, J., León, A. and Vaello-Sebastiá, A. (2011). Pricing executive stock option under employment shocks, *Journal of Economic Dynamics and Control* **35**, pp. 97–114.

Carpenter, J. (1998). The exercise and valuation of executive stock options, *Journal of Financial Economics* **48**, pp. 127–158.

Carpenter, J. (2005). Optimal exercise of executive stock options and implications for valuation, Working paper, New York University.

Carpenter, J., Stanton, R. and Wallace, N. (2010). Optimal exercise of executive stock options and implications for firm cost, *Journal of Financial Economics* **98**, 2, pp. 315–337.

Carpenter, J. N., Stanton, R. and Wallace, N. (2017). Estimation of employee stock option exercise rates and firm cost, Working paper.

Carr, P. (1998). Randomization and the American put, *Review of Financial Studies* **11**, pp. 597–626.

Carr, P., Ellis, K. and Gupta, V. (1998). Static hedging of exotic options, *Journal of Finance* **53**, 3, pp. 1165–1190.

Carr, P., Geman, H., Madan, D. B. and Yor, M. (2002). The fine structure of asset returns: An empirical investigation, *Journal of Business* **75**, 2, pp. 305–332.

Carr, P. and Linetsky, V. (2000). The valuation of executive stock options in an intensity-based framework, *European Finance Review* **4**, pp. 211–230.

Carr, P. and Madan, D. B. (1999). Option pricing using the fast Fourier transform, *Journal of Computational Finance* **2**, 1, pp. 61–73.

Chance, D. and Yang, T.-H. (2005). The utility-based valuation and cost of executive stock options in a binomial framework: Issues and methodologies. *Journal of Derivatives Accounting* **2**, pp. 165–188.

Chen, A. and Pelger, M. (2014). Optimal stock option schemes for managers, *Review of Managerial Science* **8**, 4, pp. 437–464.

Chen, M. A. (2004). Executive option repricing, incentives, and retention, *The Journal of Finance* **59**, 3, pp. 1167–1199.

Cicero, D. C. (2009). The manipulation of executive stock option exercise strategies: Information timing and backdating, *The Journal of Finance* **64**, 6, pp. 2627–2663.

Cont, R. and Voltchkova, E. (2003). A finite difference scheme for option pricing in jump-diffusion and exponential Lévy models, *SIAM Journal on Numerical Analysis* **43**, 4, pp. 1596–1626.

Cvitanic, J., Wiener, Z. and Zapatero, F. (2008). Analytic pricing of employee stock options, *Review of Financial Studies* **21**, 2, pp. 683–724.

Cvitanic, J. and Zhang, J. (2007). Optimal compensation with adverse selection and dynamic actions, *Mathematics and Financial Economics* **1**, pp. 21–55.

Dai, M. and Kwok, Y. (2005). Valuing employee reload options under time vesting requirement, *Quantitative Finance* **5**, 1, pp. 61–69.

Davis, M. (1997). Option pricing in incomplete markets, in M. Dempster and S. Pliska (eds.), *Mathematics of Derivatives Securities* (Cambridge University Press), pp. 227–254.

Davis, M. (2001). Pricing weather derivatives by marginal value, *Quantitative Finance* **1**, pp. 1–4.

Delbaen, F., Grandits, P., Rheinländer, T., Samperi, D., Schweizer, M. and Stricker, C. (2002). Exponential hedging and entropic penalties, *Mathematical Finance* **12**, pp. 99–123.

Detemple, J. and Sundaresan, S. (1999). Nontraded asset valuation with portfolio constraints: a binomial approach, *Review of Financial Studies* **12**, pp. 835–872.

d'Halluin, Y., Forsyth, P. and Labahn, G. (2003). A penalty method for American options with jump diffusion processes, *Numerische Mathematik* **97**, 2, pp. 321–352.

Dixit, A. K. (1994). *Investment Under Uncertainty* (Princeton University Press).

Duffie, D. (2001). *Dynamic Asset Pricing* (Princeton University Press).

Dybvig, P. H. and Loewenstein, M. (2015). Employee reload options: Pricing, hedging, and optimal exercise, *The Review of Financial Studies* **16**, 1, pp. 145–171.

Elliot, R. J., Chan, L. and Siu, T. K. (2005). Option pricing and Esscher transform under regime switching, *Annals of Finance* **1**, pp. 423–432.

Fleming, W. H. and Sheu, S. (1999). Optimal long term growth rate of expected utility of wealth, *The Annals of Applied Probability* **9**, 3, pp. 871–903.

Föllmer, H. and Sondermann, D. (1986). Hedging of non-redundant contingent claims, in W. Hildenbrand and A. Mas-Colell (eds.), *Contribution to Mathematical Economics: In Honor of Gerard Debreu* (North-Holland, Amsterdam), pp. 205–223.

Forsyth, P. A., Wang, I. R. and Wan, J. W. (2007). Robust numerical valuation of European and American options under the CGMY process, *Journal of Computational Finance* **10**, 4, pp. 31–69.

Frey, R. (1997). Derivative asset analysis in models with level-dependent and stochastic volatility, *CWI Quarterly* **10**, 1, pp. 1–34.

Fritelli, M. (2000). The minimal entropy martingale measure and the valuation problem in incomplete markets, *Mathematical Finance* **10**, pp. 39–52.

Frydman, C. and Jenter, D. (2010). CEO compensation, *Annual Review of Financial Economics* **2**, 1, pp. 75–102.

Giesecke, K. and Goldberg, L. (2011). A top down approach to multi-name credit, *Operations Research* **59**, 22, pp. 283–300.

Glowinski, R. (1984). *Numerical Methods for Nonlinear Variational Problems* (Springer-Verlag, New York).

Grasselli, M. and Henderson, V. (2009). Risk aversion and block exercise of executive stock options, *Journal of Economic Dynamics and Control* **33**, 1, pp. 109–127.

Grasselli, M. R. (2005). Nonlinearity, correlation and the valuation of employee stock options, Preprint, McMaster University.

Guo, X. and Zhang, Q. (2004). Closed-form solutions for perpetual American put options with regime switching, *SIAM Journal on Applied Mathematics* **64**, 6, pp. 2034–2049.

Hall, B. and Murphy, K. J. (2002). Stock options for undiversified executives, *Journal of Accounting and Economics* **33**, pp. 3–42.

Hemmer, T., Matsunaga, S. and Shevlin, T. (1994). Estimating the 'fair value' of employee stock options with expected early exercise, *Accounting Horizons* **8**, pp. 23–42.

Hemmer, T., Matsunaga, S. and Shevlin, T. (1996). The influence of risk diversification on the early exercise of employee stock options by executive officers, *Journal of Accounting and Economics* **21**, 1, pp. 45–68.

Henderson, V. (2005). The impact of the market portfolio on the valuation, incentives and optimality of executive stock options, *Quantitative Finance* **5**, pp. 1–13.

Henderson, V. and Hobson, D. (2007). Horizon-unbiased utility functions, *Stochastic Processes and Their Applications* **117**, pp. 1621–1641.

Henderson, V., Sun, J. and Whalley, E. (2018). The value of being 'lucky': Option backdating and non-diversifiable risk, Working paper.

Heron, R. A. and Lie, E. (2009). What fraction of stock option grants to top executives have been backdated or manipulated? *Management Science* **55**, 4, pp. 513–525.

Heron, R. A. and Lie, E. (2016). Do stock options overcome managerial risk aversion? Evidence from exercises of executive stock options (ESOs), Working paper.

Hirsa, A. and Madan, D. (2004). Pricing American options under Variance Gamma, *Journal of Computational Finance* **7**, 2, pp. 63–80.

Huddart, S. (1994). Employee stock options, *Journal of Accounting and Economics* **18**, pp. 207–231.

Huddart, S. and Lang, M. (1996). Employee stock option exercises: An empirical analysis, *Journal of Accounting and Economics* **21**, pp. 5–43.

Hull, J. and White, A. (2004a). Accounting for employee stock options: A practical approach to handling the valuation issues, *Journal of Derivatives Accounting* **1**, 1, pp. 3–9.

Hull, J. and White, A. (2004b). How to value employee stock options, *Financial Analysts Journal* **60**, pp. 114–119.

İlhan, A., Jonsson, M. and Sircar, R. (2009). Optimal static–dynamic hedges for exotic options under convex risk measures, *Stochastic Processes & Applications* **119**, 10, pp. 3608–3622.

İlhan, A. and Sircar, R. (2005). Optimal static-dynamic hedges for barrier options, *Mathematical Finance* **16**, pp. 359–385.

Ingersoll, J. E. (2006). The subjective and objective evaluation of incentive stock options, *The Journal of Business* **79**, 2, pp. 453–487.

Jackson, K. R., Jaimungal, S. and Surkov, V. (2008). Fourier space time-stepping for option pricing with Lévy models, *Journal of Computational Finance* **12**, 2, pp. 1–29.

Jaimungal, S. and Sigloch, G. (2012). Incorporating risk and ambiguity aversion into a hybrid model of default, *Mathematical Finance* **22**, 1, pp. 57–81.

Jain, A. and Subramanian, A. (2004). The intertemporal exercise and valuation of employee options, *The Accounting Review* **79**, pp. 705–743.

Jennergren, L. and Naslund, B. (1993). A comment on 'Valuation of stock options and the FASB proposal', *Accounting Review* **68**, pp. 179–183.

Johnson, S. A. and Tian, Y. S. (2000). The value and incentive effects of nontraditional executive stock option plans, *Journal of Financial Economics* **57**, 1, pp. 3–34.

Kabanov, Y. and Stricker, C. (2002). On the optimal portfolio for the exponential utility maximization: Remarks to the six-author paper, *Mathematical Finance* **12**, pp. 125–134.

Kalpathy, S. (2009). Stock option repricing and its alternatives: An empirical examination, *Journal of Financial and Quantitative Analysis* **44**, 6, pp. 1459–1487.

Karatzas, I. and Kou, S. (1998). Hedging American contingent claims with constrained portfolios, *Finance and Stochastics* **2**, pp. 215–258.

Karatzas, I. and Shreve, S. (1998). *Methods of Mathematical Finance* (Springer).

Klein, D. and Maug, E. G. (2010). How do executives exercise their stock options? European Corporate Governance Institute — Finance Working Paper No. 284.

Kolb, R. W. (2012). *Too Much Is Not Enough: Incentives in Executive Compensation* (Oxford University Press).

Kou, S. G. (2002). A jump-diffusion model for option pricing, *Management Science* **48**, 8, pp. 1086–1101.

Kramkov, D. and Sirbu, M. (2006). Sensitivity analysis of utility based prices and risk-tolerance wealth processes, *The Annals of Applied Probability* **16**, 4, pp. 2140–2194.

Kulatilaka, N. and Marcus, A. (1994). Valuing employee stock options, *European Finance Review* **4**, pp. 211–230.

Kyprianou, A. E. and Pistorius, M. R. (2003). Perpetual options and Canadization through fluctuation theory, *The Annals of Applied Probability* **13**, 3, pp. 1077–1098.

Lamberton, D. and Mikou, M. (2008). The critical price for the American put in an exponential Lévy model, *Finance and Stochastics* **12**, 4, pp. 561–581.

Lau, K. and Kwok, Y. (2005). Valuation of employee reload options using utility maximization framework, *International Journal of Theoretical and Applied Finance* **8**, 5, pp. 659–674.

Leung, K. S. and Kwok, Y. K. (2008). Employee stock option valuation with repricing features, *Quantitative Finance* **8**, 6, pp. 561–569.

Leung, T. (2010). A Markov-modulated stochastic control problem with optimal multiple stopping with application to finance, in *49th IEEE Conference on Decision and Control (CDC)*, pp. 559–566.

Leung, T. (2012). Sequential static-dynamic hedging for long-term derivatives, *Procedia Computer Science* **9**, pp. 1211–1218.

Leung, T. and Ludkovski, M. (2011). Optimal timing to purchase options, *SIAM Journal on Financial Mathematics* **2**, 1, pp. 768–793.

Leung, T. and Ludkovski, M. (2012). Accounting for risk aversion in derivatives purchase timing, *Mathematics and Financial Economics* **6**, 4, pp. 363–386.

Leung, T. and Sircar, R. (2009a). Accounting for risk aversion, vesting, job termination risk and multiple exercises in valuation of employee stock options, *Mathematical Finance* **19**, 1, pp. 99–128.

Leung, T. and Sircar, R. (2009b). Exponential hedging with optimal stopping and application to ESO valuation, *SIAM Journal of Control and Optimization* **48**, 3, pp. 1422–1451.

Leung, T., Sircar, R. and Zariphopoulou, T. (2008). Credit derivatives and risk aversion, in T. Fomby, J.-P. Fouque and K. Solna (eds.), *Advances in Econometrics*, Vol. 22 (Elsevier Science), pp. 275–291.

Leung, T. and Wan, H. (2015). ESO valuation with job termination risk and jumps in stock price, *SIAM Journal on Financial Mathematics* **6**, 1, pp. 487–516.

Leung, T. and Zhou, Y. (2019). Optimal dynamic futures portfolio in a regime-switching market framework, *International Journal of Financial Engineering* **6**, 4, doi: 10.1142/S2424786319500348.

Li, J. (2016). Trading VIX futures under mean reversion with regime switching, *International Journal of Financial Engineering* **3**, 3, p. 1650021.

Lie, E. (2005). On the timing of CEO stock option awards, *Management Science* **51**, 5, pp. 802–812.

Lord, R., Fang, F., Bervoets, F. and Oosterlee, K. (2008). A fast and accurate FFT based method for pricing early-exercise options under Lévy processes, *SIAM Journal on Scientific Computing* **30**, 4, pp. 1678–1705.

Madan, D. B., Carr, P. and Chang, E. (1998). The Variance Gamma process and option pricing, *European Finance Review* **2**, 8, pp. 79–105.

Maremont, M. and Forelle, C. (2006). Bosses' pay: How stock options became part of the problem; once seen as a reform, they grew into font of riches and system to be gamed, *The Wall Street Journal Eastern Edition*, p. A1.

Marquardt, C. (2002). The cost of employee stock option grants: An empirical analysis, *Journal of Accounting Research* **4**, pp. 1191–1217.

McDonald, R. and Siegel, D. (1986). The value of waiting to invest, *Quarterly Journal of Economics* **101**, pp. 707–727.

McKean, H. P. J. (1965). Appendix: A free boundary problem for the heating function arising from a problem in mathematical economics, *Industrial Management Review* **6**, pp. 32–39.

McLaughlin, T. and French, D. (2020). Why U.S. energy CEOs will get big payouts despite oil meltdown, *Reuters*.

Merton, R. (1969). Lifetime portfolio selection under uncertainty: The continuous time model, *Review of Economic Studies* **51**, pp. 247–257.

Merton, R. (1976). Option pricing when underlying stock returns are discontinuous, *Journal of Financial Economics* **3**, pp. 125–144.

Meulbroek, L. K. (2001). The efficiency of equity-linked compensation: Understanding the full cost of awarding executive stock options, *Financial Management* **30**, 2, pp. 5–44.

Monoyios, M. and Ng, A. (2011). Optimal exercise of an executive stock option by an insider, *International Journal of Theoretical and Applied Finance* **14**, 1, pp. 83–106.

Musiela, M. and Zariphopoulou, T. (2004a). An example of indifference pricing under exponential preferences, *Finance and Stochastics* **8**, pp. 229–239.

Musiela, M. and Zariphopoulou, T. (2004b). Indifference prices of early exercise claims, in G. Yin and Q. Zhang (eds.), *Contemporary Mathematics, Proceedings of the AMS-IMS-SIAM Joint Summer Research Conference on Mathematics of Finance*, Vol. 351 (American Mathematical Society), pp. 259–272.

Musiela, M. and Zariphopoulou, T. (2008). Portfolio choice under dynamic investment performance criteria, *Quantitative Finance* **9**, 2, pp. 161–170.

Musiela, M. and Zariphopoulou, T. (2010). Portfolio choice under space–time monotone performance criteria, *SIAM Journal on Financial Mathematics*.

Oberman, A. and Zariphopoulou, T. (2003). Pricing early exercise contracts in incomplete markets, *Computational Management Science* **1**, pp. 75–107.

Oksendal, B. and Sulem, A. (2005). *Applied Stochastic Control of Jump Diffusions* (Springer).

Olagues, J. and Summa, J. (2010). *Getting Started in Employee Stock Options* (John Wiley & Sons, Hoboken, NJ).

Pham, H. (1997). Optimal stopping, free boundary, and American option in a jump-diffusion model, *Applied Mathematical and Optimization* **35**, 2, pp. 145–164.

Rogers, L. and Scheinkman, J. (2007). Optimal exercise of American claims when markets are not complete, *Finance and Stochastics* **11**, pp. 357–372.

Rogers, L. and Williams, D. (2000). *Diffusions, Markov Processes and Martingales*, 2nd edn. (Cambridge University Press).

Rouge, R. and El Karoui, N. (2000). Pricing via utility maximization and entropy, *Mathematical Finance* **10**, 2, pp. 259–276.

Saly, P. (1994). Repricing executive stock option in a down market, *Journal of Accounting and Economics* **18**, 3, pp. 325–356.

Samuelson, P. (1965). Rational theory of warrant pricing, *Industrial Management Review* **6**, pp. 13–31.

Sato, K.-I. (1999). *Lévy Processes and Infinitely Divisible Distributions*, Cambridge Studies in Advanced Mathematics (Cambridge University Press).

Sircar, R. and Xiong, W. (2007). A general framework for evaluating executive stock options, *Journal of Economic Dynamics and Control* **31**, 7, pp. 2317–2349.

Sircar, R. and Zariphopoulou, T. (2005). Bounds and asymptotic approximations for utility prices when volatility is random, *SIAM Journal on Control and Optimization* **43**, 4, pp. 1328–1353.

Sircar, R. and Zariphopoulou, T. (2010). Utility valuation of multiname credit derivatives and application to CDOs, *Quantitative Finance* **10**, 2, pp. 195–208.

Sun, Y. and Shin, T. (2014). Rewarding poor performance: Why do boards of directors increase new options in response to CEO underwater options? *Corporate Governance: An International Review* **22**, 5, pp. 408–421.

Szimayer, A. (2004). A reduced form model for ESO valuation: Modelling the effects of employee departure and takeovers on the value of employee share options, *Mathematical Methods of Operations Research* **59**, 1, pp. 111–128.

Tiu (2004). On the Merton problem in incomplete markets, Thesis, University of Texas, Austin.

Villeneuve, S. (1999). Exercise regions of American options on several assets, *Finance and Stochastics* **3**, pp. 295–322.

Wilmott, P., Howison, S. and Dewynne, J. (1995). *The Mathematics of Financial Derivatives* (Cambridge University Press).

Yang, J. T. (2011). Alternatives to traditional repricing of executive stock options, *Review of Pacific Basin Financial Markets and Policies* **14**, 1, pp. 35–80.

Yang, J. T. and Carleton, W. T. (2011). Repricing of executive stock options, *Review of Quantitative Finance and Accounting* **36**, 3, pp. 459–490.

Yermack, D. (1997). Good timing: CEO stock option awards and company news announcements, *The Journal of Finance* **52**, 2, pp. 449–476.

Zamora, V. L. (2008). Characteristics of firms responding to underwater employee stock options: Evidence from traditional repricings, 6&1 exchanges, and makeup grants, *Journal of Management Accounting Research* **20**, 1, pp. 107–132.

Zariphopoulou, T. and Zhou, T. (2008). Investment performance measurement under asymptotically linear local risk tolerance, in P. Ciarlet, A. Bensoussan and Q. Zhang (eds.), *Handbook of Numerical Analysis* (North-Holland), pp. 227–254.

Zitkovic, G. (2009). A dual characterization of self-generation and exponential forward performances, *The Annals of Applied Probability* **19**, 6, pp. 2176–2210.

Index

CPSIA information can be obtained
at www.ICGtesting.com
Printed in the USA
JSHW030913280721
17337JS00002B/7